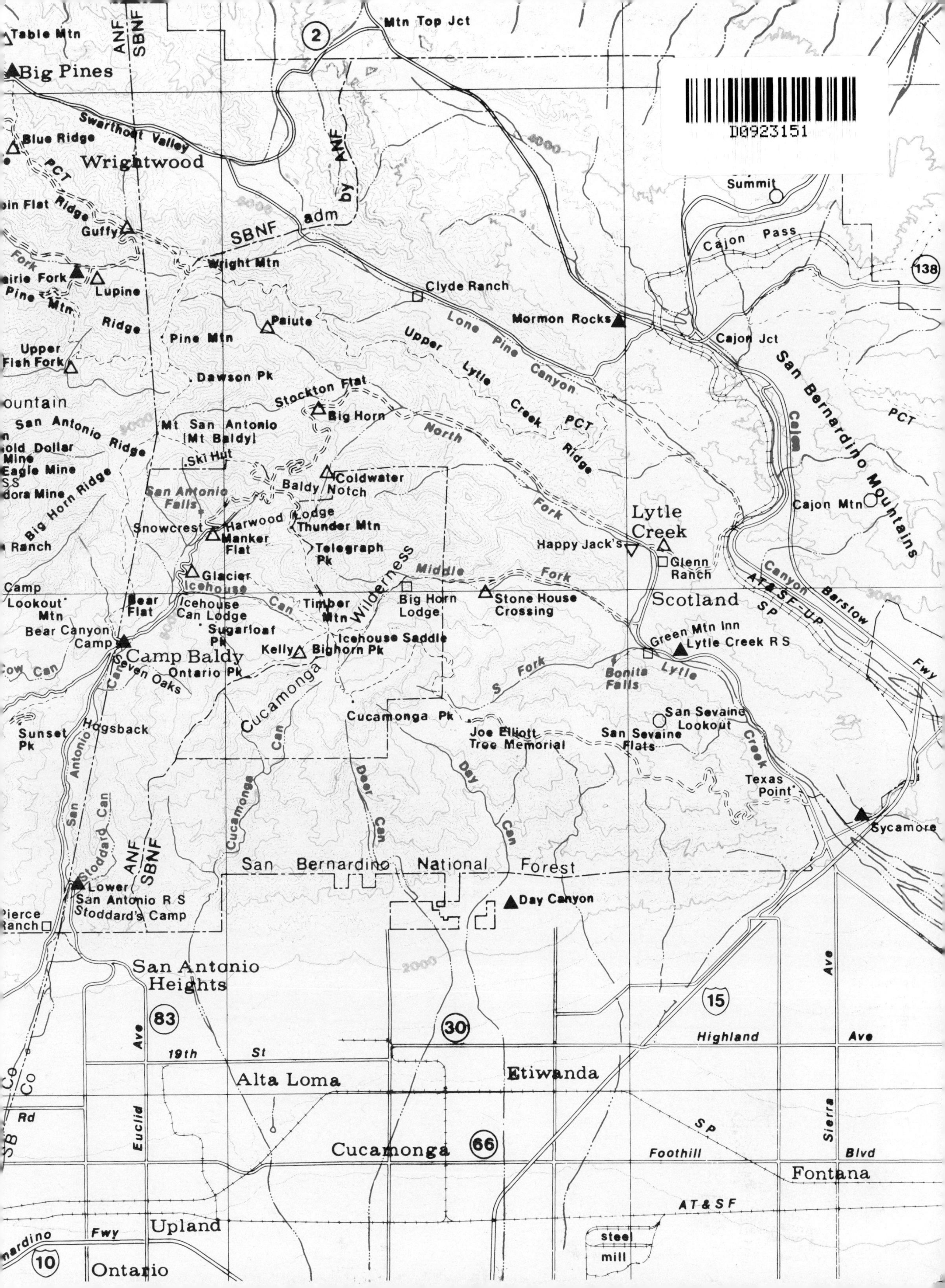
Table Mtn
ANF
SBNF
Mtn Top Jct
2
Big Pines
Swarthout Valley
Blue Ridge
Wrightwood
PCT
Ridge
Guffy
SBNF
adm
by
ANF
Wright Mtn
Lupine
Pine Mtn
Ridge
Pine Mtn
Paiute
Clyde Ranch
Mormon Rocks
Upper
Fish Fork
Dawson Pk
Stockton Flat
Big Horn
Lone Pine Canyon
Upper Lytle Creek Ridge
PCT
North Fork
Mt San Antonio
(Mt Baldy)
San Antonio Ridge
Gold Dollar Mine
Eagle Mine
Big Horn Ridge
Ski Hut
Coldwater
Baldy Notch
San Antonio Falls
Snowcrest
Harwood Lodge
Thunder Mtn
Manker Flat
Telegraph Pk
Glacier
Icehouse
Camp
Lookout Mtn
Bear Flat
Icehouse Can Lodge
Timber Mtn
Wilderness
Big Horn Lodge
Middle Fork
Stone House Crossing
Bear Canyon Camp
Sugarloaf Pk
Camp Baldy
Seven Oaks
Ontario Pk
Kelly
Bighorn Pk
Icehouse Saddle
Cucamonga
Can
Cucamonga Pk
Joe Elliott Tree Memorial
S Fork
Sunset Pk
Hogsback
San Antonio
Stoddard Can
Cucamonga
Deer Can
Day Can
San Bernardino National Forest
ANF
SBNF
Lower San Antonio R S
Stoddard's Camp
Pierce Ranch
Day Canyon
Summit
Cajon Pass
138
Cajon Jct
San Bernardino Mountains
PCT
Cajon Mtn
Lytle Creek
Happy Jack's
Glenn Ranch
Scotland
Canyon
Barstow
AT&SF-UP
SP
Green Mtn Inn
Lytle Creek R S
Bonita Falls
Lytle
Fwy
San Sevaine Lookout
San Sevaine Flats
Creek
Texas Point
Sycamore
4000
3000
2000
San Antonio Heights
83
30
15
Highland
Ave
19th
St
Euclid
Ave
Alta Loma
Etiwanda
SP
Sierra
Ave
Cucamonga
66
Foothill
Blvd
Fontana
AT & S F
Upland
Fwy
10
Ontario
steel
mill
SB Co
Rd

The San Gabriels II

The Mountains from Monrovia Canyon to Lytle Creek

John W. Robinson

Big Santa Anita Historical Society

Published by the Big Santa Anita Historical Society
7 North Fifth Avenue Arcadia, California

1st Printing – August 1983

Frontispiece: Winter on the Angeles Crest
by Roy Murphy

Logo: Ernest Benjamin Gray and son Robert Gray
on Echo Rock, Mt. Wilson, 1920.

Pacific Typesetting Company
Monrovia, California

B&K graphic arts
Printing and Lithographing
Monrovia, California

Dedicated to Kenyon De Vore . . . .

for a lifetime devotion to the San Gabriel Mountains

Acknowledgments

Of the several books I have written, this one has special meaning to me. Some of my fondest memories are of overnight hiking trips into the Mount Baldy high country, camping and boating at Crystal Lake when it was a Los Angeles County playground, throwing my first snowball at Curry's Camp Baldy in the 1930s. The eastern San Gabriels are delightful and inviting mountain country with a rich heritage. Uncovering this heritage has been time-consuming but rewarding, largely because of the generous help I have received, the new friends I have gained, who gave unstintingly of their time and effort. Without their assistance this volume would not have been nearly as complete as it is.

The individual who has given most in time and encouragement, as he did with SAN GABRIELS I, is Kenyon De Vore of Monrovia. Kenyon's great knowledge of the San Gabriels is derived from living most of his life within its folds. To Kenyon, this book is dedicated.

Those who provided invaluable historical material on the mountains include Dolores "Flo Flo" Peck, who gave me access to the late Sedley Peck's trunkful of mementos on San Gabriel Canyon; Charles G. Colver, Manager of the San Dimas Experimental Forest; Myron Hotchkiss, historian of Monrovia and its nearby mountain canyons; Bob Chapman, the sage of San Antonio Canyon; Virginia R. Harshman, historian of Lytle Creek; and Arda M. Haenszel of the San Bernardino County Museum.

Others who helped in smaller but important ways include Ruth Curry Burns and her son David Burns of old Camp Baldy, Ralph Slosson and Jack Holtz of Monrovia, Katherine Zadach of the Azusa Historical Society, Grant D. Brown of the Los Angeles County Fire Department, Stanley W. Plummer and Russell Ireland of San Dimas, Orie and Helen Trout of Glendora, J. Donald Sinclair of Aptos, Desmond Surfleet of El Monte, Dee Trent of Claremont, Glen Owens of Arcadia, Patti Wells of Big Pines Ranger Station, the late Odo Stade of Glendora, and the late William V. Mendenhall of Pasadena.

Posthumous thanks go to the late Will H. Thrall, whose work of collecting and preserving the history of the San Gabriel Mountains in *Trails Magazine* and manuscripts at the Henry E. Huntington Library were of priceless value.

The staff of the Henry E. Huntington Library in San Marino was helpful in providing access to manuscripts, rare books, periodicals and Los Angeles newspapers of the 19th century. I also thank the patient ladies of the Los Angeles, Pasadena, Azusa, Covina, Glendora, San Dimas, Pomona, Honnold (Claremont Colleges), Ontario and San Bernardino public libraries who helped track down information and provided access to local newspaper files.

Historical photographs were obtained through the generous assistance of Robert O. Dougan of the Huntington Library, David Streeter of the Pomona Public Library Special Collections, Robert Frampton of Claremont, Dee Trent of Claremont, Katherine Zadach of the Azusa Historical Society, Louise Werner of Alhambra, Charles Clark Vernon of La Mirada, Lucy Wheeler of Covina, and Julia Brown of the California Historical Society, Los Angeles.

The rangers and office personnel of Angeles National Forest deserve commendation for the many little favors they willingly granted this writer.

A special thanks goes to Maureen Cates of Chatsworth for reading the entire manuscript and spotting grammatical and spelling errors with her incredibly discerning eyes.

John W. Robinson
Fountain Valley, California
April 2, 1983

Table of Contents

PERSPECTIVE FROM A MOUNTAINTOP 8
1 EARLY PEOPLES 10
2 MISSIONS AND RANCHOS 13
3 THE GOLD OF ELDORADOVILLE 18
4 A CENTURY OF MINING 21
5 WATER STRUGGLES 45
6 MONROVIA AND SAWPIT CANYONS 73
7 SAN GABRIEL CANYON 81
8 CRYSTAL LAKE HIGH COUNTRY 105
9 DALTON AND SAN DIMAS CANYONS 115
10 THE SAN DIMAS EXPERIMENTAL FOREST 123
11 SAN ANTONIO CANYON 132
12 OLD BALDY 160
13 WILDERNESS 181
14 LYTLE CREEK 185
15 WRIGHTWOOD AND BIG PINES 196
16 THE LITERARY SAN GABRIELS 207
APPENDIX 217
BIBLIOGRAPHY 218
INDEX 223

Old Baldy.

— NILES WERNER

Perspective From A Mountaintop

The first faint glimmers of dawn lighten the eastern sky. Almost imperceptively, an arc of blueness rises from the horizon, and lesser stars begin to fade. The inky silhouettes of surrounding ridges begin to assume definition; gnarled lodgepole pines take on individual identity. Far below, the valley lights flicker and die. Eastward again, the glow behind the distant San Jacintos abruptly brightens, and a tiny point of light bursts into view. Within scant minutes the sun is airborne, casting its golden radiance on nearby crests and turning them luminous orange. Westward, the elongated shadow of our mountain stretches far down the ridgeline and across the still-black chasm of the San Gabriel River's East Fork. As the sun rises higher, the shadow hurries up the ridge and mounts the fore-slope, and soon shrinks to insignificance. A new day has come to Old Baldy.

For our man on the summit, a superb panorama unfolds. Nature's pattern of the peaks, the ridgelines, the canyons and foothills becomes readily evident, as though looking down upon a mammoth relief map. Westward, beyond the yawning gorge of the East Fork, the gray-green mass of Mount Baden-Powell looms above a cluster of sinuous ridges. Closer at hand is the rugged citadel of Iron Mountain. To the east is the jumbled mass of Telegraph, Ontario and Cucamonga peaks, their forested summits only slightly lower than Old Baldy. The brown Mojave Desert and its drab island mountains stretch northward as far as the eye can see. Southward, beyond wrinkled foothills coated with olive-green chaparral, a brownish haze veils the Southern California megalopolis.

If our summit observer had a powerful telescope, he would see, on all sides, evidence of the works of man — paved highways, fireroads, cabins, reservoirs, mine tailings. Only on the steepest slopes and highest peaks would these marks be absent. It may seem incredible that man could be attracted to so wrinkled a landscape, yet attracted he has been, and in great numbers. Few mountain ranges anywhere have been so much viewed, swarmed over, dug into, and built upon as have the San Gabriels. Indians hunted and gathered food and materials from the chaparral-clad slopes. Spaniards and Californios sought water and timber. Anglo pioneers expanded the use of water and timber, and added a feverish quest for gold. To modern man, the mountains have provided hydroelectric power, homes, recreation, and a place to find solitude and relaxation.

There is much to tell here, and this writer has spent considerable time not only in tracking down the story, but in contemplating how best to relate it. Should the book be organized chronologically, topically, or geographically? The final decision represents a compromise. The Indian and Hispanic eras, the mining saga, the water struggles are presented first as integrated chapters, primarily because these stories are better told in this manner. Then geography takes over, starting with the saga of Monrovia and Sawpit canyons and working eastward, canyon by canyon, into the Crystal Lake and Mount Baldy high country, on to Lytle Creek, and finally northward to Wrightwood and Big Pines on the desert slope of the range. A final chapter recounts the literary history of the San Gabriels, what the likes of John Muir, Charles Lummis, Mary Austin and Charles Francis Saunders have written about these splendid mountains.

Everything written on these pages is based on factual references. Because it is designed for the general public rather than as a scholarly dissertation, only the quotations are footnoted. Much of what is written here has previously appeared in scholarly form in several periodicals. Consult the bibliography.

It is hoped that *The San Gabriels II* will prove to be a worthy companion to *The San Gabriels: Southern California Mountain Country,* published by Golden West Books in 1977, which told the story of the western half of the range.

May your acquaintance with the San Gabriels' eastern high country be enhanced by what appears on the ensuing pages.

1

Early Peoples

To the Serrano Indians, who inhabited the eastern San Gabriels centuries before the European set foot in California, Mt. San Antonio (Old Baldy) was a sacred place. According to a Serrano legend, the earliest events in the creation of man occurred on the mountain: "Two brothers — Sea God and Land God — created the land, the sea, the plants and the animals. Then they decided to create man but could not agree on his form, particularly the placing of his eyes. Sea God wanted one eye in front and one in back, while Land God desired both eyes in front. One day when Sea God was away, Land God created man in his present form. When Sea God returned and saw what had been done in his absence, he became very angry and threatened to destroy his brother and man by flooding the land with sea water. At that time all the land was flat. Sea God plunged into the sea and caused huge waves to rise and roll over the land. Land God then raised the hills and the mountains to protect himself and newly-created man, thereby thwarting the evil designs of his brother. The highest mountain — where Land God and man stood — was Mount San Antonio."[1] Another legend said that the Serranos were led from the north by a pure white eagle belonging to Land God. The eagle landed first on Mt. San Antonio, and the people followed and settled there. Later the eagle flew to Mt. San Gorgonio and then to Mt. San Jacinto, each time being followed by the people.[2]

Mountains — particularly high mountains like Old Baldy — were revered and respected by the Serrano people. Not only were they the setting for numerous Indian legends, but they supplied the native people with many of life's necessities and were places of refuge. Indian rancherias (villages) were known to have been located in lower San Antonio Canyon, in Lytle Creek, and on San Sevaine Flats, the latter an oak-shaded hollow situated high on the ridge east of Cucamonga Peak. The name "Serrano" — meaning "Mountaineer" — was given by the Spaniards to these mountain folk of Shoshonean linguistic stock who lived in the eastern San Gabriel and San Bernardino mountains.

The land of the Serranos apparently extended west to the vicinity of San Dimas Canyon. West of this point, in the San Gabriel Mountains and in the flatlands to the south, dwelled the Gabrielino Indians. Anthropologists have given the name "Gabrielino" to these early people because of their assimilation into the Mission San Gabriel community. One of the largest of the Gabrielino villages was Asuksangna, located on a knoll just outside the mouth of San Gabriel Canyon. (The present city of Azusa takes its name from this aboriginal community.)

The people of Asuksangna and other nearby villages left their brush huts and paid frequent visits to the chaparral-clad mountains that towered to the north. The mountains provided the Indians with food and materials for building and hunting. For food, they hunted deer and rabbit, and gathered acorns, seeds, edible roots, wild berries and nuts. They fished in the mountain streams and dried their catches for use during the winter months. Chaparral, which clothes 80 percent of the San Gabriel Mountains, was an abundant source of many necessities. Manzanita berries were pressed for cider and the leaves were smoked. Greasewood provided arrow shafts for hunting, while yucca fibers were utilized for nets and ropes. In short, they used what the land had to offer.

There is abundant evidence that the Gabrielinos used San Gabriel Canyon. Some type of aboriginal habitation — probably a summer campsite for acorn gatherers — was located at Camp Rincon, on a forested bench just below the confluence of the West and North forks of the canyon. Graveyard Canyon, a small tributary of the San Gabriel's East Fork, was so named because of Indian burial mounds once located there, according to canyon historian Sedley

Indian hieroglyphics on boulder in San Gabriel Canyon. Gabrielino and Serrano peoples depended heavily on the San Gabriels for livelihood.
— CHARLES CLARK VERNON

Peck. Another Indian burial ground was uncovered in 1933 near Camp Bonita, farther up the East Fork. These bits of evidence suggest that there may have been a Gabrielino village somewhere on the lower East Fork.

Although the evidence is inconclusive as to whether or not Indians had permanent homes in San Gabriel Canyon, there is no doubt that aboriginal peoples were well acquainted with the region. To obtain food and materials, and to trade with tribes across the mountains, a well-used Indian footpath ascended the main fork of San Gabriel Canyon, turned west up the West Fork then north up Bear Creek, climbed to Islip Saddle on the crest of the range, and dropped down Little Rock Creek to the desert. Until recent years, signs of this ancient trade route were evident in the canyon. The most notable reminders of aboriginal activity were four large boulders bearing ancient colored markings: two in the main canyon across the river from Camp Rincon, one in upper Bear Creek and one in the East Fork.

The two boulders with red and yellow markings near Camp Rincon were allegedly discovered by Azusa pioneer-settler Henry Dalton in the late 1840s. Although the boulders were observed — and fortunately left untouched — by hundreds of miners during the 1860s and 1870s, it was not until 1883 that they were studied and recorded by a trained anthropologist. In the latter year Dr. J. W. Hoffman of the Bureau of Ethnology paid a visit to "Azusa Canon" (as San Gabriel Canyon was usually known in the 19th century) and fully described the colored pictographs on the two boulders.

It was obvious to Hoffman that the colored symbols represented directional markings for those using the cross-range trail. The first boulder showed a figure pointing toward the northwest, or up-canyon. The second boulder, about one hundred feet upstream, indicated the course of travel in greater detail: "The left hand figure appears to place the left hand upon a series of ridges, as if showing pantomimically the rough and ridged country over the mountains. The middle figure represents a gesture which in its present connection may indicate direction of the trail, i.e., toward the left, or northward in an uphill course."[3] Other markings appeared to tell of waterholes and campsites. One figure of an Indian with a weapon chasing another figure probably was a warning of hostile tribes to be encountered on the journey. Hoffman noted that the drawings appeared to be Chemehuevi in origin. The Chemehuevis lived in the Mojave Désert region, an indication that the Mojave tribes, as well as the Gabrielinos, used the San Gabriel Canyon trade route.

Unfortunately, the Camp Rincon boulders, as well as those in Bear Creek and the East Fork, have been vandalized beyond recognition. The former two were washed away or buried in the great flood of March 1938.

Before we leave the subject of the San Gabriel Canyon Indian trail, mention should be made of the distinct possibility that the route was used by desert Indian rustlers during the era of the great ranchos in Southern California (1834-1868). The late historian Robert Glass Cleland has written that "bands of Utes and Mojaves periodically swept across the ranchos from San Gorgonio to Los Angeles, killing unprotected cattle, making off with the *caballadas* (trained roundup horses), and often taking a toll in human life."[4] In 1849 Henry Dalton's Rancho Azusa, just outside the mouth of San Gabriel Canyon, was so harassed by Indian raiders that its *mayordomo* appealed to the citizens of Los Angeles for assistance. As late as 1866 a party of desert Indians armed with bows and arrows massacred the owner of Rancho San Pasqual and one of his employees within the boundaries of the present city of Pasadena. These Indian marauders struck and withdrew across the mountains with alarming swiftness. Although their main avenue of approach appears to have been Cajon Pass, it seems reasonable to assume that some of these desert renegades — particularly those who raided ranchos in the western end of the San Gabriel Valley — utilized the ancient and well-known San Gabriel Canyon route.

San Dimas Canyon, ten miles east of San Gabriel Canyon, also appears to have been an escape route

INDIAN ARTIFACTS OF SAN SEVAINE FLATS
These Mortars are at least 400 years old.

This mortar hole in the top of a granite boulder was eight feet above the ground level. The hole was ten inches across and had been much deeper but was weathered and worn away.

A granite boulder with two mortar holes. In these the Indians ground their acorns to meal with hand-operated pestles.

for renegade Indians. The Serranos, once peaceful but later resentful of Hispanic encroachment, apparently used this route. They watched as bold Ute and Mojave warriors swept over Cajon Pass from the desert to steal cattle and horses from ranchos in the San Bernardino, Pomona and San Gabriel valleys. Then, out of desperation, they changed their way of life. "The example of the daring marauders was too much for the comparatively peaceful but often hungry Serranos, who learned a similar stealth and daring. San Dimas Canyon offered them a royal pathway to beef and fast horses, and once over the ridges along Mount San Antonio their retreat led down into many a devious canyon, such as Lytle Creek, through which they could vanish."[5]

One of those victimized by Serrano marauders was Ygnacio Palomares, co-owner with Ricardo Vejar of Rancho San Jose, located at the foot of the mountains between the present-day communities of San Dimas and Claremont. Granted to Palomares and Vejar by Governor Juan Bautista Alvarado in 1837, Rancho San Jose soon was thriving with great herds of cattle, horses and sheep. The swift horses in particular were sought after by the Indians. On several occasions in the early 1840s, Serranos from San Dimas Canyon swooped down on the herds and made off with scores of the prized animals. Because of these raids, San Dimas Canyon was originally known as Horsethief Canyon. The derivation of the name "San Dimas" for the canyon is uncertain. Saint Dismas was the penitent robber crucified at the side of Christ. Legend has it that the name was first applied to the canyon by Palomares in allusion to the unrepentent Serrano robbers who stole horses from him, in the hope that they might repent their sins as had Saint Dismas, but this story cannot be substantiated by documentary evidence.

Sadly, the Gabrielino and Serrano Indians could never adjust to the coming of the white man and his aggressive ways. By the end of the 1860s these primitive peoples had all but disappeared from the eastern San Gabriel Mountains. Starvation, disease, death at the hands of the white man, removal to reservations — this was the eventual lot of these once-happy Indian mountain dwellers. They are all but forgotten today. "A few place names; a few stone mortars and tools; a few painted rocks; and the brief written accounts by explorers, missionaries and pioneers, preserving a few ideas, habits and words — these are what remain of this Shoshonean people who once ranged the mountains."[6]

1. G. Hazen Shinn, *Shoshonean Days: Recollections of a residence of five years among the Indians of Southern California* (Glendale: The Arthur H. Clark Co., 1941), pp. 34-35.
2. Ibid., pp. 35-36.
3. J. W. Powell (Director), *Fourth Annual Report of the Bureau of Ethnology* (Washington: Gov. Printing Office, 1886), pp. 156-157.
4. Robert Glass Cleland, *The Cattle on A Thousand Hills* (San Marino: The Huntington Library, 1951), p. 64.
5. Bernice Eastman Johnston, *California's Gabrielino Indians* (Los Angeles: The Southwest Museum, 1962), p. 18.
6. W. W. Robinson, *The Forest and The People: The Story of Angeles National Forest* (Los Angeles: Title Insurance and Trust Co., 1946), p. 8.

2

Missions And Ranchos

On a warm July day in 1769 Gaspar de Portola and an intrepid band of padres and soldiers, trekking from San Diego to Monterey in the most famous expedition in California history, reached the marshy banks of a river they called "San Miguel Arcangel." Father Juan Crespi, diarist of the Portola party, made the following entry for July 30:

> After we two priests had celebrated Mass with all the people present, we started about seven and descended the hill, continuing to the north-northwest . . . After traveling for an hour through a valley we came to an arroyo of water which flows among many green marshes, their banks covered with willows and grapes, blackberries, and innumerable Castilian rosebushes loaded with roses. In the midst of the verdure runs a good channel of water which when measured was found to have a volume of three quarters of a square yard. It runs along the foot of the mountains, and can easily be used to irrigate the large area of good land the valley has. The valley has a length from north to south of about three leagues, and is surrounded by ranges of hills. The one of the north is very high and dark and has many corrugations, and seems to run farther to the west.[1]

Father Crespi gives us the first written description of the San Gabriel River and, to the north a few miles, the "high and dark" San Gabriel Mountains. The party camped that night along Rio San Miguel Arcangel, probably not more than four or five miles below the mouth of San Gabriel Canyon.

With the coming of the Spaniards, life in the pleasant valleys below the mountains changed forever. Mission San Gabriel Arcangel was founded along the grassy banks of Rio Hondo on September 8, 1771. In September 1775, the padres moved the mission to its present location, one league north of the original site, for better agricultural facilities. The Gabrielino Indians were incorporated into the mission community, and within a few years all but a handful of these once-content people were serving the padres, many of them by farming mission lands and tending the large mission herds of horses and cattle that ranged along the foot of the mountains as far east as Cucamonga.

It was not long until the padres knew and gave names to the numerous streams that emit from the south rampart of the San Gabriel Mountains. The river that flowed past the mission soon became known as Arroyo San Gabriel, and the high chaparral-clad mountains from which the river emitted were called La Sierra de San Gabriel, so mentioned by Father Francisco Garces in his diary entry of April 10, 1776.[2] Two years earlier, while traveling northward with the first Anza Expedition, Father Garces made first mention of San Antonio Creek; his diary entry for March 21, 1774 reads: "Going seven leagues to the northwest, we came to an arroyo called San Antonio. Here there are many bears and sycamores."[3] Some of the place names failed to last. In mission days Big Dalton Canyon was known as "El Canon de la Boca Negra" (The Canyon with the Black Mouth), supposedly because "when the mission fathers looked at Mt. San Antonio (Old Baldy) from the mission, the oak trees, with their dark foliage, located at the entrance to the canyon, stood in deep contrast to the snow on the mountain."[4]

What did the Spanish padres call the San Gabriel Mountains as a whole? Historians have long been confused about this. Was it *Sierra Madre* (Mother Range) or *Sierra de San Gabriel?* The answer, derived after much research by this writer, is that both terms were used. *Sierra Madre,* however, was used in a more general sense, covering all the main mountain chains from northern Baja California north to the Tehachapi knot. The earliest use of the term *Sierra Madre* found by this writer was in the diary of the great Jesuit explorer-missionary Eusebio Francisco Kino. Father Kino made a number of explorations northward from his base at Mission Dolores in Pimeria Alta (Sonora, Mexico), looking for a land route to California. On November 6, 1706 he gazed westward from a hill above the

Mission San Gabriel, with Old Baldy in distance. Timber for the mission buildings were obtained somewhere in the San Gabriel Mountains, the exact location unknown. The Spaniards generally stayed clear of the mountains.
– FERDINAND DEPPE PAINTING (1832), HENRY E. HUNTINGTON LIBRARY

lower Colorado River and noticed a long chain of mountains on the western horizon. He called these *La Sierra Madre de California.*[5] In the second Anza Expedition of 1775-1776, which forged an overland route from Sonora to California, the diaries of both Fray Pedro Font and Fray Francisco Garces refer to the general mountain chains of Southern California as *Sierra Madre.*[6] It appears evident that the Spanish used *Sierra Madre* for the Santa Barbara, San Gabriel, San Bernardino, San Jacinto and San Diego ranges, possibly because they looked at these mountains as the backbone of California, from which other ranges sprang.

La Sierra de San Gabriel for the mountains north of San Gabriel Mission was used by Father Garces in his diary entry of April 10, 1776, indicating that from the earliest days the padres used this name for the mountains.[7] *Cierra de San Gabriel* is found in mission records as early as 1806.[8] Fray Jose Maria de Zalvidea, in an exploration of Antelope Valley and the Mojave Desert in 1806, specifically stated, "Beyond the valley is the mountain range of San Gabriel."[9] There is plenty of evidence that the Spaniards knew these mountains as the San Gabriels.

Although the padres provided names for the mountains and the arroyos flowing from them, they confined most of their activities to the lowlands. The mountains were useful mainly as a source of water; numerous irrigation ditches were dug from canyon mouths to mission fields. Vaqueros occasionally retrieved strayed livestock from San Gabriel and San Antonio canyons. Even with their thick leather chaps, the mission vaqueros found the dense chaparral that coated the lower slopes of the mountains uninviting.

It seems almost certain that lumber for mission buildings was obtained from the San Gabriel Mountains. The early buildings of Mission San Gabriel "were of necessity built of willow poles, or saplings, and reed, whose chinks were filled with mud."[10] However, in the construction of later mission buildings, pine timbers were used. Franciscan historian Maynard Geiger writes that, in 1788, "the roof of the church had been removed and replaced with beams of pine overlaid with earth."[11] The late Zephyrin Engelhardt, authority on the California missions, reported that much building occurred at the mission in the years 1803 and 1804 and that "all [the buildings] were roofed with pine timbers and covered with tiles."[12] Nowhere in the sparse contemporary literature concerning Mission San Gabriel is there any definite statement as to just where the lumber was obtained. But logic points to

Rancho San José, in the Pomona Valley, with Mt. San Antonio as backdrop. The rancheros used water and timber from the mountains, and herded their cattle in the lower canyons.
– ELMER WACHTEL PAINTING, LAND OF SUNSHINE

one of the nearby mountain canyons. San Gabriel Canyon is a strong candidate. It was close at hand, traversed by a well-traveled Indian trail, and possessed abundant pine timber in its upper reaches. Sawpit Canyon above present-day Monrovia is another possibility. The canyon received its name because of an ancient sawpit, dating back well before the American occupation, that was located near the canyon mouth.

The mission era drew to a rapid close with the enactment by the Mexican government of the Secularization Act of 1833. No longer were the Franciscan padres masters of the vast mission lands or the Indians who toiled on them. The end of the missions ushered in the golden age of the great private ranchos, the time of "The Cattle on a Thousand Hills."

Three great ranchos occupied the valleys and foothills below the eastern San Gabriel Mountains. West to east, they were Rancho Azusa, Rancho San Jose and Rancho Cucamonga.

Rancho Azusa, embracing the lands outside the mouth of San Gabriel Canyon, was granted to Don Luis Arenas, former *alcalde* of Los Angeles and a prominent political figure in Mexican California, in 1842. Arenas built an adobe home on the mound-like hill just east of the present-day Azusa business district. He began construction of an irrigation ditch from the mouth of San Gabriel Canyon, but accomplished little else in his short tenure. Deeply in debt, he offered to sell Rancho Azusa and his one-third interest in neighboring Rancho San Jose. He quickly found a buyer in Henry Dalton, an enterprising and ambitious newcomer to California.

Henry Dalton, born in England in 1803, set sail for South America at the age of fourteen. He spent the next twenty-five years of his life in Peru, building up a modest fortune as a merchant. He came to Southern California in 1843 and promptly bought several lots in the pueblo of Los Angeles. But Dalton's real ambition was to be a ranchero and he was not long in satisfying this desire. On December 24, 1844, he paid Luis Arenas $7,000 and became the owner of 4400-acre Rancho Azusa and Arenas' one-third interest in San Jose. Three years later he paid Hugo Reid $2,700 for Rancho Santa Anita to the west. By 1847 Henry Dalton was a major Southern California landowner, second only to Don Abel Stearns. His holdings extended along the foothills of the San Gabriel Mountains from present-day Pasadena to San Dimas. To complete his acceptance into the Mexican Californio community, he married into the prominent Zamorano family, embraced Roman Catholicism and was rechristened Enrique Dalton.

Don Enrique Dalton built his hacienda midway in his vast domain, on Rancho Azusa de Dalton. Here, on the same slight rise where Arenas had so briefly lived, Don Enrique fashioned a thick-walled adobe home. The beams, rafters and shakes for the roof were split and hewn from the trees of San Gabriel Canyon. Nearby on his feudal-like estate he erected a grist mill, winery, tannery and even a small cigar factory. There were barns, stables, corrals and a village complete with church and schoolhouse for the Indian families who labored on rancho fields. These fields stretched as far as the eye could see to the west, and eastward to the hills of Glendora, and were abundant with grain, vegetables and grape vines. For irrigation purposes, Dalton completed the Arenas ditch from the mouth of San Gabriel Canyon.

Dalton was well acquainted with "Azusa Canon," as San Gabriel Canyon was then known. His cattle and horses grazed within its lower confines. He took timber from its upper reaches. He and his friends hunted deer and bear on the wooded slopes above the canyon. In 1845 Dalton petitioned the Mexican authorities for title to the canyon and the mountains lying north of Azusa. A committee of the Los Angeles *ayuntamiento* (town council) reported favorably on his request for "the mountains and canons of Azusa stream and Boca Negra, excepting San Dimas," but the grant was never made.

Dalton's neighbors to the east were Ygnacio Palomares and Ricardo Vejas, owners of Rancho San Jose. Granted to Palomares and Vejar by Governor Alvarado in 1837, Rancho San Jose soon was thriving with great herds of cattle, horses and sheep. Verdant fields of corn, potatoes, beans and peppers were nourished by the cool waters of Arroyo San Antonio, brought from the canyon via a seven-mile irrigation ditch. Vaqueros working for Palomares and Vejar often recovered straying cattle and horses in San Antonio and San Dimas canyons and were well acquainted with the mountains.

Arroyo San Antonio served as the boundary line between Rancho San Jose and Rancho Cucamonga to the east. The name "Cucamonga" was derived from an old Gabrielino village located just east of today's community of Cucamonga. The meaning has been variously interpreted as "Sandy Place" or "Place of Many Springs." Governor Alvarado granted Rancho Cucamonga to Tiburcio Tapia, Los Angeles merchant and civic leader, in 1839. Tapia built his adobe home atop what is known today as Red Hill, and watered his cattle and corn fields from Arroyo Cucamonga and the abundant springs below the hill.

The era of the great cattle ranchos in Southern California drew to a painful close after the coming of the Anglo-Americans in the late 1840s and 1850s. High taxes, the notorious Land Act of 1851 questioning all Spanish and Mexican land grants, squatters, long court battles and a disastrous drought in the 1860s combined to ruin the rancho owners.

The industrious and aggressive Anglos who succeeded the rancheros and took their land gave more attention to the mountains that rose on the northern skyline. They not only coveted the water that poured forth from the mountain streams, but they sought mineral treasures hidden deep in back country ridges and canyons. The San Gabriels were "opened up" by prospectors in amazingly short time.

1 Herbert Bolton, *Fray Juan Crespi: Missionary Explorer on The Pacific Coast, 1769-1774* (Berkeley, 1927), pp. 143-144.

2. Elliott Coues, *On The Trail of A Spanish Pioneer: The Diary and Itinerary of Francisco Garces* (New York, 1900), I, p. 265.

3. Bolton, *Anza's California Expeditions* (Berkeley, 1930), II, p. 346.

4. Donald Pflueger, *Glendora: The Annals of A Southern California Community* (Claremont, 1951) p. 4.

5. Bolton, *Kino's Historical Memoir of Pimeria Alta* (Berkeley, 1948), II, p. 206.

6. Bolton, *Font's Complete Diary* (Berkeley, 1933), p. 122; Coues, I, p. 193.

7. Coues, I, p. 265.

8. Erwin G. Gudde, *California Place Names* (Berkeley, 1969), 3rd Ed., p. 285.

9. S. F. Cook, "Colonial Expeditions to the Interior of California: Central Valley, 1800-1820," *University of California Anthropological Records,* Vol. 16, No. 6, pp. 245-247.

10. Craig E. Salcido, *Guidebook For Mission San Gabriel* (San Gabriel, no date), p. 5.

11. Maynard Geiger, "The Building of Mission San Gabriel, 1771-1828," *Southern California Quarterly,* L, 1 (March 1968), p. 36.

12. Zephyrin Engelhardt, *San Gabriel Mission and The Beginnings of Los Angeles* (San Gabriel, 1927), p. 74.

Two views of Los Angeles with the San Gabriel Mountains in the background. The top painting, by William Hutton in 1848, shows the mountains as nebulous mounds with little attention to topographic detail. This was the usual practice in mid-19th century landscape scenes. The bottom drawing, by an unknown artist in 1857, is unique in that it accurately shows the topographic detail of the mountains. Clearly discernable are (left to right) Josephine, Strawberry and San Gabriel Peaks, the long flat ridge of Mt. Wilson, Monrovia Peak, and the dim outline of Old Baldy in the right distance. – HENRY E. HUNTINGTON LIBRARY

3

The Gold Of Eldoradoville

High in the eastern San Gabriel Mountains, between the precipitous spurs of Mount Baden-Powell and the great gray mass of Old Baldy, is born the East Fork of the San Gabriel River. Through the ages, this powerful mountain torrent has carved a deep groove through the bedrock. The river churns southward through a narrow gorge, then elbows west to join the West and North forks near Rincon. The united waters flow south into the San Gabriel Valley.

Over countless eons of geologic time, the East Fork of the San Gabriel has carried within its flow more than water. Honey-combed in the high ridges that form a horseshoe around the river's headwaters are quartz veins containing gold. Flecks of this precious metal, eroded away and washed downstream, have salted the riverbed for miles.

Gold has lured and enticed prospectors by the hundreds into the East Fork for more than a century. It has been panned, sluiced, long tommed, hydraulicked and blasted out of the canyon gravels and hillsides. Estimates of the total yield vary from around $4 million to over $13 million.

The exact date when gold mining commenced on the East Fork of the San Gabriel has not been determined. There are stories of Indians and Spanish padres digging for gold long before the arrival of the Anglo. Such tales cannot be verified and must be viewed as fanciful myths. The first American miners explored the East Fork probably in the early 1850s. It is difficult to pin down a date since prospectors, working singly or in pairs, drifted from place to place, receiving little attention unless they made a strike.

The traditional story goes that some prospectors led by a Captain Hannager, drifting down from the Kern River mines, entered the mountains via Cajon Pass and penetrated to the headwaters of the East Fork. Here they found gold and stayed to recover small amounts. First news of the strike appeared in the *Los Angeles Star* of September 21, 1854: "There has been some excitement this past week about the new gold diggings on the headwaters of the San Gabriel. We have met several persons who have been out prospecting and although they found gold of the best quality, differ very much as regards the richness of the mines. The Crab Hollow diggings are now considered the best and will pay from two to five cents to the pan. It is understood that if the river can be turned from its present bed, some rich leads may be found and big piles realized."

For five years, minor placer mining activities continued on the East Fork, with a reported average yield of six and seven dollars per day, to the man. Then, early in 1859, some prospectors struck it rich and a rush was on. By May the East Fork was being prospected over almost its entire length, and promising new discoveries were made.

The *Los Angeles Star* sent a correspondent into the canyon to report on the excitement. On May 28, 1859 he wrote, "The canyon through which the San Gabriel flows has been prospected about forty miles up, and in every instance, the 'color' has been obtained . . . All who are in operation are taking out from $2 to $10 per day to the man." By July 23, the *Star's* correspondent stated that there were 300 men working in the canyon, including a large number of Mexican miners. And many continued to pour in.

In July stage service opened to the canyon diggings. The Roberts and Williams Stage Line offered tri-weekly trips, leaving Los Angeles at 7 a.m. and arriving at the mines by 4 p.m. The fare was set at $3 to the canyon mouth and $6 to "Prospect Bar" in the East Fork.

With the large number of men working in the canyon, it was not long until a mining camp took shape to supply the miners' needs and relieve them of their gold. The *Star* of May 28, 1859 gave first mention of a rudimentary settlement consisting of "a boarding house, 2 or 3 stores, blacksmith shop, butcher shop, etc." The settlement seems to have been initially called Prospect Bar. Later it became known as Eldoradoville, and it was located four miles up the East Fork, near the confluence of that stream and Cattle Canyon.

Mining continued at a hectic pace all summer and fall. A number of companies were formed to work claims along the river and on the slopes. These mining companies were usually organized by one man, who either paid wages or agreed to split the profits with the five to twenty miners working with him. Taking advantage of technical know-how and manpower, the companies began to use more profitable methods to recover gold. The *Southern Vineyard* (August 23, 1859) described some of the methods used: "Among the most extensive mining operations upon the river are those of the Little Falls Co. and McClure & Co. The former have constructed a flume several hundred feet in length, and of sufficient capacity to carry the waters of the San Gabriel at a high stage. All the modern facilities have been brought into requisition, viz waterwheels, pumps, derricks, railroads, etc., all of which they have accomplished by their industry in the short space of three months . . . The latter of the parties named above are engaged in putting up a hydraulic pump for the purpose of washing a hill claim."

A name mentioned often as one of the leading miners in the canyon was Thomas Driver. The *Star* (November 5, 1859) reported that "The Driver claim is being worked on an extensive scale. A dam has been constructed which lays bare a large section of the river bed, which they have found quite rich . . . This company cleared $1,000 for their past week's work."

Those who know the San Gabriel River are aware of its occasional intemperate moods, when floodwaters ravage the canyon bottom. One very rainy night in late November, 1859, the miners were introduced to this vicious aspect of the river. The *Star* of December 3 described the results: "We regret to have to record the total demolition of the mining works in the San Gabriel Canyon . . . So tremendous was the force of the torrent rushing down, that it swept away as chaff all the mining works erected on the river — dams, wheels, sluices, everything, in fact. The amount of damage sustained by the miners cannot be calculated."

But the obituary was premature. Within the month, the miners were back at work, rebuilding their dams, waterwheels and sluices, and taking out as much gold as ever.

The *Star* of March 10, 1860 reported that, "There are at present eight companies engaged in bringing water by means of ditching and fluming of their claims on the different hills, so as to ground sluice or hydraulic wash, when practicable." The newspaper also announced that, as a result of a meeting of the miners at Falvey and Cullin's Store, the Eldoradoville Mining District had been formed — the first use of the name "Eldoradoville." The mining district was defined as "Commencing at the junction of the waters of the main San Gabriel River and Cattle Canyon Creek, thence following the course of the main river toward the head, two miles above the claim known as the Nevada claim, and running on both sides of the river between said points and at right angles to the river course, to the centre of the main ridge on both sides." An elaborate set of mining laws, embracing 27 items, was enacted. The *Star's* correspondent concluded his report by predicting that "The returns of gold dust from the San Gabriel will be second to those of no other river in the state."

The town of Eldoradoville sprang to life after the 1859 flood, a rowdy successor to Prospect Bar. Sedley Peck described it as "The Downieville of the South — a rough, tough miner's town." The law didn't exist here; "justice" was administered by the muzzle of a six-shooter or the blade of a knife. The *Star's* correspondent complained of Eldoradoville's lack of order (March 2, 1861): "We have frequent disturbances of the peace here, and as we have no local officers, rowdyism and sanguinary assaults are of very frequent occurrence. As there is no punishment at hand, parties get more bold in their nefarious practices. If death is not the result, there is no notice taken of the number of assaults with knife or pistol. At one o'clock yesterday morning, one Mexican or Indian killed another, by stabbing him in the breast with a knife. The apathy with which the white men received this news was, to say the least, degrading to our sense of civilized refinement. But as persons are allowed to flourish with impunity deadly weapons, of course this must be expected."

Eldoradoville boasted three stores and, according to Peck, a half dozen saloons, with their gambling and dance halls running wide open. John Robb, who

These photos show two of the early placer mining methods used by prospectors in the 1850s and '60s. The miner at left is using a sluice box to recover gold from the stream. To the right, the miners are utilizing a long tom for the same purpose. Both of these methods were used by San Gabriel Canyon miners.
– (left) MONTANA HISTORICAL SOCIETY, (right) CALIFORNIA HISTORICAL SOCIETY

allegedly spent more than sixty years in the canyon, told Peck that he "made more money by running the sawdust from the floor of the Union Saloon through his sluice box than he was able to make from real mining, so prodigal and careless of their pokes were the miners and gamblers of those days."

Suprisingly, Eldoradoville's miners showed a strong interest in politics. The crucial election of 1860 was watched with great interest by the canyon prospectors. Most of them were Democrats, with sympathies between North and South closely divided. Democratic political rallies were held in the canyon during the summer and fall months, and several candidates for county and state offices felt it worthwhile to pay campaign visits to Eldoradoville. Miners and other canyon residents turned out in full force on election day. The results, published in the *Star* of November 24, 1860, showed a clear victory for Democratic candidates. Among the presidential contenders, Northern Democrat Stephen Douglas led with 34 votes, followed by Southern Democrat John Breckenridge with 23 votes. Abraham Lincoln came in a poor third with 14 votes.

During the Civil War years there apparently was some undercover pro-Confederate activity in the canyon. Gustav Brown, an Army detective assigned to watch secessionist movements in Southern California, reported that the Knights of the Golden Circle, a secret pro-Confederate organization, had a chapter in "The San Gabriel Mines" with a membership of 27. Brown warned that the Knights had secret hideouts in the mountains, were well armed, and were prepared to open guerrilla warfare when the appropriate occasion presented itself. But no such "occasion" ever took place.

Mining continued at a hectic pace through 1861 and into 1862. The *Star* (August 17, 1861) stated that "Wells, Fargo & Co. reported the shipments of gold from their Los Angeles office during the last six months as averaging $15,000 a month," and most of it came from San Gabriel Canyon.

Eldoradoville died as it had lived – violently. During the night of January 17-18, 1862 a torrential cloudburst hit the mountains. Early the next morning a flood of churning gray water swept down the East Fork, obliterating everything in its path. As the men and women of Eldoradoville scrambled up the hillsides to safety, the shanty town was literally washed away, lock, stock and barrel, as were all the canyon-bottom works of the miners. Shacks, whiskey barrels, groceries, beds, roulette wheels, sluices, long toms, wing dams and China pumps were swept clean out of the mountains into the floodplain of the San Gabriel Valley. Where the day before there existed a town, nothing remained but mud and boulders.

Thus ended boom days on the East Fork. The miners headed elsewhere, most of them to a new gold strike along the lower Colorado River. One of them, a German immigrant named Jacob Waltz, left for Arizona, the Superstition Mountains, and immortality as the discoverer of the legendary Lost Dutchman Mine.

Although mining continued in San Gabriel Canyon until recent years, it never again approached the scale of the 1859-1862 period.

4

A Century Of Mining

The Eldoradoville gold excitement sent prospectors scurrying into other areas of the mountains. The North Fork of the San Gabriel, San Antonio Canyon, Lytle Creek and even the upper slopes of Old Baldy felt the trod of miners' boots and the thud of their tools. Streambeds were turned upside down, tunnels were bored, hillsides were washed away, and all manner of mining equipment was hauled into canyons and up precipitous slopes. The scars of many of these ventures are still visible today.

The first strike, outside of the San Gabriel's East Fork, was made on Lytle Creek, at the east end of the mountains, in early 1864. The *Los Angeles Star* of February 6, 1864 gave first news of the find: "We are informed that gold has been discovered in paying quantities on Lytle Creek west of San Bernardino. Parties at work speak favorably of the prospect. One company which has been there but a short time, after washing up, realized $75 to the hand." In the next few months, hundreds of hopeful prospectors rushed into the canyon to establish claims. The average return, according to the *Star,* was about six dollars in gold per day — a tidy wage in the 1860s.

Violence flared over allegations of claim-jumping. The *Star* (July 2, 1864) reported a fatal encounter in which Abbott, one of the original Lytle Creek miners, shot and killed a prospector named Keir when the latter refused to leave the former's claim. Abbott was charged with murder and brought into San Bernardino to stand trial; his fate is unknown.

The excitement continued into 1865. The *Los Angeles News* (April 29, 1865) reported, "The miners are engaged in working and prospecting for several miles upwards. A regular express runs three times a week from San Bernardino to Texas Point, the first mining camp in the canon . . . The Abbott claim, which was the first discovered and worked, after much expense and trouble, is still paying very good wages . . . In the Yellow Jacket claim, further up the canon, Mr. Levick, the superintendent, has been sinking a shaft in the bottom of the gulch to ascertain the depth of the bed rock. By a continuous bailing of water and working three shifts of hands, night and day, they have succeeded in reaching the bed rock just forty feet deep from the bottom of the gulch . . . More men are making good wages, and less are working upon uncertainties in prospecting, than in any other mining locality . . . Where a thousand men could work to advantage, there are now scarcely one hundred."

Texas Point, near the canyon entrance, mentioned above, became the scene of the first successful, large-scale hydraulic mining venture in Southern California. The Hardpending Company, financed by New York capital, acquired the property in 1867 and commenced installing the latest in hydraulic equipment. Under the direction of a Captain Winder, a flume five miles long was built, carrying 600 miner's inches of water from the upper canyon to Texas Point. The flume emptied into a reservoir above the mine, from which large hoses carried the water at tremendous pressure to the gold-bearing gravel and dirt. The great force thus generated literally blasted away the hillsides. Forty men, mostly Chinese from the northern diggings, were employed and the take reportedly reached $2,000 per week.

An old miner once told historian Will Thrall, "Say, did you ever see a pan full of gold? Well I never did but once and that was at Texas Point. I was there at a clean up and saw them fill a largest size gold pan, heaped up, with nuggets and fine gold. Oh boy! but that was a sight."[1]

In 1869 the Hardpending Company sold Texas Point to a company of Frenchmen headed by Louis Abadie. Abadie continued and expanded upon the hydraulic mining in the early 1870s. He is reported to have realized $50,000 for his efforts one year. Just when the Texas Point mine ceased operations is unknown, but it was sometime before 1880. A contributing factor to its demise was a dispute with the canyon placer miners over the large amount of water taken from the creek by the five-mile flume. During

The Texas Point mine near the mouth of Lytle Creek was the first larg scale hydraulic mining venture in Southern California. Water was carri to the mine via a five-mile flume from the upper canyon. Texas Point was active from 1867 until around 1880, recovering over a half million dollars in gold. This scene, ca. 1870, shows the boom guiding the heav hydraulic monitor as it sends a powerful spray of water into the gold-bearing hillside. – WILL THRALL COLLECTION

Texas Point Mine, Lytle Creek, about 1870. Gold-bearing gravels are washed through the rifled sluice box, to be recovered when the monitor is periodically shut off. – HENRY E. HUNTINGTON LIBRARY

The monitor, directed by one man, sends a powerful jet of water into the hillside, washing the gold-bearing gravels into the long sluice box.
– HENRY E. HUNTINGTON LIBRARY

seasons of little rainfall, the Texas Point flume deprived the lower canyon of all but a trickle of water, much to the disgust of the local gold panners. Some of them stole up the hillside at night and repeatedly broke the flume, causing angry arguments and at least one killing. The flume controversy, necessitating continuous repairs, along with the depletion of gold recovery from the hillside, spelled the end of the Texas Point mine.

A tall, bare cliff, to the left of the road near the entrance to Lytle Creek Canyon, marks the site of this historic mine, still plainly visible today.

Placer mining continued along Lytle Creek into the 1890s. It was probably exceeded only by the East Fork of the San Gabriel in the richness of its placer deposits. The *Star* of March 31, 1878 stated, "Lytle Creek canon has yielded over a million in gold dust, and yet a laborer can pay expenses today with a simple pan and sluice box."

The *Los Angeles Times* (July 4, 1889) sent a correspondent into Lytle Creek Canyon in 1889. He reported a good many placer deposits in the canyon, but only a few of them were being worked. The most extensive claim was being worked by George Turk, described as an enterprising mountaineer, a giant of a man who always wore a wide sombrero. For several miles below Turk's claim, the creek was described as "looking as if all the laundries in Chinatown had broken loose." A lady visitor inquired as to why the creek was so filthy. A miner answered, "Turk's washing today." "Why," exclaimed the lady, "he must get his clothes awful dirty!"

According to canyon historian Will Thrall, there were about 100 miners working the Lytle Creek placers in 1890, taking out an average of about four dollars per man per day.

The end of large-scale hydraulic mining efforts in Lytle Creek Canyon came in 1893, when a water company secured a court injunction to halt pollution of the stream. Since then, only a handful of prospectors have tried their luck along Lytle Creek, but not with any outstanding success.

After the Lytle Creek strike of 1864, the next gold discovery in the San Gabriel Mountains occurred high on the slopes of Mount San Antonio — better known as "Old Baldy." But the date that mining began on Old Baldy and the name of the discoverer remain obscure.

The traditional story goes that gold was discovered by a miner named Banks, who came across the ridge from the placer diggings in Lytle Creek to make his find just below Baldy Notch in 1862.[2] This story is probably not true.

During the middle decades of the 19th century, Southern California newspapers gave coverage to mining discoveries and developments throughout the southern half of the state. A study of these newspapers makes it possible to pin down some dates and places and discount others. The discovery of gold in Lytle Creek and the ensuing rush was extensively covered. Since Banks allegedly came from the Lytle Creek placers to make his discovery at Baldy Notch, it is unlikely that this occurred before the development of the Lytle Creek diggings in 1864. Furthermore, a search of San Bernardino County mining records reveals that the name of Banks does not appear until 1882, when he recorded his Criterion claim near Baldy Notch.[3]

A search of newspaper files reveals that the first mention of gold discoveries near Old Baldy was not made until 1870. The *San Bernardino Guardian* of September 24, 1870 reported, "Mr. F. L. Riche of Cucamonga was in town on Saturday last, and showed us some specimens of gold that reminded us of the old '49 times. The gold was coarse, hardly any of the pieces weighing less than 25 cents, and some of them ranging as high as $5 or $6 in value. He informed us that the gold came from the head of San Antonio creek, some fifteen miles from Cucamonga, and was brought to that place to exchange for provisions, etc. About a year ago, some parties found gold in paying quantities up the same creek, but as water was scarce, they did not persevere in their labors. This gold is of a fine quality, and from the statements made by the discoverers to Mr. Riche, the diggings are extensive and will pay splendid wages."

From the foregoing report, it appears that gold was discovered near the head of San Antonio Canyon in 1869, but the returns were not profitable because of a lack of water for placer recovery.

Further discoveries were made in 1871. The *Los Angeles Star* (October 24, 1871) stated, "Reports were floating around town yesterday to the effect that a rich gold lode has been found in the neighborhood of Old Baldy mountain, by a party of prospectors from this city." Unfortunately, the *Star* did not follow up this report, although very brief mention of gold and silver mining in San Antonio Canyon was made in 1872 and 1873.

Based on contemporary newspaper reports, it appears that gold was mined near Baldy Notch by persons unknown in the years 1869 to 1873. Then there was a five-year inactive period, followed by a rash of mining activity in 1878 and 1879.

The *Los Angeles Herald* of September 24, 1878 reported, "A party of eight, fully equipped with an old time miners' outfit, started from Pomona the other day for the new treasure region at the foot of 'Old Baldy,' recently discovered by Mr. Joe Clark of Pomona. They propose to get out a couple of tons of rock, which they will send to San Francisco for assay. The prospectors are all men of energy and 'go' and should the ledge come up to their expectations lively times may be looked for in that region ere long." Joe Clark, mentioned as the discoverer of the gold ledge in the above account, is the first name to be associated with mining in the Mt. San Antonio region.

In the summer of 1879, judging by newspaper accounts, activity increased at the Baldy mines. The *Herald* of May 14, 1879 described placer diggings worked by miner W. H. Bard: "They go about twenty feet to bed rock, finding there eighteen inches of pay gravel and water enough to use a rocker. The gold is quite coarse, however, and much of it is picked out with the fingers. One chunk was taken out which weighed nearly two pounds and was worth about $400."

The *Herald* of July 4, 1879 reported six companies on "Old Baldy," all busy sinking shafts and inclines and "confident of striking it rich."

Another source of information on early mining in the Mt. Baldy region is the annual reports of the U.S. Army's Wheeler Survey, an ambitious project to map the territory of the United States west of the 100th Meridian, directed by Lt. George M. Wheeler. The annual report for 1878 stated that the San Antonio Mining District was first organized in 1872 and reorganized in 1878. The report described the general location and types of mines: "Mineral croppings are found in the canon on either side of the creek; and one ledge is situated near the summit of San Antonio Peak. None of them have yet been developed to any extent. The principal mines are the Shell Bark, Gilbert, and Elmore, all placers; and the Clark, near the summit of San Antonio, and the Red, White and Blue, on the east side of the canon, both quartz." The following year (1879), Wheeler reported that "Mining in San Antonio Canon has just received an impetus from new discoveries made there, and a number of parties are at work washing or prospecting."

The early 1880's were apparently good years for the miners working on the slopes of Old Baldy. The Criterion Mine staked by James Banks and the Grubstake Mine of George Turk were filed in 1882 and extensively developed and operated for several

Hydraulic mining at the Hocumac Mine, Baldy Notch, 1894. Water for this operation was brought over from upper San Antonio Creek via a two-mile flume to a reservoir just above the mine. Full scale hydraulic mining in the Baldy area was brought to an abrupt close in 1895, when the San Antonio Water Company secured an injunction prohibiting the miners from polluting the waters of San Antonio Creek. – HENRY E. HUNTINGTON LIBRARY

years. The Criterion soon became known simply as the "Banks Mine" and was much the larger of the two operations. Both of these mines at Baldy Notch were of the placer type — the gold being found loose in sand and gravel in a gully just south of the Notch. They were worked mainly by the hydraulic process, water being discharged on the gravels at great pressure. The water supply was always a problem. The drainage area around Baldy Notch was far too small to supply more than a fraction of the water needs. A partial solution to the problem was the construction of several small reservoirs to collect water obtained from melting snow. But this technique was deficient, allowing for hydraulic operations only for short periods of each day during the months of snow-melt, mainly in May, June and into July.

Apparently a peak year for the Banks Mine was 1883. Four cabins had been built just above the mine and a rough wagon road constructed over the divide from Lytle Creek. Via this precipitous road, all supplies and equipment for the miners and their families were brought up.

In June 1884, after a severe late-season storm, the families were trapped by huge snow drifts at the Banks Mine. When word reached the Pomona Valley, a relief party of 17 men was organized, each man carrying 25 pounds of supplies for the marooned families. Bucking deep snowdrifts and felling trees to cross swollen streams, they struggled for three days to reach Baldy Notch. There, they found the snow-bound men, women and children were passing from cabin to cabin through tunnels within ten-foot snowdrifts, and their food supplies had dwindled to ten pounds of rice.[4]

The 1890s saw the climax and then the abrupt end of major gold mining ventures near Mt. San Antonio. The reopening of the Banks and Grubstake mines under new ownership, along with a rash of new claims, made the Baldy Notch area a beehive of activity during the years 1891 to 1895. In 1893, an Omaha-based concern headed by three businessmen — Holcomb, Cushion and Mackay — bought all of these claims and consolidated them into the Hocumac Mining Company — the name being deriv-

Two of the cabins at Miners' Camp, Baldy Notch, 1894. Above the cabins can be seen the dirt road that brought supplies and equipment up from Lytle Creek.
– HENRY E. HUNTINGTON LIBRARY.

ed from a combination of the beginning letters of each owner's name.

The shortage of water, long the limiting factor in hydraulic mining at Baldy Notch, was at last solved by the construction of a two-mile pipeline from the headwaters of San Antonio Creek. The wood and iron flume took in water from the 7600-foot level of the creek, about a mile above San Antonio Falls, then contoured southeastward along the slopes to a point several hundred feet above the mines, where it filled a sixty by forty-foot reservoir. "The water was brought from the reservoir, at a 'head' of 400 feet, and forced through a three-inch nozzle, so jointed that one man was able to direct the stream. Its power was prodigious, and it tore out the auriferous gravel at an impressive rate."[5] In this manner, considerable amounts of gold were recovered.

By 1894 the Hocumac Company had acquired fourteen mines in the Baldy Notch region. New pipes were put in and the wagon road up from Lytle Creek was improved. Just above the mines, and just below the crest of Baldy Notch, was a cluster of cabins known as "Miners' Camp."

Ironically, the Hocumac Company's solution to the water problem caused the company's downfall and spelled the eventual end of gold mining at Baldy Notch. The large-scale hydraulic efforts were sending down floods of reddish, muddy water, polluting the domestic water supply and clogging the irrigation pipes of Pomona Valley residents. On July 6, 1895, an injunction was served on the Hocumac Company by the San Antonio Water Company, prohibiting the miners from any further polluting or discoloring of the waters of San Antonio Creek. The end did not come right away. The Hocumac Company discovered that if hydraulic operations were carried on only for half-hour periods, the muddy water would sink into the ground before reaching the main stream in San Antonio Canyon. The company also experimented with a dry washer for removing the gold from the auriferous gravel. These limited operations were carried on during late 1895 and parts of 1896 and 1897 — just enough being recovered to average $100 for each of the fourteen claims as required by mining law and thus retain title for the Hocumac Company. But these were unprofitable, last-ditch efforts. In 1900 the Hocumac mines passed into the hands of the San Antonio Water Company, which hastily removed most of the pipeline to lessen the possibility of any future hydraulic mining that might pollute the valuable water supply of San Antonio Creek. The thirty-year saga of mining at Baldy Notch was over.

Constable James Bradford, a court officer, and Mr. Jolliffe of the San Antonio Water Company enroute to Baldy Notch to serve an injunction to halt hydraulic mining, July 6, 1895.
– ROBERT CHAPMAN COLLECTION

The cluster of cabins at Baldy Notch was known as "Miners' Camp." There were six or seven cabins just below the notch, the first built in 1882 by James Banks. The last cabin burned down in 1932.
– CHARLES CLARK VERNON COLLECTION

The dry washer, largest of its kind, built at Baldy Notch by the Hocumac Company after an injunction prevented hydraulic mining. The effort to dry wash gold from the gravels was unsuccessful, and gold mining ded in the Baldy Notch area around 1900. – HENRY E. HUNTINGTON LIBRARY.

Miner's log cabin at Baldy Notch. This one was more sturdily built than most. Dan Alexander took this post card photograph around 1926.

As the Hocumac Company was expending its last feeble efforts, new gold strikes were made high on the southeast slope of Old Baldy, a mile above San Antonio Falls. Frank Slanker, constable of Pomona, and a man named Grable discovered gold-bearing quartz veins on the ridge just west of San Antonio Creek's headwaters and only 2,000 feet below the summit of Baldy. The discovery was made in June 1897 and the following month Slanker and Grable filed claims under the titles of the Agamemnon and Penelope mines. Later, these claims and others made in the same vicinity became known as the Gold Ridge Mines. The discoveries were followed by a small rush to the area by eager prospectors and a flurry of small claims. Two ambitious prospectors, E. C. Cady and H. L. Brewer, even located a claim on the very summit of Old Baldy. The *Pomona Weekly Times* carried a series of optimistic stories about the new prospects. The issue of July 21, 1897 reported that "Messrs. Grable and Slanker have had 30 assays made of the ore of their mining claim near Old Baldy, showing an average result of $68 per ton in gold. The vein is 110 feet wide. It has been bonded to Peter Fleming for six months for $20,000." The August 4th issue contained the encouraging statement: "We hear there are over 100 people in this local El Dorado and much interest is manifested over the prospect. May this district prove richer than Klondyke." But such was not to be. A small stamp mill, believed to be a Huntington crusher powered with a Union gasoline engine, was laboriously brought up by wagon from Lytle Creek and set up near the diggings and a few buildings were constructed, but the ore was found so low-grade and the expense of recovery so high that the work was suspended after two years.

The foreman's cabin at the Gold Ridge Mine, built 1897. Gold recovery here between 1897 and 1906 was the highest such effort in the San Gabriel Mountains, only a thousand feet below the top of Old Baldy.
– CHARLES CLARK VERNON COLLECTION

Others took up the challenge. John A. Woy and C. R. Johnson, both of Pomona, worked the Gold Ridge Mines from 1900 to 1903 and managed to dig a 600-foot tunnel into the heart of the mountain, looking in vain for the elusive "mother lode." They failed to find it and sold out to a Los Angeles company in 1904. The *Pomona Daily Review* of July 19, 1904 carried an optimistic statement by one O. E. Wellborn, member of the Los Angeles company, who invested $3,000 in the Baldy mines: "There are millions of dollars of gold in the scarred and weather-beaten sides of the mountain. I have never known better prospects than up there . . . If we had about $30,000 we could open mines up there that would make the Cripple Creek and Victor properties look like thirty cents worth of dog meat." Wellborn's bombast was ridiculous. The Los Angeles company gave up after one season of fruitless search.

William B. Dewey, proprietor of the Baldy Summit Inn, caused a brief flurry of excitement when he allegedly picked up a nugget of pure gold worth $2,260 near the Gold Ridge Mines in 1911. Dewey refused to show the nugget to anyone and was accused of perpetrating a hoax in order to attract attention to his resort. Dewey insisted on his truthfulness to the end, but the nugget never appeared.

Over on the shoulder of Ontario Peak, above Icehouse Canyon, John Kelly discovered a gold prospect in 1905. He built a small cabin and worked his claim for a few years, hauling his ore down the Icehouse Canyon trail by burro-back. But the returns were insufficient to cover expenses, so the effort was abandoned. Today the spot is known as Kelly's Camp.

The ruins of the Huntington Crusher mill at the Gold Ridge Mine, near the head of San Antonio Creek, a mile above the falls. Gold was discovered here in 1897 and efforts to recover the precious metal continued, with marginal success, until about 1906.
– LLOYD COOPER PHOTO, POMONA PUBLIC LIBRARY

The dining room and kitchen at the Gold Ridge Mine, near the headwaters of San Antonio Creek, ca. 1899.
– CHARLES CLARK VERNON COLLECTION

Meanwhile, over in San Gabriel Canyon, mining continued at a pace only slightly less than the glory days of Eldoradoville. Shortly before the demise of Eldoradoville, silver was discovered in the main canyon of the San Gabriel, about four miles up from the canyon entrance. The discoverer was Francisco Zapata, and the workings became known as the Zapata Silver Mine. In April 1861 the ore was assayed at $650 in silver to the ton. But Zapata did not have the capital to develop the mine; he sold it to Dr. James B. Winston, proprietor of the elegant Bella Union Hotel in Los Angeles, in 1863. Winston poured money into his new enterprise, and extensive tunneling was initiated. Excitement reached a high pitch in 1864 when an assay of one ore pocket revealed over $3,000 in silver per ton. In 1867 operations were temporarily suspended when the main tunnel collapsed, injuring several miners. But this setback did not deter Dr. Winston; he promptly announced plans for a 1200-foot tunnel into what he believed was the "lead" vein. His spirits soared when a San

Francisco mining engineer inspected the mine and declared it possessed "a very large and fine quality of silver ore, not excelled by any ores taken from the far-famed Comstock Lode of Washoe!" But the rosy predictions of imminent bonanza failed to come true. By 1873, Dr. Winston had sunk almost $40,000 into a determined search for the elusive lead vein. He never found it. With his death in 1878 serious development ceased, although minor work continued until at least 1881. The fabled Zapata turned out to be a will-of-the-wisp.

Francisco Zapata and Dr. Winston confined their efforts to the bottom of the canyon, ignoring the rugged slopes of Silver Mountain on the west wall of the canyon. In the early 1880s, Louis Sharp, remembered today by the little bench halfway up the main canyon known as Sharps Flat, climbed the slopes and discovered promising silver veins a thousand feet above the river. He filed a claim and proceeded to dig out rich silver ore. The *Los Angeles Times* of June 29, 1882 reported excitement in town over a large nugget of pure silver from Sharp's mine on exhibit at the Pico House, Los Angeles' finest hostelry at the time.

Sharp did not have the capital to develop his claim. To exploit the silver deposits high on Silver Mountain, two well-financed mining companies were hurriedly organized.

The Kelsey Mine, on the west slope of the canyon just above today's Morris Reservoir, was opened in 1881 by Henry C. Kelsey, and for a time was believed to be immensely rich. The *Times* of January 1, 1886 described its prospects in the most glowing terms: ". . . enticing virgin silver . . . chunks from the narrow vein take a polish like a silver dollar and are almost as solid. Many specimens run $20,000 and over to the ton." It was reported that lumps of pure silver as big as man's fist had been found. Comstock king Jown W. Mackay was rumored ready to buy the mine for a million dollars. A 5-stamp steam mill was erected below the diggings, and ore was conveyed from the walls of Silver Mountain to the mill by an elaborate system of tramways and chutes. But, as usual, expectation exceeded results. The veins of rich silver pinched out or disappeared far inside the mountain, and production failed to keep pace with investment. The Kelsey halted regular operations in 1894, but was worked intermittently until 1910, and once again, briefly, in the early 1930s. Today, the old mill site is under the waters of Morris Reservoir, and the tunnels and excavations high on the mountainside are eroded and overgrown with chaparral.

A half mile down-canyon from the Kelsey was the Victoria Silver Mine, developed by an English syndicate. The Victoria opened in 1887 under the direction of English mining engineer Henry Deffy and initially showed great promise. Assays ran as high as $14,000 in silver per ton. Upwards of $60,000 was poured into the Victoria's development, including the erection of a 10-stamp mill, company store, bunk house and dining room for the 100-plus miners employed. The river was dammed just north of the mine, forming a lake of several acres. Water from the artificial lake was used to power the mill. The *Times* (September 10, 1887) predicted that the Victoria "will ultimately be one of the largest mining operations in the world." The prediction was grossly inaccurate. After only five years of operation, the mine was abandoned as a failure. The California State Mineralogist, in commenting on the Victoria's demise in 1892, stated that the mine was "a monument to mismanagement of the worst sort."

The Victoria Silver Mine, just down canyon from the Kelsey Mine, in the main canyon of the San Gabriel. Henry Deffy and an English syndicate opened the mine in 1887, pouring over $60,000 into development. The Victoria was abandoned after five years, a costly failure. – AZUSA HISTORICAL SOCIETY

Although a few rich pockets of ore were uncovered, silver was simply not present in paying quantities in Silver Mountain. It took the developers of the Zapata, Kelsey and Victoria mines many years of effort and thousands of dollars to realize this fact. The incredible saga of Nevada's Comstock silver lode was not to be repeated here.

Probably the most interesting saga in the long mining history of San Gabriel Canyon was the race in the early 1870s between Henry C. Roberts and William Ferguson to develop hydraulic works along the lower reaches of the East Fork. The efforts

The Victoria mill was on the east side of San Gabriel Canyon, connected with the silver workings by this long suspension bridge. The bridge washed out in times of high water. – HENRY E. HUNTINGTON LIBRARY

The Kelsey Silver Mine in the main canyon of the San Gabriel. Notice the wooden flume descending the mountainside behind the mill building. Henry C. Kelsey developed the mine in 1881 and for a time it was believed to be immensely rich. But silver recovery never lived up to expectations. The mill site today is under the waters of Morris Reservoir.
– AZUSA HISTORICAL SOCIETY

Henry Roberts' hydraulic mine in the lower East Fork of San Gabriel Canyon, 1871. This is the earliest known photograph of mining in the canyon. Notice the flume descending the hillside, the powerful hydraulic spray, and the riffled sluice box below.
– HENRY E. HUNTINGTON LIBRARY

of these two men represented the first large-scale, scientific hydraulic mining in the canyon.

Henry C. Roberts came into San Gabriel Canyon in 1859. He opened a stage service to the Eldoradoville mines in collaboration with a man named Williams, and after Eldoradoville's demise, he erected a store on the lower East Fork, at the later site of Follows Camp. (Roberts' store still stands at Follows Camp, the oldest building in San Gabriel Canyon.) Located on a mesa just south of the river, Roberts' store was able to survive the periodic torrents that scour the river. Roberts watched the steady stream of gold dust which came to his scales from the Cecil Graham Hill claim immediately across the river, and in 1870 decided to purchase the claim and exploit it with hydraulic machinery.

At about the same time, William G. Ferguson, Los Angeles merchant and livery stable owner, purchased a hillside claim just down-river from Roberts, on the south slope of the canyon. Ferguson also had his eye on hydraulic mining. He and several other Los Angeles investors formed the San Gabriel Mining Company and commenced exploratory work.

Hydraulic gold mining — washing down auriferous hillsides with a powerful jet of water — was an established mode of operation in the Mother Lode Country of northern California, but the process had received only fleeting use in the southern half of the state, mainly because of a chronic shortage of water. Only the largest watercourses provided sufficient flow to support major hydraulic enterprises, and then for only part of the year. Fortunately for Roberts and Ferguson, the San Gabriel was a plentiful stream for four or five months annually.

In order to, "hydraulic" effectively, the water must have great force, or "head" in miners' language. For Roberts and Ferguson, this required the construction of conduits from far up river and artificial reservoirs a thousand feet above the mines. The volume and pressure thus acquired was necessary to force water through the hoses and monitors with sufficient power to tear away the gold-bearing rocks, gravel, clay and dirt, then wash these ingredients through long sluice boxes to recover the gold.

The walls of San Gabriel Canyon are precipitous and unstable. No local surveyor or engineer could be found to undertake the task of plotting the course and grade for the conduits and supervising their construction over such difficult mountain terrain. Finally, Roberts was able to hire the services of an English engineer named Sam Hawley. Ferguson acquired the talents of a surveyor named W. W. Woodman. By the fall of 1871 the surveying was completed and the race was on.

The narrow canyon of the East Fork reverberated with the sounds of pick, shovel, hammer and blasting powder as both crews, working long shifts under the close supervision of Hawley and Woodman, hewed the ditches and built the flumes for the paralleling conduits. Roberts' flume was high on the west wall of the canyon, five miles in length. Ferguson's ditch and flume followed the east slope from four and a half miles up river.

No one knows just how it began, but a spirited rivalry erupted between the crews of Roberts and Ferguson. Some rather substantial bets were made over who would first complete their conduit and commence hydraulic mining. The two claim owners were on none too friendly terms, allegedly because

Close up of the Henry Roberts hydraulic mine, East Fork of San Gabriel Canyon, about 1873. The hillside has been water-blasted away in search of gold-bearing gravels. – HENRY E. HUNTINGTON LIBRARY

Ferguson jumped a claim sought by Roberts.

Canyon historian Sedley Peck described the great race: "Dams were built to divert the river water into settling basins where the sand, which would have quickly clogged the ditches, was removed. Conduits were blasted and hewn from the rock cliffs of the canyon, flumes on steel supports driven into sheer walls, carried on high trestles across gulches and canyons, through clay lined ditches across the high mesas, by gentle grades which soon raised the level, until the water was finally brought to the storage lakes a thousand feet above the rapidly falling canyon floor."[6]

The hectic canyon activity caught the attention of Los Angeles newspapers. The *Star* sent a correspondent into the East Fork to report on the race. On October 31, 1871 he wrote, "Times on the San Gabriel River are getting lively. Henry Roberts and Co. have finished four miles of ditch, mostly heavy work, used over 30,000 feet of lumber for fluming, got the hydraulic ready for action, and will commence piping in a day or two." On December 8 the correspondent reported, "The San Gabriel Mining Company [Ferguson] finished a ditch four miles long, covering 200 acres . . . building a suspension bridge 200 feet high to carry their flume across Cape Horn Canyon . . . A portion of the flume is suspended on the face of an overhanging cliff with iron bars drilled into solid rock."

Roberts was first to complete his conduit, considered by Los Angeles historian J. M. Guinn as "one of the most complete and substantial ever constructed in any mining camp in the state."[7]

Ferguson finished about two weeks later. Both conduits were completed in amazingly short time considering the difficult terrain.

In January 1872 both Roberts and Ferguson turned on their hydraulic monitors, accompanied by the cheers of spectators assembled for the occasion, and commenced water-blasting away their hillside

Sedley Peck, late historian of San Gabriel Canyon, and the Henry Roberts hydraulic monitor, Follows Camp. The monitor, operated by three men, directed a powerful hydraulic spray into the gold-bearing hillside. – SEDLEY PECK COLLECTION

claims. Initially their ventures appeared to be highly successful as each recovered substantial quantities of gold — $5,000 the first month, it was reported. Later they were averaging a more modest $1,000 per month, according to Peck. A problem they faced as they blasted into the cliffs was the "gophering" that honeycombed through the rocks, depriving the terrain of much gold. It was said that this gophering had been done decades earlier, by Indian miners working for Spanish or Mexican masters.

The apparent success of Roberts and Ferguson encouraged others to try their hands at hydraulic mining. The names of Matfield, Crow, Higbie, Ford, Caley and Justice appeared in the pages of local newspapers, all bent on duplicating the efforts of Roberts and Ferguson. But the most noteworthy of the later hydraulic ventures in the canyon was the famous fiasco of "Uncle" Dave Buell. Buell secured a hillside claim just down river from Roberts, but could not gain water rights to the East Fork. So after some weeks he decided to convey water to his claim from the untapped North Fork of the San Gabriel. He hired a young engineer named Simpson to survey his ditch line. To get water from the North to the East Fork, Simpson proposed a 700-foot tunnel through the ridge separating the two watersheds. Buell agreed and work commenced on the ditch and tunnel. Canyon pioneer Jim Roberts, son of Henry Roberts, described the results: "Great preparations were made for the opening of the works and visions of unlimited nuggets of gold crowded Buell's mind. Then the intake gates were opened and watchful waiting was the order of the day. But night fell and still no trace of water had appeared. Buell betook himself up along the conduit and walked through the dry tunnel. A few hundred feet from the upper portal he heard the sound of rushing waters and he discovered that Simpson had lost the grade."[8] The tunnel had been bored uphill! Simpson left in disgrace and Buell allegedly went broke and departed for Mexico. The long abandoned tunnel, partly caved in and both portals hidden in brush, still lies high above the forks of the San Gabriel.

Despite repeated breakdowns in their ditches and flumes, Roberts and Ferguson continued to work their claims. Roberts apparently was more successful; in the summer of 1873 he turned down an offer of $250,000 for his claim from a Chinese Tong in San Francisco, according to Sedley Peck.

Roberts should have accepted the offer. As it turned out, the returns in gold markedly decreased as his powerful monitor blasted deeper and deeper into the hillside. And then, legal obstacles arose. The large-scale hydraulic mining operations were sending down floods of muddy water into the populated San Gabriel Valley, discoloring domestic water supplies and clogging irrigation pipes. Valley farmers secured a court injunction against the hydraulic miners in the summer of 1874, and this was soon followed by state laws designed to prevent the pollution of domestic water supplies. Roberts, Ferguson and the rest of the canyon hydraulic miners were obliged to close down their gold-seeking enterprises, and all but minor, non-polluting hydraulic efforts ceased forever in San Gabriel Canyon.

Although overshadowed by more prosperous mining ventures elsewhere, gold recovery along the East Fork of the San Gabriel has continued almost uninterrupted into recent years. With a few exceptions, after the end of hydraulic mining in 1874, these have been small-scale efforts by individual prospectors many of whom built homes in the canyon.

Thanks to the memory of Sedley Peck, we have vivid descriptions of many of these colorful characters who mined in the canyon during this period.

Old Joe Cook, plump and long-bearded, was long a familiar figure in the East Fork. He was a miner of visionary schemes. Sedley Peck described one of his most ambitious projects: "Cook and several associates started a tunnel at Laurel Gulch with the idea of pushing through to Devil's Canyon, the plan being to take the river underground and leave the workings free from water. These hardy miners worked in deep and swiftly running, cold water, timbering with laurel logs as they went, for three heartbreaking years, but all to no avail since their tunnel developed more and more water as they went along, and their herculean efforts were doomed to failure."[9]

Prospectors entering San Gabriel Canyon, date unknown, ca. 1875. Most of those entering the San Gabriel Mountains in the early days toted firearms; grizzlies and bandits posed threats.
– AZUSA HISTORICAL SOCIETY

Miners using Long Tom in San Gabriel Canyon, date unknown. Long Toms, sluices, china pumps, water wheels, wing dams and primitive hydraulic works were all utilized by canyon miners in the 1860s. – AZUSA HISTORICAL SOCIETY

Following his tunnel fiasco, Cook devoted his efforts in behalf of a new San Gabriel Mining Company, organized in 1888 and capitalized at $1 million. Eventually the company's claims covered two miles of the East Fork below the Narrows.

William Tecumseh Heaton came into the East Fork in 1891 and, after prospecting for a while in Cattle Canyon, settled on the mesa just north of the East Fork's elbow then known as Peachtree Flat. Later it became known as Heaton Flat. He filed a claim here in 1902 and built a crude shack of stone and wood. He is said to have worked his mine "every day, rain or shine" until his death in 1924.

Oliver Justice, the lanky, long-bearded patriarch of the canyon, mined in and above the Narrows from about 1870 until his death in 1929. His grave lies on the mesa above the mouth of Iron Fork.

Alonzo Shoemaker, another bearded old-timer, mined the high bar above the small tributary of the East Fork that now bears his name. He was a familiar sight for a quarter century. In 1890 a company of four miners leased the Shoemaker claim and installed a "self-shooter" — a kind of miniature hydraulic system. The results of this unique experiment were disappointing and the effort was soon abandoned.

Fred Maley came into the canyon in the early 1890s and worked a claim at the junction of the East Fork and Cattle Canyon. He is reported to have taken out $60,000 in gold before being served with an injunction for muddying the river waters.

There was Harry Walton, "The Bee Man," who lived for twenty-five years on the little flat across the river from Camp Rincon. Every summer he sold honey to canyon visitors; in winter he worked his gold mine, driving a tunnel deep into the mountainside in quest of the elusive metal.

George Trogden was described as a close likeness of Long John Silver, "even to the rolling gait, stiff leg and bad eye." Trogden entered the canyon in 1907 as an employee of the Pacific Light and Power Company. He enjoyed it so much he stayed the rest of his days. For many years he worked a claim near the junction of the East Fork and Iron Fork, just above the Narrows. Here he built a stone house and grew his own fruits and vegetables, and was known throughout the canyon for his warm hospitality, "always ready with coffee pot and frying pan."

Every mining region had its fabled badman, and San Gabriel Canyon was no exception. He was John Knox Portwood, self-styled "King of the Canyon," prospector, claim jumper, pugilist, part-time packer, card shark and, some said, a real lady charmer. Portwood came into the canyon in 1895 and built a crude cabin in Cattle Canyon, just above its junction with the East Fork. He made his living by gold mining and occasionally running a pack train.

According to Sedley Peck, Portwood wanted to be known as a killer and boasted of the six notches carved on the handle of his six-shooter, supposedly denoting men he had killed in Virginia, Texas, Arizona and California.

Oliver "Old Hickory" Justice, the lanky, long-bearded patriarch of San Gabriel Canyon, came into the East Fork to prospect in the 1860 s. He remained the rest of his life, working a mine just below the East Fork Narrows until his death in 1929. His grave lies on a bench near the confluence of Iron Fork and the East Fork. – AZUSA HISTORICAL SOCIETY

Billy Heaton at his cabin on Peachtree Flat, today known as Heaton Flat. William Tecumseh Heaton, born in Culpepper County, Virginia in 1837, crossed the plains via wagon trail to California in the 1850s. He came into the canyon in 1891, settled on the little flat a half mile above the East Fork elbow, and is said to have worked his mine "every day, rain or shine" until his death in 1924. – CHARLES CLARK VERNON COLLECTION

George Trogden's cabin at Iron Fork, just above the East Fork Narrows, ca. 1908. Left to right, George Trogden, E.V. Lucas, Pearl Trogden (George's daughter), Ralph Follows.
– CHARLES CLARK VERNON COLLECTION

On Christmas night, 1917, after a poker game at Trogden's Iron Fork cabin, Portwood allegedly shot and killed a young German miner named Herman Miller. Portwood was arrested by a sheriff's posse after Miller's bullet-ridden body was discovered in the brush a short distance from the cabin. Before his trial, the canyon badman offered a fantastic yarn that Miller was a German spy and that the Kaiser's secret service had an espionage base in the canyon! (World War I was raging, and anti-German hysteria was at its peak in the U.S.) Portwood pictured himself as a patriotic citizen defending the cause of liberty. He told federal officers that Miller's cabin in the East Fork was often used as a rendezvous by one Franz Schulenberg, who was then under arrest in San Francisco as a German spy. According to the *Azusa Pomotropic* (January 4, 1918), the federal officers searched the Miller cabin and combed the East Fork, but found no evidence to back up Portwood's allegations. Portwood claimed self-defense at his trial and was acquitted.

Portwood died as he had lived — by the gun. On June 13, 1920, two rangers, Charles Novatny and John Dunne, called on Portwood to investigate threats the latter had allegedly made against two canyon women. The badman suddenly drew his revolver and pointed it at Dunne. The rangers ducked for cover and a gun battle ensued. When it was over, "The King of the Canyon" lay dead in the doorway of his Cattle Canyon cabin.

And there were countless other colorful prospectors who, over the years, sought a fortune in the East Fork. Among the many names are a few that stand out because of their originality — One-eyed Mountain Charlie, "Twitchlip" Kelly, "Two Gun"

"Tooch" Martin, L.A. County supervisor from 1886 to 1891, and Harry Walton at the Walton Mine across the river from Camp Rincon, ca. 1910. Walton raised bees in the canyon when he was not gold mining.
– CHARLES CLARK VERNON COLLECTION

Don Rosenkrantz, Charlie the Chink, Peg Leg Billy Coynes and Soldier Thompson. What tales the ghosts of these long-departed miners could tell!

Not all of the canyon miners confined their efforts to the river and its adjacent slopes. A few hardy prospectors scrambled high up the mountainsides, searching for the elusive "mother lode" that supposedly fed the rich placers of the East Fork. While none ever found a bonanza, many did locate quartz claims and recovered varying amounts of gold. The Big Horn high above the East Fork headwaters, the Native Son on Prairie Fork, the Stanley-Miller above the East Fork Narrows, the Allison high in Allison Gulch, the Baldora in Dry Gulch, the Eagle and the Gold Dollar far above the head of Coldwater Canyon — these represent incredible feats when you consider the elevation, rugged terrain, inaccessibility, and vulnerability to the elements. Most of these mines had a stamp or ball mill perched on a mountain shelf nearby, with heavy machinery for crushing ore. The task of lugging this machinery, piece by piece, up near-vertical slopes and hauling out tons of crushed ore required a high degree of fortitude and strenuous work. Of stern stuff these mountaineering miners were made!

The "granddaddy" of all these mountain mines was the Big Horn, perched at almost 7,000 feet on the rugged east face of Mount Baden-Powell. Charles Tom Vincent (alias Charles Vincent Dougherty), prospector and hunter who lived in a rustic cabin high in Vincent Gulch above the East Fork headwaters, discovered the gold-bearing quartz vein in 1895. He named the mine for the big horn sheep he was hunting when he made the discovery.

Vincent did not have the money to develop the mine and it soon fell into the hands of promoters. It was not long until carefully-fostered rumors were heard to the effect that the Big Horn held fabulous riches within its rocky bosom. Stories circulated that the mine was "the richest in the world . . . Its vein is a mile wide . . . There is ore so rich that it can be sent to the mint without milling." Los Angeles businessmen were told that a $50,000 investment would return millions in gold. Bank president Jackson A. Graves related how a number of prominent citizens, including Governor Henry T. Gage and U.S. Senator Stephen M. White, were on the verge of buying Big Horn stock when Graves, skeptical, urged caution. A mining engineer friend had told him that ore samples being shown about town showed evidence of "salting." To prove or disprove the fantastic claims of the Big Horn promoters, Graves and his engineer friend hiked up to the mine to check for themselves. They removed ore samples from various locations within the mine and sent them down via Ralph Follows' pack train, under round-the-clock guard to prevent any possible tampering. An independent assay in Los Angeles bore out Graves' suspicions. The assay checked out at a miniscule $1.37 in gold per ton! The Big Horn's inflated bubble was punctured.

Nevertheless, there was gold deep inside Mount Baden-Powell, if not in the quantities first proclaimed. During the years 1902 to 1910, the Lowell and California Company, a Los Angeles-based concern, invested a small fortune in developing the mine. Tunnels were bored hundreds of feet into the mountain. A 10-stamp mill was erected at the site, and a wagon road was hacked across cliffs to Vincent Saddle, then down Big Rock Canyon to the desert. Gold-bearing quartz was blasted from veins deep in the mountain, then loaded onto small ore cars and rolled out to the mill for crushing. Large horse-drawn wagons transported the crushed ore out of the mountains for processing.

In the end, the Lowell and California Company met defeat. The $200,000 in gold recovered failed to cover the high costs of development, the expected mother lode could not be located, flooding deep within the mine caused insurmountable problems, and the mill suffered a disastrous fire.

There were brief renewals of activity in 1914, when the Guggenheim interests did some exploratory work, and in the 1930s, when the American Metal Company leased the Big Horn and put in a 50-ton flotation mill, and took out several thousand tons of low-grade ore.

The discovery and development of the Big Horn caused prospectors to search out other promising quartz veins high above the East Fork. Before long, there were gold mines dotting the precipitous slopes far above the river, each with a story fully as dramatic as the Big Horn. Space limitations require only brief mention of each.

On the north slope of Prairie Fork was the Native Son Mine, worked intermittently from 1897 to 1920, never more than a marginal success.

Perched precariously on the cliffs above the East Fork Narrows was the Stanley-Miller, discovered by Gordon Stanley and Ben Miller in 1915, worked until 1939. Heavy cast-iron parts for a ball mill were somehow laboriously dragged up the precipitous mountainside and fastened by steel cables to the cliff outside the mine. The airy Wetwater Trail, terror of pack mules with its dripping water, was hacked out of the cliffs above the Narrows to gain access. The Stanley-Miller met a fierce "Gotterdammerung" in 1953, when a forest conflagration burned away the mill supports and heavy equipment came crashing down the mountainside to the bottom of the Narrows, made more dramatic by the loud din of bursting blasting caps.

Ruins of the 50-ton flotation mill building at the Big Horn Mine, perched precariously on the east slope of Mt. Baden-Powell. The American Metal Company built this mill in the 1930's with high expectations of recovering gold from deep inside the mountain. The result was failure. They were unable to locate the expected "Mother Lode" and flooding deep within the mine caused insurmountable problems.
– LLOYD COOPER PHOTO, POMONA PUBLIC LIBRARY

In 1913 John James Allison, veteran desert prospector, scrambled up the steep slopes above Laurel Gulch and, "crawling on his hands and knees," discovered the Allison Mine high on the face of Iron Mountain. Allison and his three sons expended superhuman efforts to develop their mountainside claim, utilizing an ingenious system of cables and pulleys to hoist the heavy cast-iron parts for a ball mill, rails and ore cars to their mine, and hacking out a contour trail around the cliffs and down into Coldwater Canyon, then up over the divide and down to Camp Baldy. The Allison was worked intermittently until 1942, yielding $50,000 in gold according to the California Bureau of Mines and Geology.

Adjacent to the big waterfall in Ross Gulch was the Short and Ross Mine, worked with only meager returns from 1889 until about 1910. Water piped from above the fall powered their small crusher.

Far above the head of Coldwater Canyon, just under the jagged ridge that connects Iron Mountain with Old Baldy, were the loftiest and most inaccessible gold mines of all — the Gold Dollar and the Eagle, discovered in 1909 and 1913 respectively by colorful Charlie Smith, long-time San Gabriel Canyon resident and founder of Camp Rincon. The Gold Dollar, perched near the ridgetop, had a spectacular aerial tramway that conveyed ore from mine down to mill several hundred feet below. Both mines had small ball mills perched on narrow ledges and held fast by steel cables. How this heavy machinery was hoisted so far up the mountainside defies imag-

The Big Horn Mine buildings, high on the east slope of Mt. Baden-Powell, in about 1905. The gold mine was discovered by Charles Vincent Dougherty (alias Charles Tom Vincent) in 1895 and worked by the Lowell and California Company during the years 1902 to 1910, and for brief periods by others.
– ROBERT CHAPMAN COLLECTION

ination. (Much of the machinery is still there today, a source of astonishment to the occasional hiker.)

Charlie Smith met his end in spectacular fashion. During a fierce blizzard in January 1933, an avalanche roared down on his cabin at the Eagle Mine, carrying the sleeping Charlie, his bed and his cabin all the way down the mountainside into Coldwater Canyon. He was buried in a tomb of frozen white, his remains dug out by a search party a few days later.

Following Smith's demise, George Wrockloff expended several years of strenuous effort to make the Gold Dollar profitable. He was working six claims on the mountainside in 1936.

A thousand feet below the Gold Dollar and the Eagle, in Dry Gulch, was the Baldora Mine, also discovered by Smith. Later the Baldora was taken over by Jake Widman and renamed the Widco. The mine never returned a profit, as far as is known.

Then there is the mystery mine in Alder Gulch that defies research. The cabins and equipment are still there, well preserved because of isolation from vandal-prone hikers. Who discovered and worked this mine? The records of the California Division of Mines and Geology, so complete on the other mines, are a blank here. Only the ghosts can tell.

Although none of these mountainside-clinging mines ever yielded a bonanza, one cannot help but marvel at the fortitude of those hardy souls who attempted what seemed like the impossible.

The last serious and extensive mining in San Gabriel Canyon occurred during the depression years of the early 1930s. Hundreds of unemployed men and their families drifted into the East Fork to pan, wash and dig for gold. Two shanty settlements sprang up: one, at the site of Eldoradoville, became known as "Hooverville;" the other, located downstream at Mountain View Flats, was called both "Shantytown" and "Murray Flats," the latter name derived from the self-appointed "mayor" of the group who squatted there. Families fashioned crude homes from five-gallon tin cans, cardboard, tree branches and burlap bags. Many lived in canvas tents. Some resided in their automobiles, often with a canvas canopy erected on one side. These people, on the whole, were proud and independent. They would rather dig, pan and sluice gold from the river and its adjacent slopes, recovering about $30 a month, than go on welfare. Some of their mining methods were ingenious, involving the use of pulleys, make-shift ore buckets and automatically-triggered sluice boxes. Two determined individuals even hauled a mammoth steam shovel all the way up the East Fork to a point just below the Narrows. They utilized the cumbersome piece of equipment to pick up and dump tons of sand and gravel into a large sluice box alongside the river, thereby recover-

Gordon Stanley and two hikers at the Stanley-Miller Mine, perched precariously above the East Fork Narrows, 1938. The fortitude of these cliff-dwelling miners is almost beyond belief. – J. R. MINNICH PHOTO

The main tunnel of the Allison Mine, 5,000 feet up the southwest face of Iron Mountain. John James Allison discovered this gold prospect in 1913 and, with his three sons, worked it until about 1930, with marginal success. – JOHN ROBINSON PHOTO

George Allison and pack train on the trail between the Allison Mine and Coldwater Canyon, ca. 1921. Via this route, supplies were packed into the mine and ore packed out. – ROBERT CHAPMAN COLLECTION

The main tunnel of the Gold Dollar Mine, high on the south slope of San Antonio Ridge. The mountainside gold mine was discovered by Charlie Smith in 1909 and worked by him until his death by snow avalanche in 1933. – LLOYD COOPER PHOTO, POMONA PUBLIC LIBRARY

Ore track and gasoline motor at the Gold Dollar Mine, about 1936. Gold-bearing ore from the mountainside mine was transported to the mill by a spectacular 400-foot aerial tramway. – LLOYD COOPER PHOTO, POMONA PUBLIC LIBRARY

The Eagle Mine, 700 feet below the Gold Dollar, discovered by Charlie Smith in 1913. Smith met his death here in 1933, when the cabin in which he was sleeping was carried down the mountain by an avalanche. – SEDLEY PECK COLLECTION

Flotation table at the Eagle Mine, ca. 1928. – SEDLEY PECK COLLECTION

Remains of the ball mill, Gold Dollar Mine, 1973.
– DEE TRENT PHOTO

ing appreciable amounts of gold through their unique effort.

The great deluge of March 1938 swept like a monstrous tidal wave through the canyon, completely obliterating Hooverville, part of Shantytown, and all the mining works. Thus ended abruptly the depression mining era. Although few lives were lost (there was ample warning of the rising water), only a handful of the depression miners returned to the East Fork.

In recent years, the East Fork has seen amateur weekend prospectors try their luck at gold panning. They do it mostly for fun, and if they happen to trap a speck of shining metal in the bottom of their pan, they celebrate with a can of beer. Mining in the East Fork today is predominantly a recreational activity, although with the recent increase in the price of gold, it is not beyond the realm of possibility that full-scale professional mining will return to the canyon.

High up in Cattle Canyon, an East Fork tributary that originates on the Southwest slope of Old Baldy, Ronald Curtis works a tungsten mine started by his father 30 years ago. Curtis believes there may be as much as $5 billion in tungsten ore hidden in the foreboding mountainside around the head of Cattle Canyon. He currently (1980) employs a crew of ten to work the 5,700-foot high mine and grosses about $1,800 per day. The tungsten ore is processed at a small mill built by Curtis on the floor of Cattle Canyon, then hauled out via a precipitous dirt road bulldozed a few years ago around the mountainside to the Glendora Ridge Road at Cow Canyon Saddle. Another, much poorer, road descents to the floor of Cattle and Cow canyons to join the East Fork highway. Curtis has faced and surmounted obstacles that would have long ago discouraged a less determined miner. In 1978 heavy rains damaged much of his mining equipment and washed out the

Depression miners at "Hooverville," a cardboard and canvas community of several hundred jobless prospectors at the elbow of the East Fork, 1933. – HENRY E. HUNTINGTON LIBRARY

roads. It required fourteen months for Curtis to repair and rebuild his facilities. Obstacles of a legal nature have been made by conservationists, who fear Curtis' mining activities and his bulldozed mountainside road interfere with the living and breeding habits of the 200 big horn sheep that live in the area. The mine lies within the proposed boundaries of the projected Sheep Mountain Wilderness. As of this writing, Curtis and his attorney have beaten back these court challenges by preservationist groups.[10]

Whatever one thinks of wilderness and big horn sheep, one cannot help but admire the determination and strenuous efforts of mountain miners like Ronald Curtis. Theirs is the toil that developed the West.

1. Will Thrall, "Lytle Creek Canyon from Indian Days to 1900," *Historical Society of Southern California Quarterly*, XXXII, 3 (September 1950), p. 242.

2. F. H. Manker and Dan Alexander, "At The Foot of Mt. San Antonio," *Trails Magazine* (Spring 1937), p. 7.

3. Muir Dawson, "Mining in Upper San Antonio Canyon," *H.S.S.C. Quarterly*, XXX, 1 (March 1948), p. 10.

4. Manker and Alexander, p. 8.

5. George F. Leavens, "By Way of the Devil's Backbone," *Land of Sunshine*, II (August 1896), p. 96.

6. Sedley Peck, "Colorful Old Days on the Upper San Gabriel," *Trails Magazine* (Summer 1938), p. 7.

7. J. M. Guinn, "Gold Placers of Los Angeles," *Land of Sunshine*, II (July 1896), p. 87.

8. Jim Roberts, "Hydraulic Mining in Early Canyon Days Described," *Azusa Herald*, October 20, 1937.

9. Peck, p. 8.

10. A feature story on Ronald Curtis' tungsten mine appeared in the San Gabriel Valley edition of the *Los Angeles Times*, August 31, 1980.

Water emitting from the mountains was long a subject of bitter controversy. For towns and farmers in the San Gabriel and Pomona valleys, it was a life-or-death matter. With water they would prosper; without enough of it, they were doomed to a marginal existance. – HENRY E. HUNTINGTON LIBRARY

5

Water Struggles

In all the history of the San Gabriel Mountains, nothing has caused as much controversy over long periods of time as the issue of water and water rights. Since the middle of the last century, water flowing from the mountains has been selfishly grabbed, argued about, fought over, and litigated in countless court battles. Litigation over mountain water rights alone would fill a law library. And all for good reason. Before the building of the great aqueducts from the Owens Valley, Northern California and the Colorado River, water was a very scarce commodity in Southern California. With it, farms and towns could prosper; without enough of it, they were doomed to a marginal existence.

The history of man and water from the San Gabriels is a three-part saga, involving the quest of water for domestic and agricultural use, the generation of hydroelectric power, and flood control efforts. It is a story of conflict, compromise and achievement.

During rancho days, cattle and horses roamed freely over the San Gabriel and Pomona valleys. The animals and their guardian vaqueros drank freely from the abundant streams that emitted from San Gabriel, Dalton, San Dimas, San Antonio and Cucamonga canyons. To bring the plentiful water to the heart of his Rancho San Jose de Ariba, Ygnacio Palomares dug a seven-mile ditch from the mouth of San Antonio Canyon. Luis Arenas constructed an irrigation ditch from the portal of San Gabriel Canyon to his cultivated lands on Rancho Azusa in 1843. Arenas hardly had the ditch finished when he sold his holdings to Englishman Henry Dalton in 1844. The enterprising Englishman greatly expanded the lands under cultivation, and in the early 1850s, he enlarged the irrigation ditch to 1,800 gallons a minute, twice the original capacity. Besides watering his fields, Dalton utilized the ditch to run a flour mill he built in 1854. This was the earliest water power development in Southern California.

The seeming abundance of water soon proved to be an illusion. In the years 1862 through 1864, Southern California suffered a disastrous drought. The smaller creeks turned dry as a bone, and only a trickle of water emitted from San Gabriel and San Antonio canyons. Cattle died by the thousands, and their bleached bones littered the landscape. The rancheros learned a bitter lesson that subsequent Southern Californians have learned since: there is no permanent, dependable local water supply. Water that is available must be carefully used and preserved for the droughts that hit the area every twenty years or so.

Despite the drought, the 1860s were years of growth in Southern California. The decade saw increasing numbers of people settle on the expansive lands of Ranchos Azusa, San Jose and Cucamonga. With these new settlers came higher demands on the mountain water. Whereas the streams had easily satisfied (except in times of drought) the needs of the handful of original residents, now their flows became a finite and precious commodity. Strife was inevitable.

Nowhere was this water strife more evident than on Henry Dalton's Rancho Azusa. The numerous squatters who took up residence on land claimed by Dalton helped themselves to water from Dalton's irrigation canal. They also diverted water from the San Gabriel River via their own hastily-dug ditches. Dalton was determined to uphold what he believed were his rights. In 1866 the harassed and angry owner of Rancho Azusa forcibly halted the diversion of water from his ditch to the settlers' fields. Although the settlers "knew that the water was Dalton's . . . they also knew that they had to have water to survive." In response to this dilemma, small groups of settlers "would go, well-armed, and . . . just take the water."[1] A full scale water war was averted when Dalton, perhaps realizing the futility of his position, backed down and offered a compromise. He would allow the settlers to use the water if they would enlarge the ditch to carry sufficient flow for all concerned. The settlers promptly agreed and the ditch was enlarged. Through Dalton's initiative, a three-man commission (one appointed by Dalton and two by the settlers) was established to oversee a fair division of the waters. Peace ensued, but not for long.

The resumption of conflict was caused by a shortage of water, the result of four straight years (1869-1873) of little rain. Settlers who had invested everything in their fields became desperate for irrigation water. Some settlers tore down parts of Dalton's irrigation system so that more water would flow into their fields. Dalton countered by stationing guards along his ditch. Altercations ensued that bordered on violence. The explosive situation is well illustrated by Dalton's account of his encounter with a settler who attempted to remove a dam the former had placed along the ditch: "I told him that I would break the hand that touched it; he did it and I struck his hand as hard as I could (with a walking stick). He then pushed me into the zanja and drew his pistol to fire upon me. Marcos (Dalton's ranch hand) came up and drew a pistol and ordered him to put up his pistol or he would fire upon him; he finally put up his pistol and after some words withdrew."[2]

Fortunately, cooler heads prevailed and violence was averted. Instead, the water controversies (Dalton vs. the settlers) were taken to court. What followed was a long series of conflicting legal decisions. The settlers received a boost when the Los Angeles County supervisors created the Azusa Township. The township's water commissioners, elected by the settlers, immediately launched an effort to construct a new water ditch from the mouth of San Gabriel Canyon across Dalton's land. Following several contradictory court decisions, Dalton finally lost and the new water ditch was built. At last, in 1879, Henry Dalton, grown old and financially drained from the long legal battles, gave up his fight. The Azusa commissioners were given full control over water distribution. Although Dalton's hat was finally out of the ring, the strife over water from San Gabriel Canyon was far from over.

Thousands of new settlers came into the San Gabriel Valley during the 1880 s. With the new residents came increased demands on the precious water, and the result was a new round of controversy that climaxed in the locally famous "water war" of 1887.

The renewed strife began shortly after the formation of the Azusa Water Development and Irrigating Company (henceforth referred to as the A.W.D.& I. Co.) in 1882. The new private company was founded by a segment of the Azusa settlers anxious to increase the supply of irrigation water. Almost immediately, the A.W.D.& I. Co. began excavating a development tunnel under the river from a point just inside the canyon mouth. The theory behind such a tunnel was that water percolating into the river gravels from the surface stream would collect in the tunnel and flow to its mouth where it could be readily recovered. The tunnel became a source of continuing conflict. Many Azusa residents opposed its construction, preferring instead a submerged dam below the canyon mouth to force percolating water to the surface. This internal dissent forced the company to recapitalize and sell stock outside the Azusa area. By purchasing most of the stock, a group of Covina settlers gained control of the enterprise. By 1885 the A.W.D.& I. Co. and its controversial tunnel had become a serious bone of contention and an unpopular rival to the Azusa area irrigation users.

The tunnel controversy was complicated by a flurry of lawsuits and renewed disagreement over Rancho Azusa water rights. Jonathan S. Slauson and Henry Martz, the new owners of the rancho lands (Dalton died in 1884), sued for half the water in the old Dalton ditch. Before the court could render a decision, the rancho owners and settlers arrived at a compromise, assigning 17/24 of the water to the settlers and 7/24 to the rancho. This became known as the Compromise of 1884. While the agreement resolved the essential differences among the Azusa area water users, it purposely failed to mention the A.W.D.& I. Co., now controlled by Covina settlers, whose rights to any water from the ditch were denied by the Azusans.

Meanwhile, new water ditches were being dug and the old one improved. The Duarte area water users constructed a canal from the canyon mouth to irrigate their lands west of the river. The Azusa Water District rebuilt the Dalton ditch and placed its headworks just upstream from the Duarte ditch. A group of early Azusa area settlers known as the "Old Users," who held a right-of-way across Rancho Azusa lands, leapfrogged well inside the canyon mouth to build the headworks of their "Upper Ditch" in 1886. Later that same year, the A.W.D.& I. Co., after failing to gain right-of-way through the Azusa rancho, negotiated with the "Old Users" to utilize their ditch. Well up-canyon from all these irrigation works, were the small diversion dams and ditches of the "Upper Users" — Henry Roberts, Lewis Sharp, R.W. Dawson and other canyon residents.

As long as the annual rainy season was abundant, there was enough water for all concerned. But the

Irrigation ditch near Covina, ca. 1896. Water from San Gabriel Canyon was a life-or-death matter to San Gabriel Valley settlers and farmers. Water wars between various factions were common until the Committee of nine was organized in 1889 to distribute the precious liquid fairly. – AZUSA HISTORICAL SOCIETY

middle 1880s were abnormally dry years, and as the San Gabriel River steadily diminished, year by year, each of the user groups jockeyed to assure itself its "rightful share" of water. There was not enough to go around. Conflict was the result.

The "water war" of 1887 was essentially an armed conflict pitting the Azusa and Duarte users against the Covina users, the latter represented by the A.W.D.& I. Co. Although tempers ran high, dynamite was used, and shots were fired, fortunately no lives were lost. The combatants were mostly farmers, grown desperate through fear of economic ruin if water was not forthcoming for their crops. The "war" proved to be an exercise in futility, a fact belatedly recognized by both sides. It paved the way for a final solution to the irrigation problem.

The violence began in September 1887 when a party of fifty Azusans dynamited the headworks of the A.W.D.& I. Company's development tunnel, burying two tunnel guards in the process. The two were quickly dug out, badly shaken but not seriously injured. Both sides hurriedly sent armed guards into the canyon mouth to protect their various irrigation ditches. Each side would occasionally dam up the other's headworks to assure their own water supply, and fights were commonplace. On one occasion, an unknown rifleman shot at and narrowly missed one of the Azusa guards.

News of the trouble reached Los Angeles and the *Los Angeles Tribune* sent a "war correspondent" into the canyon. On October 17, 1887 the newspaper reported, "TWO CAMPS OF ARMED MEN IN SAN GABRIEL CANYON. Force of men in the Field — The Water Captured and Recaptured."

The *Azusa Herald* later described the conflict: "Duckings, fist fights, arrests, and building up and tearing down of property continued at a merry pace. The Covina men would try to divert water into their ditch, and the Azusans would dam up the diversion ditch. A group of Covinans would suddenly arrive to seize some water, wherewith every able-bodied man in Azusa would rush to the mouth of the Canyon to defend their precious liquid."[3]

During a lull in the battle, the Azusa and Duarte users completed a new tunnel on the east side of the river. It became known as the Azusa-Duarte Tunnel and was 790 feet in length, running through the ridge at the canyon mouth to a point in the canyon above the A.W.D.& I. Co. headworks. This gave the Azusa and Duarte interests a distinct advantage over the Covina water users.

What amounted to an armed truce existed in the

Flume carrying water from the mouth of San Antonio Canyon to the Loop and Meserve Tract in Pomona, ca. 1877. To most valley residents, water, not gold, was the most valuable commodity of the San Gabriel Mountains. – POMONA PUBLIC LIBRARY

canyon during most of 1888, with occasional acts of sabotage. Extensive litigation continued in the courts as all parties tried to insure their respective water claims.

By the end of 1888 all parties were growing tired of the endless, pointless conflict and desired some kind of solution. Meetings were held to seek a compromise agreement. On January 26, 1889, representatives of all the local water interests — the Azusa and Duarte settlers, the Azusa Rancho owners, and the A.W.D.& I. Co. — signed what became known as the "Compromise of 1889." The compromise ended all disputes and divided the water, generally following allotments of earlier agreements, among the signing parties. The San Gabriel River Water Committee was created to administer the compromise agreement. The committee consisted of nine members, one from each of the nine companies or individuals involved in the agreement. It soon became known as the "Committee of Nine." (The Committee of Nine is still functioning today, 94 years later.)[4]

With harmony at last the water users were able to devote their efforts on improving the irrigation works. In 1892 their reorganized Azusa Irrigation Company, with the full sanction of the Committee of Nine, began construction of a modern water distribution system, complete with new flumes and cement pipes to replace the old dirt ditches. The Azusa-Duarte Tunnel was enlarged and extended 758 feet up-canyon. The new irrigation works were completed in 1896.

Two disputes marred the progress of the Committee of Nine in the decade after the Compromise of 1889. One involved the Vineland Water District, located where the city of Baldwin Park now stands. In 1893 the Vineland water users purchased water rights from Henry C. Roberts and built a tunnel from a point just inside San Gabriel Canyon southwestward to their fields. The Committee of Nine objected to this and constructed a redwood flume to carry water over the section of riverbed where the Vineland users' headworks was located. The flume reduced the water in the Vineland tunnel to a trickle. The unhappy Vinelanders then sent a party into the canyon and dismantled part of the redwood flume. The Committee of Nine immediately repaired the flume and dispatched armed guards into the canyon to protect it. Five years of litigation finally resulted in victory for the Committee of Nine; the California Supreme Court ruled in 1899 that the Committee had prior rights and disallowed the Vineland users' water claim.

The other dispute was with San Gabriel Canyon miners, actively involved in placer and hydraulic gold recovery since the 1850s. Periodically, the mining efforts would result in pollution of the river waters and the clogging of irrigation pipes. The problem was particularly acute during seasons of drought, when the river was low. In the late 1890s, the Committee of Nine brought suit against the canyon miners to enjoin them from polluting river water. The court enjoined the miners from using the river water any time the flow was less than the amount to which the irrigation users were entitled, and prohibited any pollution of the river.

By the year 1900, the Committee of Nine was functioning smoothly and efficiently as "lord of waters" in San Gabriel Canyon.

Disputes over water flowing from Big Dalton, San Dimas and San Antonio canyons were not as dramatic as the "war" over the San Gabriel River, but they nevertheless occurred and occasionally grew heated.

Early settlers in the Glendora area dug ditches from the mouth of Big Dalton Canyon to their homes and orchards, occasionally engaging in disputes over how much water each was entitled to from the various ditches. In 1887, the town of Glendora was founded and the Glendora Water Company was organized. Settlers pooled their interests and transferred to the new company their water rights to Big Dalton Canyon and the foothill springs. The company's first efforts were directed toward building two tunnels and cement pipes to convey the water from a mile inside Big Dalton Canyon to the homes and farms in the valley. During periodic dry years, Big Dalton Canyon had an insufficient flow to satisfy Glendora's needs. Residents were obliged to await the semi-weekly delivery of water from the San Gabriel River by means of horse and mule-drawn tanks.

Meanwhile, over the hill in Mud Springs (early name for San Dimas), the San Jose Land and Water Company was attempting to develop the water resources of San Dimas Canyon. The company met resistance from settlers who felt they had prior rights to the canyon water. In all, during the period from 1887 into the 1890s, there were twenty-two separate lawsuits over rights to San Dimas Canyon water. The most notable altercation was between attorney Richard Dunnigan of the San Jose Land and Water Company and a settler named Wicks. After a series of legal maneuvers failed to resolve the issue, Dunnigan took matters into his own hands and dispatched shotgun-toting guards into the canyon to protect company "rights". "Fort Dunnigan" was the name given to the armed camp at the canyon mouth. Wicks tried to outflank Dunnigan by springboarding into the upper canyon and laying pipe around the Dunnigan stronghold. Wicks' pipeline was a failure and was never used. San Dimas residents finally grew tired of the endless bickering and formed a compromise committee to adjudge the various and conflicting water claims. Out of this cooperative spirit emerged the San Dimas Water Company, organized at the turn of the century.

Water rights to San Antonio Creek were claimed and held almost exclusively by the Palomares family of Rancho San Jose de Ariba until 1874. The Palomares diverted a large portion of the stream via their seven-mile irrigation ditch to their cultivated fields in what is now the city of Pomona. Early settlers in the area, most notably Madison Moses Kincaid and A. A. Dexter who established residences at the mouth of San Antonio Canyon, were allowed to take what water they needed.

In 1874 Charles F. Loop and Alvin R. Meserve purchased 2,000 acres west of San Antonio Creek (between today's Pomona and Claremont) from the Palomares family. With the purchase of what became known as "The Loop and Meserve Tract" went water rights to San Antonio Creek. An elevated wood flume was constructed from just inside the mouth of San Antonio Canyon to the new tract, supplying plentiful water for domestic and irrigation purposes to the settlers who bought lots from Loop and Meserve.

The generous taking of water by Loop and Meserve disturbed the settlers on Rancho Cucamonga lands east of San Antonio Creek. The Cucamonga Water Company was organized in 1877 and claimed the right to divert and use the waters of the creek. Over the objections of Loop and Meserve, an irrigation ditch was dug southeastward from the canyon mouth and shotgun-carrying guards dispatched to protect it. Fortunately, both sides desired to avert violence and a compromise was reached. On December 8, 1877 an agreement divided the waters of San Antonio Creek equally between the two parties. A concrete division dam was built near the canyon mouth, with one flume going westward to the Loop and Meserve Tract, the other proceeding eastward to the Cucamonga lands.

New settlers poured into the Pomona Valley in the early 1880s. In 1882 Loop and Meserve conveyed most of their water rights to Cyrus T. Mills and M. L. Wicks, who in turn sold the rights to the new Pomona Land and Water Company, devoted to the building of a progressive colony on land purchased from the Palomares family. The city of Pomona was born. The new company proceeded to improve the water supply from San Antonio Canyon, building a new intake inside the canyon mouth, a redwood flume and cement pipe to convey the precious water to Pomona.

A spirited rivalry erupted almost at once with two new colonies on Rancho Cucamonga lands, organized by two brilliant, ingenious Canadians. George Chaffey and his brother William came from the province of Ontario, Canada in 1880 and settled first in Riverside. In 1881 they purchased the Garcia Ranch portion of Rancho Cucamonga, subdivided it, and founded the colony of Etiwanda. They incorporated the Etiwanda Water Company and proceeded to take water from nearby Day Canyon. The following year the Chaffey brothers purchased another, larger section of Rancho Cucamonga and began the subdivision they named Ontario, after the province of their birth. The Chaffeys took over the San Antonio Creek water rights of the old Cucamonga Water Company and proceeded to develop and improve the flow to their new subdivision. Pomona became concerned over sudden increased water-taking activity on the east side of San Antonio Canyon and sent gun-toting guards to the division works to insure that the Chaffeys didn't infringe on Pomona's right to half the water. To ease the threat of a water war, the Chaffeys and the Pomona Land and Water Company met and agreed to abide by the 1877 compromise, giving each party half of the surface water flow of San Antonio Creek.

Here George Chaffey's ingenuity came into play. The agreement with Pomona divided equally the surface water flow but said nothing about the subterranean flow. (Tapping underground stream flow was unknown in Southern California at the time.) Acting on a Spanish saying that "the rivers of California run bottom upward," Chaffey drove a tunnel into the canyon bed, the work being done by Chinese labor at wages of $1.75 per day, and struck a strong underground flow after penetrating 2,850 feet. A cement pipeline was built to bring the subterranean flow to the surface and join it with the surface flow, thereby securing an abundant supply of water for the Ontario Colony. Chaffey's tunnel is still in use today, supplying water to San Antonio Heights residents.

In November 1882, before completing his tunnel, Chaffey deeded his rights to San Antonio Canyon water to the newly-formed San Antonio Water Company, incorporated to supply the water needs of Ontario and the surrounding area, in exchange for 160 shares of stock. This new company was destined to jealously guard its water interests in San Antonio Canyon right up to the present day.

The San Antonio Water Company proceeded to rebuild and enlarge the tunnel, pipe and flume system that brought canyon water to Ontario. New concrete headgates were installed just beneath the Hogsback, the great rock hill barrier that for many years blocked easy entry into the upper canyon. To avoid friction with Pomona and the westside water users, agreement was reached in 1897 giving complete control of San Antonio Canyon water to the San Antonio Water Company; in return Pomona was guaranteed its half of the surface flow below the canyon entrance. Litigation by a number of canyon residents and land owners, and later by the U.S. Forest Service modified some of the Company's canyon water claims, but essentially the San Antonio Water Company remained "king of the canyon waters." And it exercised this "kingship" forcefully in zealous defense of its water rights.

Canyon water pollution was a major headache of the San Antonio Water Company. For years San Antonio Canyon had been a favorite camping area for valley residents, many of whom were careless in their sanitation practices. The *Pomona Progress* of August 15, 1889 complained that filth thrown into the stream by campers was endangering the water supply: "It is a common thing for horse manure to go floating down the stream and into the pipes that supply Chino and Ontario." The newspaper warned that the canyon might soon be closed to campers.

Closing the canyon to campers and visitors is just what the San Antonio Water Company attempted. In 1901 and 1903 the Company placed a locked gate across the road at the canyon entrance, but each time the gate was removed by Los Angeles County officials who claimed that the road was a public thoroughfare.

To further discourage visitors, the San Antonio Water Company began buying up all the usable land in the canyon it could get its hands on. By 1905 there was little canyon-bottom land not owned by the Company.

It appeared the public might soon have nowhere to go in San Antonio Canyon when Charles Baynham, a young Pomona College graduate, discovered a loophole. In 1906, looking over Forest Service maps, Baynham discovered forty acres of forested streamside land about two miles up-canyon from the Hogsback. He filed on the land and announced plans to convert the site into a resort camp.

The San Antonio Water Company was stunned by Baynham's filing on land it had neglected to lay claim, and was determined to stop him. In May 1906, the water company again placed a locked gate across the San Antonio Canyon road and dispatched armed guards to protect it. No one was allowed to enter the canyon without the water company's permission.

This set the stage for an epic battle, pitting the San Antonio Water Company, the city of Ontario, and San Bernardino County officials on one side, and Baynham, the City of Pomona, and Los Angeles County on the other. In June 1906, acting on a complaint from Pomona citizens, the L.A. County supervisors sent county road inspector I. W. Wire to remove the gate. Accompanied by some 200 Pomona and Claremont citizens, Wire tore down the gate and reopened the canyon road. Two water company guards were powerless to stop Wire and his angry mob. Next day the water company sent in a strong force of armed guards and replaced the gate. Whereupon Wire drove back to the canyon and, after a scuffle with the water company guards, again removed the gate. Fortunately, cool heads prevailed and no shots were fired, even though both parties were fully armed. After removing the gate, Wire was arrested by the company guards, forcibly taken to Upland across the county line, and charged with "malicious destruction of property." (The boundary between L.A. and San Bernardino counties crosses the lower reaches of San Antonio Canyon; the disputed gate was just inside L.A. County.) Released on bail, Wire charged that his arrest was illegal, in that San Bernardino County deputies had no right to charge him with an offense committed in L.A. County. Anger ran high on both sides. A Pomona newspaper reported, "Feeling on this side of the county line is so worked up over what might be termed the high-handed proceedings of the San Bernardino deputy guards of the water company, that it would only take a spark . . . to precipitate a possibly serious fight."[5]

The San Antonio Canyon gate dispute ended up in court, with each county suing the other to uphold or deny the water company's right to close the canyon road. In a series of conflicting decisions, the San Antonio Water Company was adjudged the owner of the road, while Baynham was given the right of access to his proposed resort. In the end, the water company was enjoined from keeping people out of the canyon. After assurances by all parties concerned that efforts would be made to keep San Antonio Creek free from pollution, the water company gave up its fight and, in 1908, opened a toll road into the canyon. Thus began the popular resort era in San Antonio Canyon (covered in a later chapter).

Dr. Cyrus G. Baldwin, Pomona College president, envisioned the use of hydroelectric power from San Antonio Canyon to light up Pomona. In 1891-1892 his San Antonio Light and Power Company built a power plant in the canyon just below the Hogsback, bringing vision into reality. – POMONA PUBLIC LIBRARY, SPECIAL COLLECTIONS

HYDROELECTRIC POWER

Hydroelectric energy — harnessing water to produce electricity — was unknown in Southern California prior to 1882. In that year, the ingenious Canadian, George Chaffey, installed a small dynamo near the mouth of Day Canyon above Etiwanda. The dynamo, powered by the down-rushing current of the mountain stream, provided electricity for an arc light atop Chaffey's Etiwanda ranch house. Every night, the strange white beam flashed across the colony, arousing curiosity and wonderment.

Chaffey's experiment with a dynamo and arc light was just a forerunner to larger projects ahead. In 1891 Dr. Cyrus G. Baldwin, president of Pomona College, proposed the building of a hydroelectric plant in San Antonio Canyon. Baldwin had visited the canyon on numerous occasions with camping parties and had noticed the waterfall plunging over the Hogsback. Here was the potential to generate electricity, he thought, power that would provide Pomona with electric lights and operate a street railroad between that city and the college town of Claremont. He also envisioned the possibility of supplying electric power to the nearby communities of Ontario, Chino and even San Bernardino.

The upper end of the San Antonio Light and Power Company's tunnel through the Hogsback, immediately after completion in 1892. The tunnel diverted water from San Antonio Creek through the mountain, dropping 412 vertical feet in 1,300 linear feet to the power house immediately below the Hogsback.
– POMONA PUBLIC LIBRARY, SPECIAL COLLECTIONS

Dr. Baldwin presented his hydroelectric proposal to the Pomona Board of Trade (forerunner to the Chamber of Commerce). The Board gave him an enthusiastic endorsement and promised financial backing for his idea. The plan was relatively simple. It called for the boring of a 1,300-foot tunnel through the Hogsback to serve as a steep flume dropping the creek 400 feet to a powerhouse below. High voltage lines would transmit the generated current to Pomona and other points.

In November 1891 the San Antonio Light and Power Company was organized with Baldwin as president and Arthur W. Burt of Ontario as general manager. Capital was supplied by a number of Pomona and Ontario businessmen. First problem faced by the new enterprise was procuring equipment. There was no comparable installation anywhere in the West that might serve as a model. Dr. Baldwin went East to consult with the Westinghouse Company, and after an initial negative response, persuaded George Westinghouse to not only provide the equipment for the powerhouse and transmission lines but also to install it under the supervision of Westinghouse engineers and guarantee it for a year.

Hurrying home, Baldwin and his Westinghouse consultants set the wheels in motion to divert San Antonio Creek and construct the powerhouse. Water was diverted by a dam above Hogsback into a pipeline 2,370 feet long which led into the 1,300-foot inclined tunnel. After a 412-foot drop through the Hogsback, the water emerged at the powerhouse. This building was a concrete structure 66 feet long and 30 feet wide built into the side of the mountain. It housed the latest model Westinghouse circular dynamo, capable of generating more than 5,000 volts of electricity

On November 28, 1892, just a year after its organization, the San Antonio Light and Power Company transmitted its first electric power over a 5,000-volt high tension line, lighting up arc and incandescent lights fourteen miles away in Pomona. A month later another switch was thrown and electricity flowed to San Bernardino 28¾ miles away. So efficient was the plant's operation that early in 1893 transmission was stepped up to 10,000 volts. Operating expenses were lower than expected, making it possible to supply electric current for less than competing steam installations.

The tunnel through the Hogsback in operation, 1894. – POMONA PUBLIC LIBRARY, SPECIAL COLLECTIONS

The original power house of Baldwin's San Antonio Light and Power Company, ca. 1898. The solidly-built structure housed a Westinghouse circular dynamo capable of generating 10,000 volts of electricity. The power thus generated was transmitted to Pomona. – POMONA PUBLIC LIBRARY, SPECIAL COLLECTIONS

The interior of the San Antonio Light and Power Company's power house, showing the Westinghouse dynamo.
– POMONA PUBLIC LIBRARY, SPECIAL COLLECTIONS

William G. Kerckhoff, Los Angeles businessman, was the leading name in hydroelectic power development in Southern California. With Henry O'Melveny, he founded the San Gabriel Power Company in 1894 to generate power from San Gabriel Canyon. In 1902 he expanded his hydroelectric efforts under the banner of the Pacific Light and Power Company, tapping streams from the San Bernardino Mountains to the High Sierras. – HENRY E. HUNTINGTON LIBRARY

The San Antonio powerplant was a model of generating efficiency. Its performance exceeded all expectations. But the one factor Dr. Baldwin and the Westinghouse engineers could not control was nature. And here, Dame Fortune proved fickle. 1898 and 1899 were years of drought, dry beyond any previous record. San Antonio Creek was reduced to a small trickle, with insufficient flow to power the dynamos below the Hogsback. To fulfill contracts, stockholders were obliged to come up with additional funds to build a supplementary steam plant. By 1900, Baldwin's company was hopelessly in debt. The powerhouse and transmission lines were finally sold to William G. Kerckhoff's San Gabriel Electric Company.

Kerckhoff, like Baldwin, was a pioneer in Southern California hydroelectric power development. Over the years, his became *the* leading name in the hydroelectric field, while Baldwin's name faded into near obscurity with the passage of time. Kerckhoff, a young and enterprising Los Angeles businessman, first became interested in hydroelectric energy as a possible power source for an ice-making plant in Azusa, in which he had invested in 1888. Early in 1891 Kerckhoff went to the office of prominent Los Angeles attorney Henry O'Melveny with a proposal to build a hydroelectric plant in San Gabriel Canyon. O'Melveny liked the plan, became a partner, and rounded up other investors. Two engineers were hired to survey a conduit route. By year's end, 1891, they had mapped an eight-mile conduit route along the east wall of the canyon, and had located a site for a power plant just outside the canyon mouth.

Kerckhoff and O'Melveny quickly discovered that obtaining the necessary water rights was a major stumbling block. The Committee of Nine, fearful of losing precious irrigation water, was a tough and stubborn bargaining agent. It would require five years of difficult negotiation to reach agreement.

Meanwhile, Kerckhoff and O'Melveny went on with their hydroelectric power plans, confident that some kind of accommodation with the Committee of Nine would be reached. They incorporated the San Gabriel Power Company in May 1894. In 1896 they gained the services of electrical engineer A. C. Balch, one of the best in his field. Balch was made a full partner and took over management of the canyon project. In May 1897 the San Gabriel Power Company, with several new investors, was reincorporated as the San Gabriel Electric Company, capitalized at $500,000.

Construction work proceeded smoothly, under the guidance of Charlie Smith of Azusa. The sound of pick and hammer reverberated from canyon walls as the large conduit, beginning eight miles up canyon, was hewed from solid rock and tunneled through promontories. The conduit reached the east canyon portal 500 feet above the powerhouse, built at the base of the mountain southeast of the canyon mouth. The hydroelectric plant was designed to produce 2,000 kilowatts when operating at full capacity. No longer were Kerckhoff and O'Melveny content to produce power solely for the Azusa ice-making plant; their goal now was to transmit electricity to Los Angeles.

But these efforts would come to naught if negotiations failed with the all-powerful Committee of Nine. The main divisive issue was the amount of water salvaged by the hydroelectric conduit. Naturally, the water being diverted belonged to members represented by the Committee of Nine. The San Gabriel Electric Company, however, claimed to be instrumental in saving a great quantity of water which normally would have been lost

William G. Kerckhoff purchased Baldwin's debt-ridden San Antonio Light and Power Company in 1901 and temporarily renamed it the Sierra Power Company. He abandoned the original powerhouse below the Hogsback and built a new one with three times the generating capacity a mile down canyon. This 1904 view shows Kerckhoff's Sierra Power Plant and part of the stream diverging works in lower San Antonio Canyon.
– POMONA PUBLIC LIBRARY, SPECIAL COLLECTIONS

through evaporation and percolation, had the water been allowed to flow in the river bed. After months of discussion, the Committee finally conceded that ten percent was the actual quantity of water salvaged by the conduit, and granted this amount to Kerckhoff. The last obstacle was surmounted by this agreement signed in March 1898. By June 30, 1898 power was being transmitted from San Gabriel Canyon to Los Angeles, and Kerckhoff's dream was realized.

Kerckhoff was not content to rest on his laurels. He was determined to make his San Gabriel Canyon powerplant number one in Southern California. To reduce water waste and increase the plant's efficiency, The San Gabriel Electric Company in 1900 constructed a submerged dam 300 feet long and 73 feet deep seven miles up-canyon. Its purpose was to reduce the underflow of the river and allow more water to enter the conduit intake. The subterranean dam failed to noticeably increase the water intake. The problem was finally solved by increasing the capacity of the conduit to 36,000 gallons per minute.

Kerckhoff's interest in hydroelectric development extended beyond San Gabriel Canyon. He was the leading pioneer in expanding this power source throughout Southern California. To this end, he acquired hydroelectric plants and promoted new development wherever he deemed it profitable. In 1901 he purchased Baldwin's San Antonio Power and Light Company, acquired control of the Mentone Power Company near Redlands, and, with O'Melveny and others, incorporated the Kern Power Company near Bakersfieled. Kerckhoff briefly renamed his enlarged enterprises the Sierra Power Company. In San Antonio Canyon, he abandoned Baldwin's old Hogsback powerhouse and built a new, enlarged hydroelectric plant a mile down-canyon with triple the capacity of the original. On March 6, 1902 all of Kerckhoff's hydroelectric ventures were merged into the Pacific Light and Power Company, capitalized at $10 million.

Kerckhoff's San Gabriel Electric Company's powerhouse just outside the mouth of San Gabriel Canyon, ca. 1898. Notice the conduit descending the hillside to build up "head" to turn the dynamos. – HENRY E. HUNTINGTON LIBRARY

The Pacific Light and Power Company (which soon became known simply as P.L. & P.) immediately looked toward expansion of hydroelectric facilities in San Gabriel Canyon. In July 1907, a 14-man survey and engineering crew was sent into the East Fork, the largest of the three main streams of the San Gabriel River. Here, just below the rugged Narrows, the P.L. & P. hoped to erect a power plant fed by a three-mile conduit to bring water from the upper reaches of the gorge. One of those employed in this exploratory work was George Trogden, who liked the canyon so well he remained the rest of his life, living in a rustic stone canyon at Iron Fork. In 1911 the natural stillness of the Narrows was broken by the shattering din of jackhammers, hewing a level flume-bed out of the west wall of the Narrows high above the river. Although the bed was completed, neither the flume nor the power plant was ever built. Today, hikers walking the "P.L. & P. Trail" above the Narrows follow this old flume bed.

The P. L. & P. concentrated its efforts in operating the conduit and powerhouse at the mouth of San Gabriel Canyon, utilized largely as a generating system for Henry E. Huntington's electric railway lines in and around Los Angeles. In time, Huntington's Pacific Electric Company gained the controlling interest in the P. L. & P., while Kerckhoff devoted his main efforts on the colossal hydroelectric system on the San Joaquin River in the Sierra Nevada.[6]

Meanwhile, others attempted to emulate William Kerckhoff's hydroelectric achievements in the San Gabriels. Most successful was the Ontario Power

Interior of Kerckhoff's San Gabriel Electric Company powerhouse, ca. 1898. – HENRY E. HUNTINGTON LIBRARY

Company, organized in 1902 to provide electric service to the Ontario colony. Ontario's Number 1 plant was completed in San Antonio Canyon late in 1902, its Number 2 plant in 1919, and Number 3 plant in 1922. Together, the three powerhouses provided enough electrical energy to light up Ontario, Upland and several other nearby communities.

Not so successful were a number of hydroelectric ventures in San Gabriel Canyon. Several Los Angeles businessmen incorporated the Electric Power Company in 1892 and announced their intention of building a powerhouse near the Forks to supply electricity to Los Angeles. By March 1893 five miles of ditches, flumes and tunnels were completed, and 100,000 pounds of machinery was sitting in Azusa awaiting shipment up-canyon. But the enterprise was never completed. Costs exceeded expectations, technical problems were encountered, and the Committee of Nine proved a stubborn adversary. The Electric Power Company gave up its efforts in 1903.

The Crystal Lake Irrigation and Power Company was incorporated in 1897. The company paid R. W. Dawson, North Fork land-holder, $5,000 with $15,000 promised later for water rights to Crystal Lake, and planned to pipe water from the lake down to a pair of powerhouses in the North Fork — one at Sycamore Flats (today's Coldbrook Public Campground), the other at the mouth of Bichota Canyon. The ambitious plan was abandoned when it was belatedly discovered that Crystal Lake was fed by run-off water only and there was insufficient water in the North Fork drainage to power a hydroelectric operation.

The brief but energetic saga of the P. L. & P. came to a close in 1917, when the company merged with the giant of electric power development in the southern half of the state, the Southern California Edison Company. Ten years later, in the fall of 1927, Edison purchased the Ontario Power Company. For a time the Edison Company operated all the major powerhouses in the canyons of the San Gabriel Mountains. In 1933 it sold the San Gabriel Canyon power system to the city of Pasadena in conjunction with the latter's Morris Dam project. Pasadena maintained the old conduit, relocating the sections displaced by the construction of San Gabriel and Morris dams, and operates the power plant on the outskirts of Azusa to this day.

FLOOD CONTROL

Those familiar with the long-term climate of Southern California know that the weather, year to year, varies considerably. A cycle of normal precipitation, lasting several years, may be followed by seasons of drought or flood. Climate records, dating back to mission days, reveal that rainfall high enough to cause serious flooding occurs about six times a century.[7] Precipitation in the mountains is always much heavier than in the lowlands, and the result is that normally peaceful mountain streams turn into raging torrents. Canyon bottoms are swept clean and there is flood damage in the valley below. Mountain rampages such as this occurred in 1862 (the demise of Eldoradoville), 1868, 1884, 1914, 1916, 1938 and 1969.

All of these years except the last saw the San Gabriel River, Big Dalton, San Dimas and San Antonio creeks overflow their banks and do damage in the communities below the mountains. Harnessing the streams emitting from the San Gabriel Mountains was discussed by the Los Angeles County Board of Supervisors as early as 1893, but no concrete action was taken for many years. The floods of 1914 resulted in renewed agitation for effective flood control, and the following year the Los Angeles County Flood Control District was formed. That flood control was an urgent necessity was again demonstrated by a destructive flood in January 1916. Two months later, County Flood Control engineer John W. Reagan submitted a $3,600,000 flood control plan to the supervisors. Reagan's proposal included control projects for the San Gabriel River, Big Dalton Canyon and San Dimas Canyon. Early in 1917 the Board of Supervisors submitted to the voters a $4,450,000 bond issue to provide for flood control dams on watercourses emitting from the south side of the San Gabriel Mountains. The bonds emerged victorious by the barest of margins: 51% to 49%. Opponents contested the result, and it was not until January 1918 that the election was validated by the court and serious work toward harnessing the mountain streams could begin.

Chief engineer Reagan commenced work almost immediately on a proposed dam just inside the mouth of San Dimas Canyon. Engineering studies were made, blueprints were drawn up, and construction of the $560,000 concrete dam began in November 1920. The structure, the first of its kind in the San Gabriel Mountains, was completed in September 1922 and dedicated the following April in an impressive ceremony attended by more than 500 persons.

San Dimas Dam and reservoir have been in operation for more than a half century. The dam itself is 130 feet high, 430 feet wide, and contains 50,000 cubic feet of concrete. The reservoir behind the dam is one mile long when filled and has a storage capacity of 1,820 acre-feet. It effectively controls the entire San Dimas watershed of sixteen square miles.

San Dimas Dam shortly after completion in 1922. The first of the modern flood control dams built in the San Gabriels. – SAN DIMAS HISTORICAL SOCIETY

Big Dalton Dam, built by the Los Angeles County Flood Control District in 1927-1929, is a modern multiple-arch structure, more resembling a beautiful piece of sculpture than a simple flood control barrier. This picture was taken in June 1941, when the reservoir was filled to capacity. – HENRY E. HUNTINGTON LIBRARY

Only in 1938 and 1969 did the reservoir water level reach high enough to overflow the spillway, but the overflow was of short duration and resulted in minimum damage to the valley below.

The dam in Big Dalton Canyon was not built as quickly nor as easily as San Dimas Dam. It required the utmost effort of the Glendora Chamber of Commerce, the strong support of Supervisor Prescott F. Cogswell — often called the "father" of Los Angeles County flood control — and a new bond issue to get the project under way. And even then there were long delays.

The $4,450,000 bond issue of 1916 proved wholly inadequate to finance the multitude of dams and channels planned for the south side of the San Gabriel Mountains, so a new $32,361,000 flood control bond issue was submitted to the county voters in May 1924. Among the projects promised if the bond was approved was a dam for Big Dalton Canyon, to cost $650,000. The voters approved the expenditure and the way appeared open for rapid construction of the Big Dalton structure.

Engineering studies and drilling for bedrock commenced in late 1924. A dam site was chosen two miles up the canyon, and excavation was begun early in 1926. A month later construction was halted when engineers discovered that the bedrock under the dam was unstable. Engineers proposed a new site 400 feet up-canyon, then reversed themselves and decided to use the original location. The newly-laid foundation was torn out and excavation went deeper to solid bedrock. A further delay occurred when engineers could not agree on what type of dam to build. After studying the feasibility of an earthen dam, the builders rejected this and decided upon a revolutionary multiple-arch structure, to be the first of its kind in Southern California.

At last, in November 1927, ground was broken and Big Dalton Dam was underway. Under the guidance of E. C. Eaton, Reagan's successor as chief flood control engineer, work proceeded rapidly on the unique seven-arch structure. Crews worked six days a week as the white concrete rampart, more resembling a beautiful piece of sculpture than a simple flood control barrier, rose dramatically from the canyon floor. Two workers lost their lives when a landslide buried their steam shovel in October 1928. The dam was finally completed and dedicated in August 1929. Since then, Big Dalton Canyon has been effectively harnessed against nature's occasional wet rampage.

Big Dalton Dam is 161 feet high and 480 feet wide across the top. Its storage reservoir has a capacity to hold 1,500 acre-feet of water. Only twice has it been fully tested, holding back the angry torrents of 1938 and 1969 and earning the thankful respect of Glendora residents. Today, half a century after completion, Big Dalton Dam remains the most splendid man-made structure in the San Gabriels.

Upstream side of Big Dalton Dam, 1934.
– U.S. FOREST SERVICE

At the same time Big Dalton Dam was going up, the County Flood Control District constructed a concrete dam near the mouth of Sawpit Canyon above Monrovia, ending the flood threat to that thriving community.

Saved for the last were the big dams in San Gabriel Canyon, largest and potentially most destructive watercourse in the San Gabriel Mountains. One might suppose that these dams would be given first attention by the County Flood Control District, so devastating were the floods that emitted from this gorge. But seemingly endless legal obstructions, engineering mistakes and financial uncertainties, topped by a scandal in the highest level of county government, delayed the completion of the three dams for almost twenty years. The San Gabriel did not give up her "water rights" easily.

As early as 1916, county flood control engineer John W. Reagan proposed a dam in San Gabriel Canyon. While the county supervisors and other interested parties wrangled over the proposed barrier, several experimental wire and brush check dams were built in the lower canyon. The method used was to drive piles into the riverbed, secure wiring to the piles, and fill the area behind the wires with brush. These miniscule "dams" were an exercise in futility. A grand jury report in 1921 condemned them as useless. It would require efforts of a much more substantial nature to control the San Gabriel River.

Facts About San Gabriel Dam

San Gabriel Flood Control Dam, located 11 miles up San Gabriel Canyon from Azusa, the Gateway, is the largest dam in the world. It is the largest public improvement ever undertaken by Los Angeles County, excepting only the building of public roads. The cost, $25,000,000, is equal to that of the Los Angeles Aqueduct and is also equal to the expenditure of the City of Los Angeles for the harbor at San Pedro.

The Dam will contain 4,000,000 cubic yards of concrete, compared with 5,000,000 cubic yards of concrete used in the construction of the Panama Canal and 3,000,000 cubic yards to be used in Boulder Dam on the Colorado River.

After several years of negotiation, work on the dam commenced in January, 1929. Five to seven years will be required to complete the project. The Dam will have an impounding capacity of 240,000 acre feet of water, but as this is primarily a flood control and not a storage project, it is possible this amount of water will not be impounded, for some time.

The Dam is 425 feet high from stream bed to top; 500 feet high from bed rock to top; 2400 feet wide at top; 900 feet wide at bottom; 407 feet thick at bottom and 20 feet thick at top. It is what is known as a gravity type dam, depending on its enormous weight for its stability. Some of the most prominent engineers in the West have been employed in an active or an advisory capacity in working out the plans. Four contracting firms joined forces in order to provide facilities for the construction work.

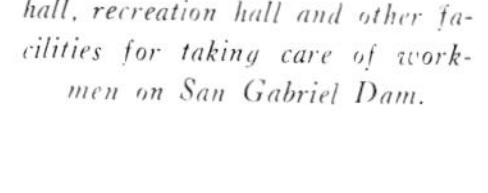

Bunk houses for 800 men, dining hall, recreation hall and other facilities for taking care of workmen on San Gabriel Dam.

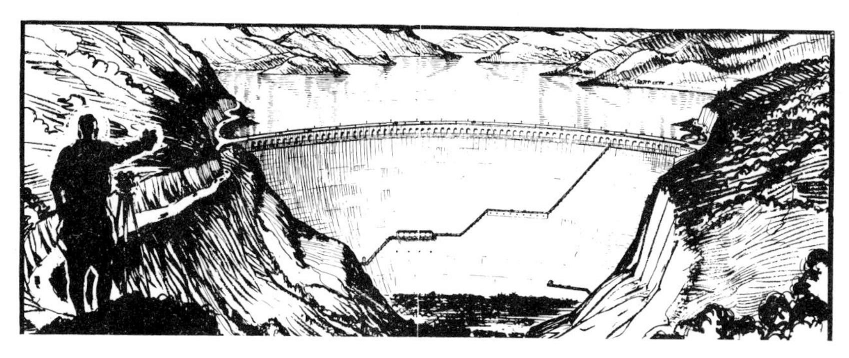

Publicity for the mighty San Gabriel Forks Dam put out by the City of Azusa in 1929. If completed, it would have been the world's largest at the time.

In 1921, after completing an engineering study of possible dam sites in San Gabriel Canyon, Reagan announced a proposal to construct a concrete dam 425 feet high and 1,700 feet across, to be located in the main canyon just below the confluence of the West and East forks. This "Forks Dam," as it became known, would be the world's largest concrete structure and would create a reservoir of eight square miles.

At the time, the only route up the canyon was a poor dirt road, annually washed out and repaired, that crossed and recrossed the river without benefit of a bridge a dozen times — totally inadequate for transporting construction materials for the dam. To remedy this problem, Reagan proposed that the county build a standard gauge rail line from the Santa Fe tracks in Azusa up-canyon twelve miles to the dam site.

But again, construction was delayed by legal obstacles, financial uncertainties and conflicting engineering studies. The main objection to building the canyon railroad came from the city of Pasadena, which wanted to erect its own dam in the lower canyon. In 1926 Los Angeles County filed an application with the Department of the Interior (most of the canyon was federal land) to build the railroad up the canyon floor. The Interior Department initially ruled against the rail line, citing Pasadena's objections, then reversed itself and approved the canyon railroad. By year's end, legal obstacles were finally out of the way, the county taxpayers had approved a $25 million bond issue to build the dam, and construction was at last ready to begin.

Work crews under Superintendent R. H. Travers of the Nevada Construction Company, contractors for the canyon railroad, hurriedly graded a roadbed out of Azusa and into San Gabriel Canyon. Other crews followed the graders, laying wooden ties and spiking down steel rails. Within a month three miles of the line were completed and blasting crews were gouging a tunnel through the horseshoe ridge a mile inside the canyon mouth. Once through this obstacle, the railroad took shape rapidly. By July 1927, eight miles along the east floor of the canyon were finished and a trestle was under construction to move the line to the west side of the river for the final four miles. The canyon railroad was completed in September 1927, and Superintendent Travers proudly turned it over to Los Angeles County. All was in readiness now, many thought, to begin construction of the great Forks Dam.

Construction city, housing over 600 workers, for the San Gabriel Forks dam project, 1929. Below the city is the upper terminal of the San Gabriel Canyon railroad, built to bring in equipment and supplies to build the dam. The forks dam was never completed; a massive landslide caused the abandonment of the project.
– LOS ANGELES COUNTY FLOOD CONTROL DISTRICT

World's largest electric shovel loading debris onto flatcar at Forks Dam project, 1929.

But the canyon railroad lay idle for more than a year. New hassles erupted over the size and cost of the dam. A board of consulting engineers recommended that the barrier be lowered in height from 425 to 385 feet. Chief flood control engineer E. C. Eaton, who had succeeded Reagan in 1926, insisted on the original height. While the county supervisors argued over this, a taxpayers' suit demanded all work be stopped until a complete cost analysis could be made. The supervisors first voted to lower the dam to 385 feet, then reversed themselves and opted for the original high dam. The taxpayer group was finally placated when the supervisors promised that the cost of the dam would not exceed $25 million.

While all this was going on, a disaster took place along the Santa Clara River in Ventura County that had implications toward the building of the Forks Dam. During the night of March 12, 1928, the newly-completed St. Francis Dam, part of the Owens Valley Aqueduct system, gave way. The resulting torrent swept all the way to the sea and claimed over 400 lives. The supervisors immediately ordered Eaton and the consulting engineers to review the plans for the Forks Dam to make certain a similar disaster would not occur in San Gabriel Canyon. And within a year, new state regulations would tighten dam-building standards throughout California.

Reassured by Eaton that the dam site was safe, the supervisors called for bids on the Forks Dam in July 1928. In November the contract was awarded to the lowest of six bidders, the San Francisco firm of Fisher, Ross, McDonald and Kahn. The construction contract was signed on December 7, 1928, and the San Francisco firm announced that work would proceed at once. After years of delay, it appeared that the great dam was about to become reality.

By February 1929 work was in full swing. The San Gabriel Canyon railroad was ferrying in men, equipment and materials around the clock. A construction camp the size of a small city, built to house a work force of over 600, sprang up just below the dam site. So as not to block canyon travel, a new "high line" road was carved in the west canyon wall, climbing high over the top of the dam-to-be. By March two of the world's largest electric shovels were in operation, and the first cache of black powder was exploded on the west wall, loosening tons of earth and rocks. Powerful jet streams of water were directed at the loose material, washing it to the canyon bottom to be loaded on railroad flatcars and hauled away. In this manner, 600,000 tons of dirt and rock had been removed by June.

Operations were at a peak when, on the afternoon of September 16, 1929, misfortune struck. "Accompanied by a roar and rumble that could be heard for miles, an enormous earth movement carrying 100,000 tons of rock and earth from an approximate height of 400 feet crashed into the pit of excavation," reported the *Los Angeles Times* (September 17, 1929). A landslide had crumbled the west wall, negating months of work. Water and power lines were destroyed, and several hundred feet of the railroad was buried. Fortunately no lives were lost; chief engineer Eaton had noticed signs of impending earth movement the previous day and had ordered the men away from the threatened area.

No one realized it at the time, but the landslide spelled the end for the Forks Dam. Work was suspended while engineers studied the west abutment. Their report, given to the supervisors in October, stated that a safe dam at the proposed height of 425 feet could not be built at the Forks site because of unstable rock conditions.

The final demise of the Forks Dam project occurred following an investigation by engineers of the State Department of Water Resources, authorized by the state legislature as a consequence of the St. Francis Dam disaster. The state engineers concluded that "the dam proposed . . . cannot be constructed without creating a menace to life and property." As a result, the State of California, on November 26, 1929, revoked the Los Angeles County Flood Control District's permit to build the Forks Dam.

The Forks Dam fiasco wasted almost three million dollars of the taxpayers' money. And the bitter aftertaste did not end with the final abandonment of the project. Not only was the county condemned for gross engineering mistakes, but charges of bribery and corruption at the highest level of county government crept into the picture. Following a grand jury investigation, it was revealed that $80,000 had been "transferred" from the San Francisco firm of Fisher, Ross, McDonald and Kahn to the personal account of Los Angeles County Supervisor Sidney Graves while the contract was being negotiated. Supervisor Graves was indicted, tried and convicted of accepting a bribe, and in 1933 sentenced to a term in San Quentin Prison. The contractors were indicted for offering the bribe but never brought to trial. A civil damage suit for $2.6 million was filed by the county supervisors against the contractors; it was settled in 1936 with the county recovering $737,986. Reagan and Eaton of the County Flood Control District were exonerated of any criminal wrongdoing, but their reputations as competent engineers were sullied as had been William Mulholland's after the St. Francis Dam disaster. So ended what county supervisor John Anson Ford called "the darkest episode" in the history of Los Angeles County government.

Morris Dam, built by the city of Pasadena to supplement it s water supply, rises in white majesty, September 1933. To the left is the spillway under construction. The 10-million dollar bulwark was completed in less than two years and named in honor of Samuel Morris, chief engineer of the Pasadena Water Department.
– PASADENA WATER DEPARTMENT PHOTO

The Forks Dam fiasco failed to deter Pasadena from building its dam in lower San Gabriel Canyon. Pasadena's motive was water. Since its birth in 1873, Pasadena had obtained its water from the Arroyo Seco and other nearby streams above the city. By 1920 these local water sources were insufficient to meet the growing city's needs, and Pasadena began searching for additional supplies. After a three-year investigation by Samuel B. Morris, superintendent of the Pasadena Municipal Water Department, attention was focused on San Gabriel Canyon. Here, Morris believed, was the only practical source for Pasadena's increasing water requirements. Acting on Morris' recommendation, the City of Pasadena filed an application with the California Division of Water Rights to appropriate the flood waters of the San Gabriel River in March 1923.

Morris' plan called for a concrete dam four miles up the canyon to store water, and a 17-mile conduit along the foothills to bring the water to Pasadena. The proposed dam, located near the junction of Pine Canyon and the main canyon, became known as the Pine Canyon Dam.

Almost immediately, Pasadena found itself the target of strenuous protests. This opposition came not only from the Committee of Nine, but also from the more powerful San Gabriel Valley Protective Association, organized in 1919 to safeguard the rights of water users from Azusa to Whittier. Much to the chagrin of the S.G.V.P.A. and the Committee of Nine, the State granted Pasadena permission to build its dam and conduit in July 1928.

A new aspect entered the picture in November 1928 with the creation of the Metropolitan Water District of Southern California. The intention of the new M.W.D. was to build an aqueduct from the Colorado River to the Los Angeles basin, thus providing ample water supplies to thirsty Southern California. Although Pasadena was a charter member of the M.W.D., Morris felt that the city should continue its Pine Canyon Dam project because Colorado River water could not be delivered

Morris Dam under construction, September 1933. In the background can be seen the new "high line" highway up San Gabriel Canyon, great improvement over the old canyon-bottom road.
– PASADENA WATER DEPARTMENT PHOTO

Morris Dam and reservoir immediately after completion, 1934. Pasadena used the reservoir to supplement its water supply until the completion of the Metropolitan Water District's aqueduct from the Colorado River in 1941. Morris Reservoir was used by the M.W.D. for water storage until 1977, when it was turned over to the L.A. County Flood Control District. – PASADENA WATER DEPARTMENT PHOTO

in time to meet the impending shortage.

In May 1929 the Secretary of the Interior granted Pasadena the right to build a reservoir on federal lands in San Gabriel Canyon. A month later Pasadena voters overwhelmingly approved a $10 million bond measure to authorize construction of the dam and conduit.

The S.G.V.P.A. and other San Gabriel River users as far away as Long Beach made plans to resist what they considered the Pasadena "water grab." A mammoth court struggle appeared likely. In March 1932, as Pasadena was moving in material and equipment to start work on the Pine Canyon Dam, the S.G.V.P.A. filed suit in superior court to enjoin construction. Thirty-nine plaintiffs, representing almost every city along the San Gabriel River from Azusa to the sea, were parties in the suit. The plaintiffs alleged that the Pasadena dam would deprive them of water rights, retard growth, and that such a dam posed "a great threat to lives and property down river," this latter fueled by memories of the St. Francis Dam disaster.

There was one avenue toward possible compromise that might avoid a long and costly legal battle that neither side really wanted. This was the fact that Pasadena wanted San Gabriel River water only for a limited time – until the M.W.D. aqueduct from the Colorado River was completed and able to deliver water to the city. With this factor in mind, Pasadena and the numerous plaintiffs began negotiations aimed at reaching a possible compromise in April 1932, the same month that Pasadena broke ground for her Pine Canyon Dam.

Ground-breaking ceremonies were held at the Pine Canyon sit on April 26, 1932. Within a few weeks, excavation work was in full swing, with over

Morris Dam with valves and spillway open, 1965.
– LOS ANGELES COUNTY FLOOD CONTROL DISTRICT

300 workers busily employed. The *Azusa Herald* of August 5, 1932 described the dam site as "a veritable beehive of industry. Hundreds of workmen with steam shovels, fleets of trucks, blasting crews and overhead tramways rush and roar above the shouts of foremen calling orders to their men. Down into the rocky depths beneath the San Gabriel River, a great gaping hole is being deepened daily. The crews are seeking a bedrock that will satisfy state engineers of the safety of the dam's foundation. Into the walls of the mountain on either side, great rifts are being gouged out and into these tons of cement will be poured to anchor the huge water barrier." By October, the great white bulwark began to rise slowly from the canyon's bowels as crews worked around the clock to beat the freshets of winter.

While construction was in full swing, Pasadena and the San Gabriel River water users reached a settlement of their dispute. In a pact signed on June 27, 1934, Pasadena was allowed to complete the dam and use San Gabriel River water until Colorado River water became available through the M.W.D. In return, Pasadena agreed to relinquish all rights to San Gabriel River water once water from the Colorado arrived.

The Pine Canyon Dam, rising in white majesty 325 feet above the canyon floor, was completed in January 1934. Ex-president Herbert Hoover was the featured speaker at an impressive dedication ceremony on May 26, 1934. The great bulwark was christened "Samuel B. Morris Dam," in tribute to Pasadena's water engineer chiefly responsible for its construction. Morris, about to retire, gave a moving tribute to his fellow workers, then turned the valve wheel that sent the first water flowing toward Pasadena.

San Gabriel Valley residents soon discovered that Morris Dam was a beneficial blessing rather than a millstone around their necks, when, in January 1934 and again in the winter of 1936, the barrier held back floodwaters that would otherwise have played havoc in the valley.

Colorado River water became available to Pasadena in June 1941. Consequently, on August 1, 1941 Pasadena relinquished title to Morris Dam and reservoir to the M.W.D.

Morale in the Los Angeles County Flood Control District was badly shaken by the Forks Dam failure and the ensuing bribery scandal. Nevertheless, the pressing need for flood control protection caused the county supervisors to order surveys to locate new dam sites in San Gabriel Canyon. Consequently, chief engineer Eaton came up with a plan to build three new dams in the canyon — one in the main canyon two miles below the Forks, one in the West Fork, and one in the East Fork near Camp Bonita. The cost was estimated at $21 million, an amount remaining in the county treasury originally earmarked for the Forks Dam. The supervisors, after hearing reports from a special board of consulting engineers, approved the new dams for the main canyon and the West Fork (known as Dams No. 1 and No. 2, respectively), but rejected the proposed East Fork dam.

The state engineer approved the plans for Dam No. 2 in January 1932, and two weeks later the supervisors called for bids. In March a $2 million construction contract for the West Fork barrier was awarded to the Macco and Lewis construction companies, joint low bidders. Within a month 300 men were at the site, a workmen's camp was hurriedly built, and heavy machinery was being hauled up from Azusa. The first shovelful of dirt was turned on April 15, 1932.

Dam No. 2 was running right on schedule, but Dam No. 1 was not. The design for the latter structure, to be the major flood control dam in San Gabriel Canyon, was altered several times. Instead of a concrete dam as first proposed, it was decided to make it a rockfill dam, the world's largest. With the plans finally agreed upon, Dam No. 1 was approved by the state engineer in June 1932. A month later the Secretary of the Interior gave his approval for the use of public lands as a reservoir, and the last state and federal obstacle to starting construction was surmounted. In December 1932 the construction contract was awarded to the West Slope Construction Company of Chicago, low bidder at $8,600,527.

The foundation for San Gabriel Dam #1 is laid as the great earthen dam begins to take shape, December 1936. Following the Forks Dam fiasco, the L.A. County Flood Control District resurveyed the canyon and chose a new dam site two miles down canyon from the forks. – LOS ANGELES COUNTY FLOOD CONTROL DISTRICT

The West Slope Construction Company rushed in 300 men and commenced work on the diversion tunnel and hillside quarry in February 1933. The ground-breaking ceremony was held on March 3rd, and a few days later the first blast of dynamite was heard as far away as Azusa. By June, 10,000 cubic yards of rock per day were being quarried from the canyonside and moved to the dam site, and the huge earthen barrier began to rise from the canyon floor. 600 men were hard at work.

With two big dams going up in the main canyon — Pasadena's and Flood Control No. 1 — the old canyon-bottom road could no longer be used. The short-lived railroad from Azusa to the Forks was abandoned shortly after Pasadena started work on Morris Dam. To provide a new, permanent and washout-free road, the supervisors authorized the expenditure of $1,300,000 to build a "high line" road along the west slope from the canyon mouth to the Forks. The contract for the new highway was given to the Guy F. Atkinson Company and work commenced in July 1932. In a year of blasting, grading and paving, the road was completed.

Electric shovel and dump truck loading earth at the quarry adjacent to San Gabriel Dam#1, August 1936. Thousands of tons of earth were moved from the hillside quarry to fill the great earthen dam.
KENYON DEVORE PHOTO

San Gabriel Dam #1, built by the L.A. County Flood Control District, immediately after completion, 1937. – CORNELIUS SMITH PHOTO

Widened and improved in recent years, it is today the main highway up San Gabriel Canyon.

Dam No. 2 in the West Fork reached its specified height of 270 feet in November 1933. Finishing touches, including a concrete face, required two more years. In December 1935 the completed barrier was christened Prescott F. Cogswell Dam, in honor of the county supervisor who had been a pioneer in calling for flood control efforts.

With Morris and Cogswell dams in operation, only San Gabriel Dam No. 1 remained to be completed. But obstructions came up in 1934 that for a time threatened a reenactment of the Forks Dam fiasco. Engineers feared that the huge rock quarry on the hillside immediately east of the dam was unstable. An earth movement could send tons of loosened rock down on the dam and on hundreds of workers. The dam design was also criticized. As a result, the supervisors ordered all work on the dam suspended pending a thorough investigation.

Cleves H. Howell, former engineer of the Upper Rio Grande reclamation project and, more importantly, with an impeccable reputation, was brought in by the supervisors as a consulting engineer. After a 2½-day study, Howell criticized not only the dam design, but stated that the dam's west abutment was unsafe and threatened a possible landslide. Shades of the Forks Dam! As a reward for his investigative efforts and because of his reputation as one of the foremost flood control engineers in the country, Howell was appointed chief engineer in January 1935.

In July 1935 Howell and his engineers completed a new design, calling for a rock-fill dam composed of six separate vertical zones, each filled with a different type of rock. A spillway was called for, something the old design did not have. It would be first necessary to remove several hundred thousand cubic yards of rock from the dam's original foundation, then start from scratch.

Finally, in August 1935, work on the dam was ready to resume. By October, 250,000 cubic yards of old fill had been removed and replaced, and the giant earthen barrier began to rise. Crews worked feverishly to build the dam high enough to resist winter rains. By early 1936 there were 650 men on the job. To help settle the fill rock, a mammoth tamping machine, built originally for dike work in Holland, was brought in. Workmen nicknamed it "Leaping Lena." In September the crews set a record for one day's work: 28,000 cubic yards of rock, weighing 50,000 tons, were dumped onto the dam in two eight-hour shifts.

On July 21, 1937 the final load of rock was dumped on the structure during the dedication ceremony. Governor Frank Merriam spoke, as did numerous county officials. Chief engineer Howell proudly described the giant rock-fill dam, filled with

Water pouring over the spillway at San Gabriel Dam during the March 1938 flood. The canyon dams proved their worth during this worst flood in the recorded history of the San Gabriel Mountains, holding backs torrents that otherwise would have wrecked havoc in the San Gabriel Valley.
– HENRY E. HUNTINGTON LIBRARY

10,641,999 cubic yards of earth and rock, as "Hell for stout." At last, the San Gabriel was flood-tamed.

The finishing touches to San Gabriel Dam required another two years. The spillway, the penstock and the great needle valves were completed by November 1938. The state engineer formally approved the completed structure in November 1939.

The completion of San Gabriel Dam No. 1 (The "No. 1" was soon dropped) could hardly have come at a more opportune time. Five days of heavy rainfall, commencing on February 27, 1938 and not letting up until March 3, resulted in the greatest flood in the recorded history of San Gabriel Canyon. At its height on March 2, 36,450,000 gallons per minute were flowing into the reservoir. (This contrasts with 18,000,000 gallons per minute in 1916, the previous high.) Water poured over the spillways at both San Gabriel and Morris dams. For a few hours, a wild rumour that the dams were collapsing, caused by a break in radio communication with the dams and rapidly rising waters in the river, panicked Azusa. The canyon dams remained intact but did not prevent the river from overflowing its banks — 27,810,000 gallons per minute flowed past Azusa during the flood peak — but they did prevent a catastrophe. Had the dams not been there, the resulting torrent would have certainly inflicted mortal damage to a much larger portion of the San Gabriel Valley.

Only twice since the record flow of 1938 has water poured over the spillways of San Gabriel and Morris dams. This occurred in January 1969, and again a month later. The trio of barriers — Cogswell, San Gabriel and Morris dams (the latter was transferred to the County Flood Control District in 1977) — have effectively controlled the once rampant river.

San Antonio Creek was late in being harnessed by a major dam, despite repeated floodings to surrounding areas. The disastrous 1938 flood caused over $2 million in property damage and prompted demands that some type of flood control system be implemented. Long delayed help finally came from Congress. After the 1938 flood Congress approved federal aid to harness San Antonio Creek, but World War II intervened. In 1950 Congress authorized $500,000 towards dam construction, and raised this

Prescott Cogswell (1859-1960), known as "The Father of Flood Control" in Los Angeles County. As a county supervisor, he worked tirelessly for the construction of dams in San Gabriel Canyon. Cogswell Dam, on the West Fork, built in 1932-35, honors him today.
– DAVE VANDEVOET PHOTO

Laying the foundation for San Gabriel Dam #2 (Cogswell Dam), September 1932. Rock was quarried in Devils Canyon for this flood control barrier in the West Fork of San Gabriel Canyon.

– LOS ANGELES COUNTY FLOOD CONTROL DISTRICT

Cogswell Dam under construction, 1933. Concrete is being poured over the rock base at the bottom of the dam.

– LOS ANGELES COUNTY FLOOD CONTROL DISTRICT

Cogswell Dam upon completion, 1935.

– LOS ANGELES COUNTY FLOOD CONTROL DISTRICT

West Fork, San Gabriel River from north slope of Monrovia Peak. Cogswell Reservoir and Dam below, Mt. Baldy on skyline. Looking northeast. – JOHN ROBINSON PHOTO

amount to $1,700,000 three years later. The U.S. Army's Corps of Engineers was ordered to do the job. A huge earth-fill barrier, 160 feet high and 3,850 feet across, was erected at the canyon mouth by the Army Engineers during the years 1953 to 1956. San Antonio Dam was dedicated by the Corps of Engineers on May 12, 1956.

1. *Azusa Herald and Pomotropic,* October 20, 1937. This was a special issue of the newspaper devoted to San Gabriel Canyon.

2. Henry Dalton, "Daily occurrences at the Azusa," July 7, 1870, logbook quoted in Keith Vosburg, *Azusa, Old and New* (Azusa, 1921), p. 17.

3. The *Azusa Herald and Pomotropic,* October 20, 1937.

4. This account of the San Gabriel River water war and resulting compromise is based largely on Alfred Clark, "The San Gabriel River: A Century of Dividing the Waters," *Southern California Quarterly,* LII, 2 (June 1970). Clark also wrote a much longer treatise entitled "War Over The San Gabriel," senior thesis, California State Polytechnic College, Pomona, 1968. A copy of this informative paper is in the Azusa Public Library.

5. The story of the San Antonio Water Company's fight to close San Antonio Canyon to the public is covered in many undated newspaper clippings contained in the valuable Frank Wheeler Scrapbooks, 3 volumes, in the Honnold Library, Special Collections Department, Claremont Colleges.

6. See Henry W. O'Melveny, *William G. Kerckhoff: A Memorial* (Los Angeles, privately printed, 1935), for a fine summary of Kerckhoff's many hydroelectric enterprises.

7. Harry P. Bailey, *The Climate of Southern California* (Berkeley, 1966), p. 69.

Monrovia Canyon Creek. – MYRON HOTCHKISS PHOTO

6 Monrovia And Sawpit Canyons

From the San Gabriel Valley, 5409-foot Monrovia Peak looms high on the northern skyline, blanketed with olive-green chaparral and a scattering of spruce and pine. The astute observer standing in the valley below can readily make out two deep grooves on the south face of the mountain — Monrovia Canyon to the left, Sawpit Canyon to the right. The two canyons, both nourished by sparkling creeks, begin high on the mountain's southwest and southeast slopes, respectively, then join in the foothills to form a massive natural V.

Just below the junction of the two canyons, near Emerson Flat, was once a large man-made sawpit, a hole in the ground in which one sawyer crouched to assist another at ground level to jointly operate a large handsaw. In this crude manner, logs hauled down from the mountain were hewed into lumber for building purposes. Sawpit Canyon takes its name from this old sawpit, long since disappeared. The origin of the sawpit is a mystery. It was there when the earliest settlers came into the canyon in the 1870s, and appeared old at the time. Legend says it was dug by Spanish padres and their Indian neophytes to furnish lumber for the construction of San Gabriel Mission, according to the late Monrovia historian John L. Wiley. The story cannot be verified but it makes good sense, since Sawpit Canyon was one of the closest sources of timber to the mission.

It was to Emerson Flat and its sawpit that Hibbard Rankins, his wife Polly and their four children came in 1874. The Rankins family, having journeyed from Wisconsin to California, built a little cabin in the canyon, planted vegetables and a fruit orchard, and cut wood in the sawpit. It was this latter enterprise that provided the close-knit family with its main livelihood. They hauled the wood to Los Angeles and sold it, the round trip by wagon taking two days. They kept bees and sold honey as an additional source of income. The Rankins children attended school in Duarte and walked the entire distance from their canyon home to school and back every day, remembered a Duarte old-timer.

Tragedy — one of the saddest episodes in the long saga of the San Gabriel Mountains — struck the Rankins family in 1877. The oldest child, Albert, age 19, was apprenticed to a blacksmith in San Gabriel, and somehow he contacted typhoid fever. He died after a short illness on March 6. While the family was still in mourning, both girls, Estella, age 13, and Polly, age 16, came down with the dreaded disease. They died within a week of each other, on April 19th and 25th. Heartbroken, their lives shattered, Mr. and Mrs. Rankins buried their three children on a little rise above the cabin and marked the grave with a triple tombstone that included the childrens' names, ages, and dates of death engraved in the marble. The bereaved parents and their sole surviving child, Ernest, then returned to Wisconsin.

A few years later the little cabin was destroyed by fire and flood, but the marble gravestone remained, overgrown with brush, an object of curiosity to later canyon visiters.

Years later, Ernest Rankins returned to the scene of his family's tragedy and removed his brother and sisters' remains to a cemetery in Monrovia. Still later they were again removed and taken to their final resting place, Mountain View Cemetery in Pasadena. Ernest Rankins, seemingly haunted by the sad fate of his kin, returned to the canyon time and again until his death in Los Angeles in 1914.

The next name associated with Monrovia and Sawpit canyons was L. H. Emerson, who filed on land just below the junction of the two canyons and built a stout log cabin in the middle 1880s. Emerson is mainly remembered because of his fight over water rights with the new city of Monrovia, founded by William P. Monroe in 1886. The community laid claim to the water of Monrovia and Sawpit canyons and built a reservoir at the canyon mouth in 1887. Pipelines from the small reservoir supplied the precious liquid to the residents and farms of the new community. Emerson diverted some of the water for his own use, thereby lessening the city's supply. Monrovia secured an injunction preventing Emerson from diverting water, and a long legal battle ensued. The city won in the end, and Emerson left

The triple gravestone for the three Rankin children — Polly, Estella and Albert — who tragically died within a week of each other, from typhoid fever, in 1877. The Rankin family were the first known settlers of Monrovia Canyon, living in a cabin at Emerson Flat and sawing and hauling wood for a living. Albert M. Cook, former Monrovia Canyon Park guard, is standing next to the gravestone in this 1950 photo.
— RALPH SLOSSON PHOTO

for greener pastures. He did leave his name, however, to the little oak-shaded flat just below today's Monrovia Canyon Park.

Monrovia's interest in the beautiful wooded canyons north of the city was not confined to water. As early as 1890, citizens rode the rough trail into Monrovia Canyon to picnic and camp. A favorite spot was the sloping glen just above Emerson Flat, replete with magnificent canyon live oaks and leafy sycamores, nourished by a bubbling creek. A half mile further up the canyon was Monrovia Canyon Falls, a silver spray of falling water overarched with oaks and spruces. Some summer weekends as many as a hundred persons enjoyed the sylvan sanctuary of the canyon, some bringing tents and remaining a week or more.

In 1913 a road was constructed by volunteer effort up the canyon to the popular picnic and camping area. Over 250 trees, mostly pines, were planted to replace those washed away by flood. The City of Monrovia incorporated the canyon and began maintaining the picnic grounds as a city park. On April 15, 1913 this became Monrovia Canyon Park, today one of the most idyllic city-maintained parks in the southern foothills of the San Gabriels. A small museum, displaying the area's natural and human history, is located there.

Far up near the head of Sawpit Canyon, close under the southern ramparts of Monrovia Peak, is a sloping forested bench known as Deer Park. It received its name because of the abundance of deer that roamed the mountain slopes in the 1880s. Grizzly bears were present there, too. The little high-mountain flat became a popular hunters' camp. One of the main attractions of Deer Park was the gushing springs of icy-cold water that emitted from the mountainside just above the park. The water flowed in abundance through the camp, and formed the headwaters of Sawpit Canyon. In 1887 L. H. Emerson, W. H. Mace and a man named Fields formed the Deer Park Development Company and

Ben Overturff, Monrovia building contractor, discovered the beautiful forest cove known as Deer Park in 1905, and his life was never the same afterwards. From 1907 until 1948, he was proprietor and host of Deer Park Cabin, a popular little trail resort in Sawpit Canyon. He died in 1954.
— MYRON HOTCHKISS COLLECTION

Deer Park Cabin, high up in Sawpit Canyon, about 1928. The little trail resort was a favorite weekend and holiday hangout for many valley residents from 1907 until 1948. Ben Overturff was the genial host, and Mrs. Overturff's famous lemon pies were featured.
– MYRON HOTCHKISS COLLECTION

laid claim to the water there. Their plans to develop the water source were frustrated by the City of Monrovia, which claimed all the water in Sawpit Canyon and went to court to defend its claim. In 1894 William N. Monroe, founder and leading citizen of Monrovia, constructed the first burro trail up Sawpit Canyon to Deer Park, and the spot became more popular than ever with hunters and campers.

The history of Deer Park down through the years is tied predominantly to one man — Ben Overturff, one of Monrovia's most colorful figures. A native of Selma, Iowa, Overturff came to Monrovia in 1901 and for many years was a successful building contractor. He was also a deputy sheriff of Los Angeles County and active in local fraternal organizations.

Around 1905 Ben Overturff, during a hunting trip into the mountains, discovered Deer Park and his life was never the same afterwards. He fell in love with the idyllic glen high on the slope of Monrovia Peak and spent many weekends camping and hunting there. He took out a Forest Service lease in 1907 and, working weekends, toting building supplies up the canyon via burro, erected a wooden lodge underneath the tall oaks. It was not long until Deer Park Lodge became a favorite weekend retreat for many valley residents, drawn there as much by the genial hospitality of Ben Overturff as by the sylvan surroundings. In 1911 Overturff constructed a new, sturdier, more spacious lodge, using the canyon boulders as his main building material. The original wooden building he converted into a barn for his burros and saddle horses. Deer Park became more popular than ever. Even today, a half century later, old-time Monrovia residents vividly remember Ben Overturff and his string of three loaded burros, plodding up Canyon Avenue every Friday, toting supplies up to his weekend resort. Guests arriving at Deer Park Lodge would usually find a pot of beans on the stove, and several of Mrs. Overturff's delicious lemon pies on the table.

Monrovia Peak during the great mountain holocaust of 1924, taken from the Mt. Wilson Observatory. The fire, which started in San Gabriel Canyon, burned west, ate a horseshoe path around Monrovia Peak and into Sawpit Canyon, before finally being halted by the determined efforts of a thousand fire-fighters. – CHARLES CLARK VERNON COLLECTION

Deer Park Lodge managed to survive two of nature's fiercest onslaughts in the San Gabriels — flood and fire. No one who was at the resort on the weekend of January 24-25, 1914 ever forgot the horrendous storm that battered the mountains. It began early Saturday afternoon when violent wind and sheets of rain hit the slopes of Monrovia Peak, and peaceful little creeks suddenly became angry torrents. Huge boulders crashed downhill and trees two and three feet in diameter were uprooted like matchsticks. Ben Overturff feared the end was coming: "The sound of the boulders and rocks crashing together as they were hurled down the stream sounded like a thousand steel riveters all going at once, and the impact shook the mountain and the cabin. The noise was deafening, and mingled with the roar of the waters and the rumble of huge stones could be heard the crack and snapping of trees. It was the most awe-inspiring sound I ever heard in my life."[1] All night and the next day the rain fell, although the ensuing storm was not as violent as that first onslaught. The new Deer Park cabin, made of stone, was not badly damaged, but the old wooden barn was in a shambles and many of the great oaks were uprooted.

The storm left much of Sawpit Canyon looking like a battleground. W. A. Chess, descending from Deer Park after it was over, could hardly believe his eyes: "The trail is gone. The shady nooks are no more, and there is scarcely a live tree left along the watercourse, or even in the floor of the canyon. Desolation and destruction is everywhere."[2]

Fortunately, nature's restorative powers are ever at work, and it was not many years before Sawpit Canyon's trees and foliage were lush and green again.

Ten years later the second of nature's mountain scourges threatened Deer Park and Sawpit Canyon. The great mountain fire of September 1924, worst in the recorded history of the San Gabriels, erupted in San Gabriel Canyon on August 31 and burned rapidly westward through the crackling-dry chaparral. The flames raced through Roberts Canyon and then Fish Canyon, and after six days approached Monrovia Peak and the head of Sawpit Canyon on a broad front. Monrovia's water supply was threatened, and every available man was pressed into service to fight the holocaust. A fire camp was established at Deer Park under the direction of forest ranger Victor Vetter, housing 175 firefighters, most of them volunteers. The crews hurriedly cut firebreaks from the head of Fish Canyon around the east flank of Monrovia Peak to Sawpit Canyon. Just when the fire appeared near control, flames jumped the fireline north of Monrovia Peak and ate their way northward into the West Fork-Devils Canyon region, as well as south towards the Monrovia Canyon-Sawpit Canyon watershed. A desperate struggle ensued to save the Monrovia watershed. Still the blaze crept forward, burning over Monrovia Peak and down into the head of Sawpit Canyon, forcing the evacuation of Deer Park. The mountains on fire presented a terrifying spectacle in the valley below. "At night a spectacle grand but appalling

Jack Holtz of Monrovia at Deer Park cabin ruins, 1980. Jack plans to rebuild the historic cabin as a nature study center. – JOHN ROBINSON PHOTO

was presented. Flaming mountain sides stretched in a lurid line from Monrovia to San Gabriel Canyon. In its stupendous extent the scene dwarfed any pyrotechnic display ever staged by man. The flames swept a path over a half-mile high and five miles long — a mountain range on fire, with hissing flames leaping skyward as though thrown with fury from the bowels of the earth."[3] William Greeley, Chief Forester of the United States, hurried out from Washington, D.C. to Monrovia to direct the fire-fighting struggle. As the holocaust moved relentlessly down Sawpit and Monrovia canyons, the city of Monrovia itself was believed in peril; evacuation plans were drawn up. Miraculously, just when all appeared lost, the winds died down, newly-cut firebreaks held, and on September 18, almost three weeks after it erupted, the great holocaust was declared under control.

As a result of the 1924 fire, the Forest Service initiated a program to build fireroads and firebreaks throughout the range. A dirt fireroad was carved up Sawpit Canyon in 1925, and firebreaks were blazed on all the ridges, even over the top of Monrovia Peak. The San Gabriels would never be quite the same again.

By some fortunate quirk of fate, Deer Park was spared although the fire burned most of the surrounding slopes and most of upper Sawpit Canyon. It was not long until Overturff was back in business, guiding his familiar burro train up the canyon every weekend, rain or shine. The late 1920s were the peak years for Deer Park Lodge, with guests crowding the little resort and camping nearby in the canyon. Mrs. Overturff's cooking chores were sometimes so heavy that she would remain at Deer Park weekdays while her husband was in town managing his contracting business.

The halcyon days of Deer Park, as with most of the mountain resorts, drew to a close in the 1930s. The years of depression cut down the number of guests willing to make the weekend trek up-canyon, making it difficult for the Overturffs to make ends meet. The great flood of March 1-2, 1938, although sparing Deer Park Lodge, wreaked havoc on the canyon trail, making it almost impossible to reach the resort. No sooner had the trail been put back in first-class condition than World War II erupted, and people had more important things to do than enjoy mountain retreats. Overturff closed his resort for the duration, although continuing to use the lodge as a weekend retreat for his family and friends. After the war, he hoped to reopen Deer Park as a resort, but his plans were frustrated by the City of Monrovia, which owned water rights to Sawpit Canyon. The city placed a locked gate at the canyon entrance to discourage the public from using the

Sawpit Dam, upstream face, 1980. The concrete barrier, built by L.A. County Flood Control District in 1928-29, has effectively harnessed the floodwaters of Sawpit Canyon. – JOHN ROBINSON PHOTO

canyon. Ill health forced Overturff to leave Deer Park Lodge for good in 1948. He died in 1954. Once-beautiful Deer Park Lodge fell prey to vandals, causing the Forest Service to demolish the buildings in 1958. Only the foundation and lower walls of the lodge remain today. However, it appears possible that Deer Park will enjoy a rebirth. Jack Holtz of Monrovia has obtained the city's sanction (Monrovia annexed Deer Park in 1957 as part of the city watershed) to rebuild the cabin as a nature study center. He hopes to start work in the near future.

Sawpit Canyon has undergone much change in recent decades. The biggest change is Sawpit Dam, a 160-foot high concrete barrier just inside the canyon mouth erected by the Los Angeles County Flood Control District in the years 1928 and 1929. To get around the dam, the City of Monrovia, which owns watershed rights to the canyon, and the Forest Service relocated the canyon road high on the southeast slope. The Forest Service then extended the Sawpit Canyon road up to the Sawpit-Fish Canyon Divide to join with the network of fire roads around Monrovia Peak. The lion's share of this fire road construction was done by the Civilian Conservation Corps (C.C.C.), a federal program to employ young men victimized by the depression, in the years 1933 to 1942. The young men were housed in the Monrovia C.C.C. Camp, located just below the canyon mouth in May, 1933.

In the lower reaches of Sawpit Canyon, a mile above the dam, is the Tallman H. Trask Boy Scout

Monrovia C.C.C. Camp near the mouth of Monrovia Canyon, 1934. CCC Boys from Monrovia Camp and 17 other camps in the Angeles did a considerable amount of road and trail building and forest conservation work during the 1930's.
– JACK MCCASKILL COLLECTION

The Hardy Harris cabin at Stone Cabin Flat in upper Fish Canyon, 1919. Harris and several schoolboys built the cabin in 1911, using boulders from the streambed. Harris and his friends used the cabin as a private retreat, hunting and fishing in the surrounding country. Only the lower walls are standing today, but the idyllic spot in upper Fish Canyon will always be known as Stone Cabin Flat.
– LOUISE WERNER COLLECTION

Spring Camp, high on the west shoulder of Monrovia Peak. The name derives from an all-year spring that flows there. Around the turn of the century, Spring Camp was often used by hunters. 200 fire-fighters were based there to battle the great holocaust of 1924. This 1926 picture shows the tents of the Forest Service line camp, the base for building firebreaks and fireroads in the Monrovia Peak area.
– GLEN OWENS COLLECTION

Camp. Trask was an executive of the San Gabriel Valley Council of the Boy Scouts of America from 1919 until his retirement in 1955. The camp occupies the site of the 160-acre Harrison Ward Ranch, obtained by the City of Monrovia in a tax-delinquent sale and then leased to the scouts. Since its dedication in 1972, Trask Camp has provided a memorable outdoor experience to thousands of San Gabriel Valley boy scouts.

In contrast to Sawpit Canyon, Monrovia Canyon has remained relatively pristine and unspoiled. The ¾ mile walk from Monrovia Canyon Park up to the waterfall is a delightful stroll under a green canopy of live oak and sycamore. There is a rough trail on up-canyon to a second fall, equally as scenic. Monrovia Canyon is one of the very few in the south front of the San Gabriels that retains wilderness charm of past ages.

Although located in neither Sawpit nor Monrovia Canyon, mention should be made of Spring Camp, a delightful shady dell high on the west buttress of Monrovia Peak. The camp's name derives from an everflowing spring of icy-cold water located there. In the early days, Spring Camp was often used by hunters seeking the big game that roamed the area. An old trail, now impassable, climbed up the East Fork of Big Santa Anita Canyon to the camp. The spot was used as a fire camp during the great 1924 holocaust. From 1925 until about 1929, the forested dell was a Forest Service "line camp," housing a crew of 200 rangers and C.C.C. boys building fire roads and firebreaks in the Monrovia Peak area. A contingent of conscientious objectors was stationed at Spring Camp during World War II to maintain the fire roads and breaks and build new ones. Since then, the camp has been abandoned, except for occasional visits by Forest Service work parties doing trail maintenance.

Reverend Edward Payson Rankin, founder of the Yucca Hiking Club, with Richard Lejon Johnson, the club's second president, ca. 1933. Rankin retired as a Presbyterian minister and moved to Monrovia in 1923. To prove that you're only as old as you feel, he climbed Monrovia Peak on his 78th birthday and continued to do so every year until his 90th birthday, placing Old Glory on the summit. After his death at the age of 92 in 1937, the U.S. Board on Geographic Names, honoring a request of the reverend's many friends, named the prominent summit just southwest of Monrovia Peak *Rankin Peak*. For a number of years after Rankin's passing, the boy scouts made an annual pilgrimage to the summit to raise the flag.
– MYRON HOTCHKISS COLLECTION

1. John L. Wiley, *History of Monrovia* (Pasadena, 1927), p. 139.

2. *Monrovia Daily News*, February 2, 1914.

3. Wiley, p. 225.

Monrovia Peak after a winter snowfall, 1971. The picture was taken from Gold Hill to the southwest, just above the town of Monrovia. – MYRON HOTCHKISS PHOTO

The outdoor chapel at the Tallman H. Trask Boy Scout Camp in Sawpit Canyon, 1972. Since the camp's dedication in 1972, thousands of young boys of the San Gabriel Valley Council of the B.S.A. have enjoyed a week in the wilderness there. – MYRON HOTCHKISS PHOTO

7

San Gabriel Canyon

"In the old days, before hydroelectric development and flood control dams, the San Gabriel River flowed even in summer all the way to the mouth of the canyon above Azusa. There was no other trout stream in southern California that could compare with it. The water was clean and clear, alternating between sparkling riffles and darker pools. Wherever the floods of winter had not scoured the boulders, alders and sycamores graced the banks, casting their shadows athwart the stream. The old wagon road wound its torturous way in the canyon bottom, crossing and recrossing the rocks and river, and only seemed to make progress if it reached some bench or flat a little above the stream level and lined out across the sandy earth."[1]

This picture of San Gabriel Canyon in the 1890s was drawn from memory by Stuart O'Melveny, son of Henry O'Melveny, one of the first to partake in the recreational delights of the canyon. In those days, mountain trout abounded in the sparkling waters of the river and its major tributaries. It was the lure of these speckled beauties that drew many an angler into the canyon.

As far back as the 1850s, when gold miners toiled in the East Fork and the town of Eldoradoville was in its brief glory, the canyon of the San Gabriel was known for its fabulous fishing. A correspondent for the *Los Angeles Star* (July 9, 1859) wrote: "This is really a beautiful canon, and a more contented set of miners I have never seen . . . . Should you think of visiting the mines at any time, . . . I will promise you a mess of mountain trout which abound in the river."

During the last three decades of the 19th century, San Gabriel Canyon was known throughout Southern California for its abundance of mountain trout. The *Star* of June 8, 1870, in describing an eight-day hunting and fishing trip into the canyon by a party of Los Angeles businessmen, stated, "They caught eight hundred fine trout, many of which measured from twelve to sixteen inches in length, the entire lot averaging nine inches." The lower West Fork seemed to offer the best fishing. A Pasadena historian has written that "The waters of the West Fork were so loaded with fish that in 1892 Frank Bolt, president of the San Gabriel Valley Bank, caught 100 trout in one pool and then became so carried away with his success that he fell in. In the same year, a lady fell into the San Gabriel River and caught a trout in her bustle."[2] The *Pasadena Evening Star* (June 3, 1896) reported, "To W. S. Wright belongs the distinction of landing on his recent trip the largest trout ever known to have been caught in the San Gabriel. It measured 17½ inches in length and was caught on a rod and reel." Some anglers let their enthusiasm and greediness go too far. The *Pasadena Weekly Star* (July 23, 1890) complained that "Parties in the San Gabriel Canyon who are taking trout by dynamite or any method but the hook, ought to know that the penalty for such an offense is very severe. It is not a sport. It is barbarous and it is a crime against the State and should be stopped."

By the late 1880s, the unrestricted greediness of hundreds of fishermen was resulting in marked depletion of trout in the canyon. To remedy this situation, the State Fish and Game Commission limited the catch per angler to fifty trout a day and began stocking the river with fish from as far away as Mount Shasta and Lake Tahoe. The *Pasadena Union* (October 29, 1887) gave first notice of this new practice: "Yesterday 10,000 young Tahoe trout were planted in the San Gabriel River. When these speckled beauties get their growth — seven or eight pounds — sport in the San Gabriel Canyon will be better than ever." Stuart O'Melveny remembered that "The small trout were sent from Shasta in milk cans. I note in my father's diary that on August 31, 1899, he met the train from the North carrying 25,000 fingerlings to be planted, and it was his custom to attend to this each year."[3] The replenishing of trout from northern California lakes and streams continued into the 1930s.

Before the turn of the century, San Gabriel Canyon was renowned throughout Southern California for its trout fishing. This picture shows California Governor Henry Markham in his angling camp on the lower West Fork in 1896. – HENRY E. HUNTINGTON LIBRARY

Trout were not the only form of wildlife in San Gabriel Canyon. The region was infested with rattlesnakes, and many a traveler returned to civilization with a snakeskin and rattles as mementos of his close brush with danger.

The canyon had its share of bear stories, too. The upper reaches of the West, North and East forks were abundant with mean-tempered grizzly bears until just after the turn of the century. Newspapers often reported harrowing contests pitting man against beast. Few persons would penetrate deep into the mountains without a trusty rifle and plenty of ammunition.

Grizzlies were particularly fond of raw beef. In the 1870s, Cornelius Potter, pioneer white settler of Camp Rincon, was obliged to remove his cattle from Pine Flat, at the headwaters of the North Fork, because predator grizzlies were decimating his herd. A decade later Henry Roberts was forced to hire many gun-toting vaqueros to escort his cattle into high-country grazing areas; it was not uncommon for Roberts' cowboys to shoot and kill as many as a half dozen grizzlies on a single two-week trip to Pine Flats or Prairie Fork.

To protect fishermen from enraged grizzlies in the West Fork, early-day forest rangers Jess Sevier and Bill Bacon placed a number of steel bear-traps in the canyon. One day in 1900 a mammoth female grizzly was caught near the junction of Valley Forge Canyon and the West Fork. When the frenzied beast caught sight of the rangers, she jerked free of the trap and charged. Altogether she took nine slugs before being felled just a step away from Ranger Bacon. Her carcass reportedly weighed 1,300 pounds.

Pasadena historian Hiram Reid related how Bear Canyon, a tributary of the lower West Fork, received its name: "In 1891 or '92 two or three hunters camped in the upper part of the canyon. One night a bear was caught by the hind foot in a heavy steel trap which they had set. He gnawed off his own leg and hobbled away on the bleeding stump, leaving his foot in the trap. The hunters soon discovered this in the morning, and following the bear's bloody trail, shot him. They nailed the entrapped foot up on a tree at their camp, and I saw it there two years later. From this incident that portion of the West San Gabriel has ever since been called Bear Canyon."[4]

Although the grizzlies were extinct in San Gabriel Canyon by about 1903, deer hunting continued as a major recreational activity for valley residents. Pine Flat, at the head of the North Fork, became a popular hunters' camp. Weekends and holidays saw as many as fifty or sixty rifle-toting sportsmen roaming the slopes in search of venison. But again, unrestricted killing decimated the herds until they neared extinction. As a result, the Forest Service, in 1915, declared Angeles National Forest a game preserve and prohibited hunting in all but a few isolated areas on the north side of the range. A colorful — and wasteful — era came to a close.

It was inevitable, with the hordes of fishermen, hunters and vacationers in the canyon, that some enterprising entrepreneur would take advantage of the opportunity to cater to the canyon visitors. Eventually, as we shall see, a number of public resorts sprang up in the canyon, but credit for the first goes to William Potter and his Mountain View ranch in the lower East Fork. Potter, known to his friends as "Lying Bill" for the tall tales he enjoyed telling, built his pretentious ranch house in 1878, and soon thereafter planted fruit trees and vegetables on the river-side property. It was not long until he began allowing canyon vacationers to camp on his property for a small fee and selling them

William "Lying Bill" Potter's Mountain View Ranch, in the lower East Fork of San Gabriel Canyon, ca. 1888. Potter's ranch was the first tourist resort in the canyon, catering to weekend and holiday visitors. It was a favorite hangout of "the busted lung brigade." – HENRY E. HUNTINGTON LIBRARY

fruits and vegetables. By the mid-1880s, "Potter's Ranch," as it was generally known, was a thriving hostelry. The *Azusa News* (September 14, 1889) reported not only "swarms of people camped . . . who hail from all parts of the United States," but also that Potter's Ranch was becoming a favorite hangout of "the busted lung brigade," consumptives who had moved into the canyon to regain their health. After Lying Bill's death in 1903, his son Hayes Potter enlarged the resort and was the congenial host into the 1920s.

Potter's Mountain View Ranch set the stage for a number of other resorts in San Gabriel Canyon, many of them started by addicts of trout fishing. One of those who enjoyed the fishing delights of the canyon, time and again in the 1880s, was Henry O'Melveny, a Los Angeles attorney and insurance executive. O'Melveny became so enthralled with the trout-abundant river that, in 1889, he talked a number of Los Angeles businessmen into organizing the Creel Club, dedicated to angling, gourmet eating and fellowship. A clubhouse site was selected just below Persinger Flat on the east bank of the river, nine miles above Azusa. Building materials were hauled to the site, but a flood in December 1889 washed everything away before construction could begin. After the storm, Bates and Mary Persinger, original residents of the little flat, packed in a new load of lumber and supplies, and a rather spacious and homey cabin was completed in early 1891. The Creel Club was an immediate success, and new members were added every year. "Our outings were generally for the weekend," recalled Los Angeles banker Jackson A. Graves, "but frequently with an extra day or two thrown in. We were liberal in entertaining our friends. Our guest book, if in existence, would show the names of all the red-blooded men of Los Angeles of the period, who loved an outdoor life."[5] Fishing was the first priority, but congenial talk and good eating were not far behind. "Famous dishes were cooked, corks were pulled from bottles of good wine, and the occasional tinkle of an old guitar was followed by a merry song," remembered Stuart O'Melveny.[6] For most of its years, the club

Mary and Bates Persinger and their home on Persinger Flat in San Gabriel Canyon, ca. 1890. The Persingers farmed, hunted and fished in the canyon for some thirty years. – HENRY E. HUNTINGTON LIBRARY

The original Creel Club cabin in San Gabriel Canyon, built in 1880. Los Angeles attorney Henry O'Melveny organized the Creel Club, dedicated to "angling, gormet eating and fellowship," in 1889. Many leading Los Angeles citizens were members. In this 1895 photo, O'Melveny is the right-hand man on the roof. Mary Persinger, club manager and cook, stands directly below. – CHARLES CLARK VERNON COLLECTION

The Creel Club cabin after the addition of a second story in 1910. Mary Persinger standing in front. The cabin was located just below Persinger Flat on the east side of the canyon, 9 miles up from Azusa. – HENRY E. HUNTINGTON LIBRARY

was managed by Mary Persinger, who ably served as "cabin boss, stewardess, chief and general supervisor." The Creel Club broke up in the 1920s and met its final demise in 1932 when the property was purchased by the Los Angeles County Flood Control District. Today the old club site lies under the waters of San Gabriel Dam reservoir.

Not to be outdone by the Creel Club founders, a party of young Pasadena businessmen, in 1891, selected a sylvan site along the lower West Fork opposite Bear Canyon for their Pasadena Bait Club. A year later they had completed their rustic log cabin and the club was in business. One rainy night in the '90s, the members were aroused by a clamoring at the door, which upon being opened, admitted Professor T.S.C. Lowe of the Mount Lowe Railway and California Governor Henry H. Markham. Lowe and Markham had become lost in the storm and were suffering from exposure and fatigue. The distinguished guests were made comfortable before a roaring fire "and further fortified with a drink from a jug of whiskey which had been buried in the earthen floor for such an emergency."[7] Governor Markham became an honorary member of the Pasadena Bait Club and, on one fishing excursion, "proved to be the most fortunate angler in the party, having landed 98 fish in about six hours, besides throwing a number of smaller ones back into the stream." The old club house was used until 1922,

The fireplace in the Creel Club cabin. Many joyful gatherings of Los Angeles businessmen were held here. – CHARLES CLARK VERNON COLLECTION

The Covina Outing Club cabin in Bear Creek, about 1910. Seven Covina businessmen founded the club in 1906 and used the stone cabin as a base for hunting and fishing. The club disbanded in the late 1920 s and the cabin was used as a supply station by the Forest Service until being dismantled in the 1930 s. – CHARLES CLARK VERNON COLLECTION

when a new site was selected and a new cabin built two miles farther up the West Fork. The original cabin was burned in the great fire of 1924, "leaving only the old stone chimney, a monument to the memory of many happy outings in the old days."

The Covina Outing Club built a substantial stone club house at the forks of Bear Creek, two miles up from the West Fork, in 1906. The seven Covina businessmen who founded the club "found in this secluded spot wonderful fishing and hunting and the big stone cabin sheltered many a happy outing of the members, their families and friends." The club disbanded in the late 1920s and the cabin was used as a supply station by the Forest Service.

The Sunset Club of Los Angeles held annual outings at Potter's Mountain View Ranch during the early 1900s, its members enjoying a week of fishing, hunting and camaraderie.

Henry O'Melveny, founder of the Creel Club, fell totally in love with San Gabriel Canyon and its angling delights. In 1897 he purchased George Islip's old property on the west bank of the river, seven miles up from Azusa, and here built a comfortable frame home he named "The Crag." As he grew older, he spent more and more of his time there, tending his exquisite garden of daffodils and tulips and entertaining famous guests. Among those making visits to The Crag were such notables as Henry E. Huntington, Charles Lummis, George Patton, Sr., William Kerckhoff, Harry Chandler, Harrison Gray Otis, Frederick Holder and Henry Van Dyke. O'Melveny continued as the genial host of his canyon lair until 1932, when he was obliged to relinquish the property to the City of Pasadena for the building of Morris Dam. Today, the site of so many happy weekends lies under the waters of Morris Reservoir.

Potter's Mountain View Ranch and the various fishing clubs were the early resorts in San Gabriel Canyon, but they were neither the largest nor the most famous. That honor belonged to Follows Camp, founded by Englishman Ralph Follows in 1896.

The building of Follows Camp, located three miles up the East Fork on a broad bench south of the river, epitomized the miracle recovery story of Ralph Follows, who had once been given only a few months to live. Follows was critically ill with tuberculosis when his brother, Jack Follows, a sailor on the Liverpool to San Francisco run, learned of the supposed therapeutic powers of San Gabriel Canyon. Jack persuaded his brother to leave England and come to the canyon. Arriving in Azusa in 1891, the two brothers rented a cabin on the old Ferguson property in the lower East Fork. Ralph's health improved almost immediately, and it was not long until he was well enough to go into business. His little cabin became a short-order restaurant serving canyon travelers and miners. In 1896 Follows purchased the Henry Roberts property just upstream from the Ferguson place and began building a resort camp. The following year he married Jennie Heaton, daughter of canyon miner William Heaton.

Ralph and Jennie Follows had a knack for the resort business, and it was not long until Follows Camp was the largest and best known hostelry in San Gabriel Canyon. "Good home cooking, a genial friendliness and welcome, good fishing and glorious scenery were the attractions." An early camp brochure boasted, "Camp life at Follows Camp is spent in real comfort. The tents are all good size, well floored, cozily furnished and are kept spotlessly clean. Where guests may prefer, homelike rooms may be reserved. The camp is provided with bath tubs, shower baths and plunge bath — and every modern arrangement has been incorporated to insure perfect sanitation and health throughout the camp. Pure mountain water is pumped by a private water plant which Mr. Follows has installed at enormous expense. Mountain fruits and vegetables, rich milk and fresh eggs are produced on the premises. The table is always supplied with fresh meats and seasonable delicacies, and ice is brought up daily on the stage."

Ralph Follows and Jennie Heaton Follows, wedding picture, 1897. The twosome had a knack for the resort business and quickly turned Follows Camp into the major hostelry in San Gabriel Canyon.
– SEDLEY PECK COLLECTION

One might think that Follows, once a consumptive himself, would be sympathetic with those suffering from tuberculosis. Such was not the case. He was adamant about barring anyone with the disease from his camp. His brochures conspicuously stated, "NO CONSUMPTIVES ADMITTED. This rule is absolute and no deviation from it will be made!"

To haul guests up the torturous twelve-mile canyon road, Follows initiated the famous four-horse Follows Stage. Via this conveyance, thousands of vacationers from all over the West made the trip in. The camp could accommodate as many as 200 guests at one time in its numerous cabins and tents. Quite a number of Western movies were shot in and around Follows Camp, with Ralph Follows and his four-horse stage, hired hands and even guests often appearing as "extras." Such early-day film stars as Mabel Normand and Fatty Arbuckle appeared in silent movies with a Follows Camp setting.

Ralph Follows' major headache during the years of his camp's popularity involved the maintenance of the canyon road. It washed out almost every winter. Mrs. Jennie Follows related in later years: "His life story was one of trying to keep that road open so he could pack people and things through, and out again. It meant appearing before the county board of supervisors and asking the Azusa merchants for help. Now it is possible to go in half an hour the distance it took a four-horse stage 3½ hours to travel. It was necessary then, though, to ford the stream some forty times, and even in the best weather that was not an easy trip. In times of high water it was impossible."[8] When the canyon road was impassable, the only route from Azusa to Follows Camp was to take the old Woods Trail over the mountain, an all-day, narrow and steep passage via shank's mare.

In the later years of the camp, Follows operated a livery stable not far from the Santa Fe station in Azusa. Guests debarking from the train would be met at the station by Follows or one of his stage drivers and transported the fifteen torturous miles to the resort, either via the four-horse stage along the canyon road, or on horseback over the mountain via the Woods Trail.

Ironically, the rebuilding and paving of the canyon road in 1925, which Ralph Follows had long urged, spelled the eventual downfall of Follows Camp. The first automobile had reached the resort in 1904, but the trip in was a hair-raiser. No more. By the end of 1925 autos were a common sight at

An early photo of Follows Camp, ca. 1897. It wasn't long until the two tourist tents in the foreground were supplemented by many more cabins and tents. Henry Roberts' store, built before 1868, is just beyond the tents. – SEDLEY PECK COLLECTION.

Follows Camp, ca. 1914. Housekeeping tents for up to 100 guests surround the green. The resort was then at its height of popularity. – SEDLEY PECK COLLECTION

The famous four-horse Follows Camp stage, with Ralph Follows standing on right. Thousands made the stage trip from the Santa Fe Station in Azusa to the resort every year.

the camp. "The coming of the automobile made the trip to Follows Camp too easy, the romance was gone and soon the camp languished and died," lamented Sedley Peck. In 1926 Ralph Follows was killed in an automobile accident near Redlands. Jennie Follows kept the resort open for a few more years, but her toil was not worth the effort. People were not willing to stay overnight when they could drive in and out of the canyon so quickly. The end of Follows Camp as a tourist resort came with the depression. The tents were removed; the cabins were rented to canyon residents. Today, the once-famous resort, many of its buildings still intact and occupied by permanent residents, sits quietly above the tumultuous waters of the East Fork.

Second only to Follows Camp as a popular tourist resort in San Gabriel Canyon was Camp Rincon, located on a forested bench just south of the confluence of the West and North forks. "Come to the Rincon," ads proclaimed, "The Gem of San Gabriel Canyon." Set in a sylvan cove, alongside the sparkling, trout-abundant river, Camp Rincon during its heyday was truly one of the most appealing resorts in Southern California. "There is nothing in all nature so beautiful as the moonlight evenings under the live-oaks. The campers gather for dancing at the big open-sided dance hall, and there are masque balls, candy pulls, popping corn in the coals of a dying campfire, and pool and billiard playing. In the afternoon there is the big concrete plunge to swim

Follows' Four-Horse Stage nearing canyon mouth on old San Gabriel Canyon road, ca. 1914.
– SEDLEY PECK COLLECTION

William Heaton and Ralph Follows at Follows Camp, ca. 1919. – SEDLEY PECK COLLECTION

Cornelius Potter riding "Branding Iron" near Camp Rincon, ca. 1895. Potter was one of the earliest white settlers in San Gabriel Canyon.
– HENRY E. HUNTINGTON LIBRARY

in, mountain walks over the trails, a few sets on the splendid cement tennis court, and trips to Painted Rock, Fern Falls, Cold Brook, and through the long mountain tunnel. If you prefer the simple life, the day can be spent in hammocks and swings," read a 1911 camp brochure.

The Rincon, with its bubbling springs, verdant growth and splendid overarching oaks, had always been a favorite rest haven for canyon travelers. Indians camped there in the early days. In the 1860s Cornelius Potter, brother of Mountain View's William Potter, filed a 160-acre claim to the area, brought in honey bees and pastured cattle. But it remained for Charlie Smith of Azusa to turn this superb streamside glen into a resort. Smith leased the Rincon property from Potter in 1897 and almost overnight converted it into a popular tourist hostelry, complete with store, hotel, cabins, tents, swimming pool, dance floor and tennis court. By 1905 the general store at Camp Rincon was the largest such establishment in the canyon, offering the vacationer and miner everything from food and spirits to clothing and fishing gear.

To bring guests to Camp Rincon, Charlie Smith borrowed an idea from Ralph Follows and initiated the four-horse Camp Rincon Stage. Visitors were carted in daily from Azusa during the spring and summer months. "Our comfortable stage will meet the morning Santa Fe train, give guests a delightful ride over a picturesque mountain road, and return in time for the 4:45 Santa Fe local . . . . Rates per day $2, per week $10," read an advertisement in the *Azusa Pomotropic* (August 24, 1905).

Camp Rincon became a stock company in 1906, with Potter selling the property to four businessmen. Smith stayed on as manager for two more years, then was succeeded by Raymond Briggs. The halcyon days of the shady hostelry continued into the 1920s. Like Follows Camp, the automobile proved to be Camp Rincon's nemesis. Easy access took away some of the back country luster of the resort, and it experienced a gradual decline in popularity. Burt Luckey briefly revived the camp in the early 1930s, and to draw attention to his resort installed the first neon lights in the canyon. From 1933 to 1935 Luckey shared the glen with 194 boys of the Federal Government's Civilian Conservation Corps, who used Camp Rincon as a base from which to build new roads, trails and firebreaks.

The disastrous flood of March 1-2, 1938 overnight wiped out all but a few buildings at the camp, and turned the once-beautiful green sanctuary into a scene of utter devastation. By then it was L.A. County property, the county having acquired it during the construction of the flood control dams. The county leased what remained of the camp to Clara Schmidt, who vainly attempted to rebuild it as a tourist resort. The end came with World War II, when travel in the canyon was severely curtailed. Today, what remains of the glen (half of it has disappeared into the river's floodplain) is an Angeles National Forest ranger station.

Nestled snugly on a little bench halfway up the North Fork was Sycamore Flat, named for the stately sycamores that lined Coldwater Creek. The spot was a favorite hunters' camp until R.W. Dawson

Duncan "Stuttering" McNabb standing in front of Cornelius Potter's original Rincon cabins, ca. 1895. Potter homesteaded the little flat near the confluence of the West and North forks in the 1860's. – HENRY E. HUNTINGTON LIBRARY

Pamphlets proclaiming the merits of Follows Camp and Camp Rincon.

The Rincon, near the forks of San Gabriel Canyon, has always been a favorite haven for canyon visitors. In 1897 Charlie Smith of Azusa leased the glen from Cornelius Potter and almost overnight turned it into a popular tourist hostelry, complete with store, hotel, cabins, tents. It became known as Camp Rincon. Today, only a ranger station remains at the spot.

Hotel Rincon included a general store, the largest commercial establishment in San Gabriel Canyon. Photo taken about 1905. – SEDLEY PECK COLLECTION

filed a claim in the 1880s. In 1900 Dawson leased the flat to A.A. "Doc" Beatty for resort purposes. Beatty built a rough road up the North Fork from Camp Rincon and opened a rustic hostelry he called "Squirrel Inn" in 1901. The inn was a hit from the start, particularly because of a beautiful waitress named Nellie Hawkins. Never a gal like Nellie; from 1901 until about 1906, she charmed and attracted miners, hunters, campers — just about every mountain man for miles around. Nellie is long gone now, and the doors of Squirrel Inn have been closed for a half century, but the popular waitress will never be forgotten. Her name is eternally transfixed on Mount Hawkins, looming high over the North Fork.

In 1904 R. W. Dawson took over the management of the resort he owned, changed its name to Coldbrook Camp (spelled Cold Brook on some camp advertisements), and secured a U.S. Post Office under that name. With the help of M.M. "Dad" Dougherty, Dawson turned the camp into a thriving resort. Coldbrook Hotel was completed by 1907, and numerous cabins and tents were spotted among the graceful sycamores and alders. The resort attracted many notables, among them John and Ethel Barrymore and cartoonist Jimmy Swinnerton. Author Charles Francis Saunders described Coldbrook as "a cheerful little village in summer of canvas tent-houses, past which Soldier Creek, as hearty, exuberant a water as you often encounter, goes brawling to the San Gabriel."[9] A brochure for the camp described the varied activities for the guests' enjoyment: "Amusements at Cold Brook Camp are many, including special dinner parties, dances, masquerade balls, candy pulls, pop corn around the campfire, moonlight strolls to the old mine, quoit pitching, swinging, boating on Crystal Lake, croquet and tennis. Hunting and fishing are the season's most popular sports. The mountains are full of deer, squirrel, foxes and other game, and our streams are yearly stocked with fish for the pleasure of our guests."

In 1913 Coldbrook Camp was sold to three Covina men — W.O. Custer, W.P. Watts, and C.B. Casey — who promptly added improvements, including an electric generating power plant powered by the falls just above the camp, to provide lighting and run nightly motion pictures.

A constant problem was the narrow, zigzagging road that climbed from Camp Rincon to the North Fork resort. The route washed out almost every winter and had to be hurriedly repaired to allow access for the summer crowds.

Coldbrook's heydays continued well into the 1920s; then, as with the other canyon resorts, attendance gradually declined. The little resort, under the guidance of Mr. and Mrs. Robert F. Hill, struggled on until 1938.

In 1935 most of the Coldbrook property was leased to the Civilian Conservation Corps. Two hundred and fifty young men of the C.C.C.'s 1950th Company, the "Fighting Fifties" as they proudly called themselves, abruptly transformed Coldbrook

The store at Coldbrook Camp, well up the North Fork of the San Gabriel, ca. 1905. The woman and man standing together in right center are Mrs. and Mr. R. W. Dawson, proprietors of the resort.
– SEDLEY PECK COLLECTION

The Coldbrook stage, crammed with visitors, prepares to leave the resort for the tortuous ride down canyon to Azusa, ca. 1906. – HENRY E. HUNTINGTON LIBRARY

Mock hold-up of the Camp Rincon stage, 1908.
– SEDLEY PECK COLLECTION

SOUVENIR OF

Cold Brook Camp

THE BEAUTIFUL MOUNTAIN RESORT

On the Ice Cold Head Waters of North Fork

SAN GABRIEL CAÑON

R. W. DAWSON, Proprietor

Department A. AZUSA, CALIFORNIA

The C.C.C. Camp at Coldbrook, home of the "Fighting Fifties," as the 1950th C.C.C. Company was known. 1937 photo. From 1933 to 1938, the C.C.C. boys based at Coldbrook did a tremendous amount of road and trail building and forest conservation work in the canyon. – HENRY E. HUNTINGTON LIBRARY

Camp into a military base. Barracks were erected, a parade ground and sports area was cleared, and the road improved. The men worked five days a week on Forest Service-directed projects, chiefly fire control work and campground construction. Weekends were periods of relaxation and sports. The "Fighting Fifties" fielded teams in basketball, baseball and boxing. In 1937 the Coldbrook C.C.C. boys were transferred to Cucamonga and the little sycamore-shaded flat was suddenly still.

Plans were in the works to expand the resort, using the C.C.C. buildings, when the flood of March 1938 hit with devastating impact, causing the final abandonment of the camp. After World War II, the Forest Service took over and built a ranger station and the Coldbrook Public Campground of today.

Halfway up the mountainside between Coldbrook Camp and Crystal Lake is a little verdant glen nourished by falling springs, known as Little Cienega in the early days. Here, in 1931, Frank Headlee fashioned a small resort featuring housekeeping cabins, a swimming pool and trout dinners. It was first called La Cienega, then Headlee's, and finally Falling Springs Resort, the name it holds today. Just off the winding road to Crystal Lake, it attracted a small but dedicated band of enthusiasts who would return time and

The Coldbrook stage descending the North Fork road, 1910. The route from Camp Rincon up to Coldbrook Camp was precarious and needed repairs after every storm. – SEDLEY PECK COLLECTION

Henry C. Roberts' stables in Azusa, across street from the Santa Fe depot, ca. 1902. Roberts standing in doorway, on right. On horse to right is son Charles Roberts. Bates Persinger sits on burro to left. To his right, standing with loaded mule, is "Two-Gun" Don Rosencranz.

Roberts operated this livery stable for many years, providing transportation to the San Gabriel Canyon mines and resorts. – MARGARET BUSH COLLECTION

Henry C. Roberts home at the mouth of San Gabriel Canyon, ca. 1900. Roberts claimed 160 acres here in 1859 and struggled for two decades to gain title from Henry Dalton. His original home, built in 1859, burned; this second home was built in 1874. For some forty years, Roberts was a leading figure in San Gabriel Canyon, operating stage service, supplying the mines, and doing hydraulic mining himself.
– MARGARET BUSH COLLECTION

Flo Flo Peck standing before Henry Roberts' old store and stage station at Follows Camp, San Gabriel Canyon. This building may be the oldest man-made structure in the San Gabriel Mountains, erected by Henry Roberts sometime before 1868. It is used as a storehouse today, although Mrs. Peck hopes to turn it into a canyon history museum.
– MRS. SEDLEY PECK COLLECTION

Fisherman adjusts his reel at Camp Bonita, 1914. This small resort at the East Fork's elbow was a favorite of anglers. – SEDLEY PECK COLLECTION

Jay Gardner Scott founded a delightful little resort at the junction of the East Fork and Cattle Canyon in 1909. Called Scott's Camp at first, it became famous as Camp Bonita, the delight of fisherman until its demise in the great flood of 1938.

again. In 1939 Headlee sold out to Mr. and Mrs. Robert Hill, the last proprietors of Coldbrook Camp before its demise in the 1938 flood. In the late 1940s Falling Springs was taken over by Ben and Virginia Bierke, who enlarged the resort by adding more cabins and recreational facilities. Today, Falling Springs is the only privately-owned resort on the North Fork. Delightful during the summer months when the surrounding mountainsides are dry, Falling Springs retains the quiet charm of yesteryear.

Nestled among the oaks and sycamores at the junction of the East Fork and Cattle Canyon was a beautiful little resort founded by Jay Gardner Scott in 1909. Scott originally called his resort Scott's Camp, but soon changed the name to Camp Bonita. A small lodge and store were built and tents were erected alongside the river. Fishing at this elbow of the East Fork was ubelievably good, and it was not long until Camp Bonita became a favorite haunt of anglers. Scott left for Arizona about 1912 and was succeeded by a progression of owners. In 1914 Henry Willard took over as the host, and under him Camp Bonita reached its zenith of popularity. Three times a week, and more often when the traffic demanded, the Camp Bonita stage would bring dozens of happy fishermen and campers to this verdant hostelry alongside the rushing stream. Unfortunately, the camp's streamside location made it susceptible to the periodic flooding that hits San Gabriel Canyon. The resort was damaged several times by high water during the 1920s and early '30s. The end came in March 1938, when all the cabins and most of the tents were washed away in the worst torrent in the recent history of the canyon.

A mile and a quarter downstream from Camp Bonita was Williams Camp, founded by Jim Williams in 1913. Williams became known throughout the canyon for his "home brew" during the prohibition era, an activity that apparently escaped the eye of the usually vigilant "feds." Imbibers, along with the usual coterie of campers and fishermen, kept Williams' little tent camp well attended during the 1920s and into the 1930s. Jim Williams, however, did not have his heart in his resort. He was more involved with his various mining claims, which included a tin mine up nearby Horse Canyon and several marginal gold prospects.

Camp Williams was acquired by Lyle and Ramona Johnson in the early 1950s. The Johnsons turned the old resort into a combination campground, trailer park, picnic area, store and restaurant. In the 1960s the Hunter family took over, and they in turn were succeeded in 1976 by Grace Melton, who runs the resort today.

The old Ferguson property downstream from Follows Camp is now known as Shady Oaks, or Follows Camp West. For many years it was a

The original log cabin built by John P. Weber in 1906, in Coldwater Canyon. Weber's Camp was a small but popular mountain hostelery from 1906 until 1924.
– JAMES B. McNAIR PHOTOGRAPH

private retreat for the Ferguson family. After World War II it was briefly a religious retreat called "Beulah Land." In the early 1950s Tony Galleta bought it, gave it the name Shady Oaks, and built a campground, picnic area and store. Since 1979 it has been owned by Joe Davidson.

The record for the shortest life of any resort on the East Fork goes to Branscome Camp, once located alongside the river just east of Follows Camp. Branscome laid out his camp too close to the tumultuous waters of the East Fork in 1913. He paid for his mistake the following year, when the little resort was totally washed away.

Two small resorts in Coldwater Canyon, a tributary of the East Fork, need to be mentioned.

One of the most beautifully-situated hostelries in the mountains was Weber's Camp, founded by John P. Weber in 1906. Deep in Coldwater Canyon, shaded by oak, spruce and pine, Weber's Camp was a delight to its small but loyal clientele, many of whom returned year after year. The resort consisted of three main buildings and a half dozen housekeeping tents alongside the icy-cold creek. To supply his guests with fresh fruits and vegetables, Weber cleared several patches of forest and planted crops. His apple and pear orchard high on a sloping bench required superhuman effort on his part. The hostelry was at its zenith of popularity when John Weber

John P. Weber and his dog "Reb", 1913. Weber came into Coldwater Canyon in 1906 and founded a small resort. His most ambitious achievement was building a trail to the summit of Old Baldy.
– ROBERT CHAPMAN COLLECTION

Until Angeles National Forest was proclaimed a game preserve in 1915, Weber's Camp was a favorite hangout for hunters. Here, John P. Weber (sitting to left) and two hunters pose before skins of mountain lion, sheep and bear caught in the wilds above the camp. – ROBERT CHAPMAN COLLECTION

The dance pavilion at Weber's Camp, 1913. The little resort in Coldwater Canyon had a small but loyal clientele. – ROBERT CHAPMAN COLLECTION

died in 1920. His niece, Gertrude Lutz, managed the camp for several years, but things just weren't the same without the charismatic Weber. The end for the isolated little resort came in 1924.

A half mile upstream from Weber's Camp, close under the spurs of San Antonio Ridge, was the Widman Ranch. Jake and Flora Widman came in the day of their marriage, June 9, 1919, and stayed fifty years, until Jake's death on May 17, 1969. They built a log cabin and planted a fruit orchard. In the middle 1920s they erected more small cabins and took in paying guests. Widman's was a favorite retreat for those who relished a wilderness setting deep in the mountains.

Those who know San Gabriel Canyon, or have read previous chapters in this book, are aware of the recurrent floods that have plagued the canyon. Not generally known is that another danger has also played a significant role in the canyon's history — fire. Since the 1870s, forest and brush conflagrations have destroyed much of the canyon watershed and greatly contributed to the severity of the floods. These fires generated demands for government action to save the watershed and resulted in the establishment of the San Gabriel Timberland Reserve — forerunner of today's Angeles National Forest — on December 20, 1892. To guard against fires and enforce Forest Service regulations, a ranger force was created in 1898. The first ranger stationed in the main San Gabriel Canyon, and the

The Widman cabin in Coldwater Canyon, ca. 1923. Jake Widman homesteaded her in 1913. In 1919 Jake and his bride Flora came in on their wedding day and stayed fifty years, until Jake's death in 1969. – JAMES B. McNAIR PHOTOGRAPH

Jake Widman with a mountain lion he shot outside his cabin, ca. 1920. – ROBERT CHAPMAN PHOTOGRAPH

only ranger in the region for many years, was Irving D. Carter. Carter set up headquarters at Camp Rincon and patrolled the North and East forks regularly. In 1900 the first ranger station built with government funds ($70) in California was constructed by Lewis Newcomb twenty miles up the West Fork. Rangers Bill Bacon and Jess Sevier were stationed there in the early days.

Unfortunately, the creation of a government forest reserve and the employment of rangers failed to solve the fire problem. Minor conflagrations broke out in 1896, 1900 and 1913, followed by the great holocaust of September 1919. The 1919 fire erupted on September 12th near the Narrows of the East Fork, allegedly caused by a miner burning trash. The blaze, fanned by 25 mile-per-hour winds and 90-degree temperatures, quickly spread westward and crossed the ridge into Bichota Canyon. Another fire broke out in Big Tujunga Canyon, twenty miles west, on September 15th, and Angeles National Forest officials were faced with a major crisis. By September 25th the East Fork fire had advanced westward into the North Fork, sending up huge clouds of smoke that darkened the sun. Two thousand men, recruited from all over Southern California, were on the line fighting both fires, and the Mount Wilson Observatory was considered in peril. In the San Gabriel Valley, churches held prayer meetings seeking divine aid. Their prayers were apparently answered. On September 26th it began to rain. For two days rainfall pelted the San Gabriel Mountains and when the storm ended the twin conflagrations were out. Fortunately, the mountain camps had been saved by the strenuous work of fire crews, but 60,000 acres of valuable San Gabriel River watershed were destroyed. In all, over 150,000 acres of timber and brush land were blackened in what Angeles National Forest Supervisor Rush Charleton called "The greatest fire we have ever known in Southern California."

The 1919 blaze was just a prelude to the terrible mountain holocaust of 1924, which began in San Gabriel Canyon and spread westward into the heart of the range. The fire erupted at O'Melveny Flat in the main canyon on Sunday afternoon, August 31, 1924. It was caused by the careless throwing of a match by a camper. The conflagration spread with lightning quickness through the dry chaparral and timber. It crossed the ridge into Fish Canyon, burned up the West Fork into the almost inaccessible heartland of the San Gabriels to the slopes of Mount Waterman. Two thousand men from all over the Southwest were on the fireline and succeeded in saving most of the mountain resorts in the fire's path. One tongue of the fire, however, crept up the East Fork, destroyed most of Mountain View, and was stopped just short of Follows Camp by the backbreaking efforts of Ralph Follows and his make-shift fire crew. The fire burned into the back country north of the West Fork until finally doused by rains in mid-October, blackening over 90,000 acres of valuable watershed.

The fires clearly revealed the need to improve fire control techniques in Angeles National Forest. Charleton stated the main problem: "The greatest difficulty in fighting the fires was the lack of roads over which to transport supplies to the men." As a result, the Forest Service in 1925 initiated a crash program to build fire roads and firebreaks. Also, more rangers were employed and stationed in the mountains. The Rincon ranger station was enlarged, and a new one was built below Camp Bonita in the East Fork. Stringent fire regulations went into effect at resorts and campgrounds. It is a tribute to the Forest Service that, through these efforts, never again did a fire in San Gabriel Canyon spread so far or cause so much damage to watershed and property.

Road construction in the mountains, given impetus by the Forest Service after the 1919 and 1924 fires, was long overdue in the minds of those who lived or managed resorts in the canyon. Until the 1930s, the canyon roads were abominable. "Store your auto at our Azusa garage," read a Coldbrook Camp advertisement in 1911, "and the stage will carry you to the camp." Indeed, the average motorist risked his automobile and sometimes even his life to negotiate the torturous San Gabriel Canyon road. The route followed the canyon bottom and was unpaved, very rough in places, and crossed the river without benefit of bridge 19 times between Azusa and Camp Rincon. "As the entire road construction was in the bottom of the canyon, each year's flood season would render it useless and after the spring freshets had subsided, the work had all to be done over," recalled Cornelius Smith, canyon historian and secretary of the Azusa Chamber of Commerce. Maintaining the primitive road was jointly financed by the canyon resort owners and the Azusa Chamber of Commerce. "A yearly sum of between two and three thousand dollars was raised and expended on the canyon road without a single penny coming to our aid from outside sources," continued Smith.

"Finally, through the untiring efforts of the Chamber of Commerce a prison camp was established at the mouth of the canyon and a road above high water grade was slowly constructed by prison labor with shovels and wheelbarrows. This was the first prison camp established in the county and from this beginning much road work has been done in the country in a like manner.[11]

The Camp Rincon Stage, crossing the last ford of the San Gabriel on its journey from the Santa Fe Station in Azusa to the resort camp, ca. 1910. The rough road up the canyon forded the river some twenty times. – SEDLEY PECK COLLECTION

It was obvious that any major highway construction in San Gabriel Canyon would require financial support from outside the local area. With this in mind, the Azusa Chamber of Commerce in 1914 proposed the building of a "San Gabriel Canyon Scenic Drive." The original idea was an all-year route from Azusa to the Forks, but Los Angeles County officials went one better. The County Road Department proposed a route up the canyon, over the crest of the mountains, and down Big Rock Creek to Antelope Valley. Unfortunately for San Gabriel Canyon boosters, strong competition for a cross-range highway came from Pasadena, which wanted an Arroyo Seco route. Through 1914 and much of 1915, a verbal battle raged between the supporters of the two proposed scenic routes. The Auto Club threw its support behind Pasadena, and eventually the county and the state opted for the Arroyo Seco route that later became the Angeles Crest Highway. The county supervisors did, however, authorize a paved highway up San Gabriel Canyon as far as the Forks.

It was a long time before the canyon highway became reality. After the 1919 and 1924 fires, forest supervisor Charleton urged that work on the new all-weather canyon road be speeded and proposed $127,000 in federal funds for construction if the county would put up a similar amount. The county believed the state should provide half the funds, and the highway project became bogged down in a financial morass. As a temporary substitute, the county did pave the old canyon-bottom route as far as the Forks, and improved the dirt roads to Camp Rincon and Follows Camp in 1925.

Plans for construction of major dams in San Gabriel Canyon — one by the County Flood Control District and the other by Pasadena — created a need for a new "high line" highway up the canyon in the early 1930s. A high, washout-free route had been talked about in previous years, but the cost was considered prohibitive. Now, necessity became the mother of creation. Surveys were undertaken by county engineers in 1930, and construction got underway in January 1932. The "high line" thoroughfare was a cooperative effort of four agencies — the Los Angeles County Flood Control District, the City of Pasadena, the Forest Service and the State of California each sharing the cost. The total expenditure was $1,300,000, a hefty sum for the depression-laden 1930s. The route snaking high along the west canyon wall, required an

The Los Angeles County Board of Supervisors fording the San Gabriel on a inspection tour of the canyon road, ca. 1912. It was decades before the Board agreed to build an all-year highway up San Gabriel Canyon.

immense amount of excavation, as much of the rock proved to be decomposed, the slope was steep, and recurring slides necessitated frequent repairs. The preliminary roadway was blasted through and graded to the Forks by the end of 1933, although it was not paved and ready for public use until 1935. Widened and improved in recent years, it is still the only highway up the main canyon.

From the Forks, the county planned to build two roads into the steep, rugged headwater regions of the San Gabriel. Work was begun in 1929 and completed in 1931 on a winding, hairpin highway from Camp Rincon up the North Fork to the county's new Crystal Lake playground. The other roadway, begun in 1929 but never completed, followed a route up the deep chasm of the East Fork. County prison crews did the lion's share of construction work as the narrow paved highway, following the bowels of the canyon, slowly snaked its way north to the Narrows. Here, where the walls of the East Fork close in and form the deepest gorge in Southern California, a concrete bridge was built and a tunnel chiseled out of the sheer rock. The scenic highway was originally planned to continue to the head of the East Fork, then zigzag up over Blue Ridge and down to Wright-

Follows Camp auto stage passing a washout on the old canyon road, ca. 1917. Washouts like this happened every year, requiring constant repair work.
– SEDLEY PECK COLLECTION

The entrance to San Gabriel Canyon, 1914. "Badman" John Knox Portwood on wagon. The Associated Chambers of Commerce of the San Gabriel Valley erected this sign to promote a proposed cross-mountain highway from Azusa via the canyon to Antelope Valley. Pasadena supported an Arroyo Seco route. The latter route was chosen in 1919, and fifteen years later became the Angeles Crest Highway. San Gabriel Valley boosters had to wait until 1961, when Highway 39 was finally blasted through the Islip Saddle, for their mountain thoroughfare dreams to become reality. – HENRY E. HUNTINGTON LIBRARY

The Bridge to Nowhere, Narrows of the East Fork. The modern highway span, part of a proposed route up the East Fork, was completed just before the great flood of March 1938. The highway was washed out, but the bridge remains, a monument to man's folly.

wood. It never made it. On the night of March 1-2, 1938, an unprecedented rainstorm hit the mountains, causing a savage torrent to boil down the East Fork. Literally overnight, the East Fork highway was chopped to pieces. Damage was so extensive that the new roadway was abandoned. Since 1938, "The Bridge to Nowhere," visited only by hikers, has stood as a mute reminder of the power of mountain water.

The idea of a road up the East Fork was revived after World War II. In 1954 the county road department, again utilizing inmate labor, began construction of a new highway up the most spectacular chasm in the San Gabriels. This time, to avoid the flood hazards of the canyon, the roadway was to be etched high along the west wall. Original plans called for completion to Vincent Gap by 1977. Working daily shifts, the prisoners of County Detention Camp Number 14 had four miles of highway carved out of the mountainside and graded by 1969. Then the county ran into opposition from budget-cutters and from conservationists who wanted to preserve the upper East Fork in its wilderness state. Work abruptly stopped, and not a shovelful of dirt has been turned on the mountainside highway during the last decade. The excavation scars remain an ugly stain high on the west slope of the canyon, a defacing monument to plans that went astray.

The East Fork Bridge, affording all-year access to the East Fork resorts, upon completion in 1949. – AZUSA HISTORICAL SOCIETY

Roads in the East Fork are in constant need of repair. The canyon is a natural flood channel, as the Eldoradoville miners learned in 1862 and countless others have discovered since. – WALT WHEELOCK PHOTO

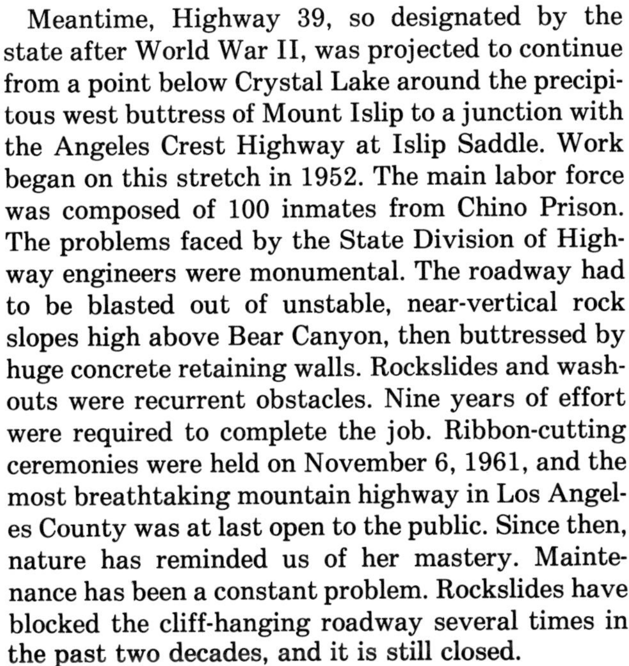

Meantime, Highway 39, so designated by the state after World War II, was projected to continue from a point below Crystal Lake around the precipitous west buttress of Mount Islip to a junction with the Angeles Crest Highway at Islip Saddle. Work began on this stretch in 1952. The main labor force was composed of 100 inmates from Chino Prison. The problems faced by the State Division of Highway engineers were monumental. The roadway had to be blasted out of unstable, near-vertical rock slopes high above Bear Canyon, then buttressed by huge concrete retaining walls. Rockslides and washouts were recurrent obstacles. Nine years of effort were required to complete the job. Ribbon-cutting ceremonies were held on November 6, 1961, and the most breathtaking mountain highway in Los Angeles County was at last open to the public. Since then, nature has reminded us of her mastery. Maintenance has been a constant problem. Rockslides have blocked the cliff-hanging roadway several times in the past two decades, and it is still closed.

Today, San Gabriel Canyon is easily accessible via well-graded, paved highway. Every weekend sees crowds of sightseers, picnickers, campers, hikers and offroad vehicle enthusiasts crowd the canyon roads. Most of the old resorts are long gone, others are only shades of their former selves, catering to a different, more mobile clientele. The old San Gabriel remains a prime vacation haunt for thousands of Southern Californians.

1. Stuart O'Melveny, Foreword, in W.W. Robinson, *The Forest and The People* (Los Angeles, 1946), p. v.
2. Henry Markham Page, *Pasadena: The Early Years* (Los Angeles, 1964), p. 161.
3. Stuart O'Melveny, *It's Best to Divide With Friends* (Los Angeles, 1955), p. 13.
4. Hiram Reid, *History of Pasadena* (Pasadena, 1895), p. 410.
5. Jackson A. Graves, *California Memories* (Los Angeles, 1930), p. 244.
6. O'Melveny, *It's Best to Divide With Friends,* p. 4.
7. Cornelius Smith, "The Old San Gabriel and Some of Those Who Made Its History," *Trails Magazine* (Summer 1936), p. 10. See also Henry O'Melveny, "The San Gabriels: Sportsmen's Rendezvous of Half a Century Ago," *Westways* (May 1944).
8. *Azusa Herald,* October 20, 1937.
9. Charles Francis Saunders, *The Southern Sierras of California* (Boston, 1923), p. 47.
10. Cornelius Smith, "Early Canyon Road-Building Activity," *Azusa Herald,* December 26, 1935.

Newman's El Encanto, just inside the mouth of San Gabriel Canyon, built by Miller and Henrietta Newman in 1920-21. Miller Newman was a forest ranger and his home was used as a ranger station, known as Camp One, in the 1920s and '30s. The Newmans opened their home to private parties for dinner and dancing in 1934, featuring Henrietta's home cooking. Success was immediate and El Encanto became a true restaurant in 1938. It continued as a popular spot until Mrs. Newman sold it in 1957. Since 1965 Byron and Donna Hinkley have been the genial hosts. It is now known as Hinkley's El Encanto.
– MARGARET BUSH COLLECTION

Henrietta Roberts Newman, daughter of Henry Roberts, and her husband Miller Emil Newman, founders of Newman's El Encanto in San Gabriel Canyon. Miller Newman was a forest ranger who patrolled the canyon regularly from the early 1920s until his death in 1952.
– MARGARET BUSH COLLECTION

8
Crystal Lake And Its High Country

High under the 8,000-foot summits of Mounts Islip and Hawkins, just below the main crest of the San Gabriels, lies a forested basin replete with Jeffrey and sugar pine, white fir, incense cedar and big cone spruce. Springs of sparkling cold water gush from mountainside recesses, watering the basin and forming the headwaters of the San Gabriel River's North Fork. Just southwest of the basin, without an outlet, nestles a little silver dollar-shaped lake, the only natural lake in the San Gabriel Mountains.

Pine Flat and Sycamore Lake, as the basin and its nearby body of water were known in the early days, attracted hunters as early as the 1860s. Grizzly bears, mountain lions and deer abounded in the high country. In fact, the little round lake was "a favorite haunt of the grizzlies, who appear to prefer its waters to those of the stream in the canyon below," according to an anonymous visitor who reported his experiences to the *Los Angeles Star* (October 2, 1871).

Grizzlies were a constant menace to early visitors to Pine Flat. Cattle grazed there in summer by Cornelius Potter and Henry Roberts were often attacked by the hungry behemoths. They extracted such a heavy toll that Potter was obliged to remove his herd, while Roberts, more stubborn, hired rifle-toting vaqueros to guard his animals. Pasadena historian Henry Markham Page related a close man vs. bear incident of the brothers Ben and Ed Hahn, who visited Sycamore Lake in the 1880s: "The trip to the lake was made without accident and plenty of game, including deer and mountain lions, were killed. Bear signs were found to be numerous, and Ed Hahn had the fortune to come face to face with a grizzly. As he was armed with nothing more deadly than a shotgun, the interview was short, Ed terminating it by flight, in the course of which he fell into a stream several times."[1] Page also related an incident in May, 1892 when "a Spaniard in the North Fork of the river came across so many bear tracks that he tied his donkey to a tree and hurried to a camp nearby for a gun, so that he could be ready should he meet a bear. When he returned, all that remained of his burro was its head still tied by the halter to the tree. The animal and all the provisions he carried had been eaten."[2]

There is evidence that very early timber cutting took place at Pine Flat. The *Star's* writer of October 2, 1871 reported many stumps of large pines, which he claimed were "felled many years ago to furnish a portion of the lumber used in the construction of the Mission of San Gabriel." Was Pine Flats the lost source for San Gabriel Mission timber? Or was the timber taken out years later by miners in San Gabriel Canyon to shore up their works? Just who did the early lumbering at Pine Flat may forever remain a mystery.

Pine Flat and its nearby lakelet was such delightful mountain country that it was not long until settlers laid claim to the area. In 1873 three men — W.P. Barnes, Oliver Justice and E.L. Burdick — filed on quarter sections of Pine Flat with the intention of building cabins there, but nothing ever came of their plans. R.W. Dawson, pioneer settler of Sycamore Flat halfway up the North Fork, first visited the lake in 1876 and soon thereafter laid claim to it. (Dawson apparently first called it Sycamore Lake. There are no sycamores there; he probably gave it that name because he owned Sycamore Flat.)

Judge Benjamin Eaton of Pasadena visited the little lake in 1887. "The water is clear as a crystal and the party found it good to drink," he commented. Eaton also saw resort possibilities: "The locality would be accessible for a mountain railroad, and if provided with such facilities it could not fail to become a popular resort."[1] Needless to say, nothing ever came of his railroad suggestion. His mention of the crystal purity of the water was heeded, however. It was not long until Sycamore Lake became known by the name it holds today — Crystal Lake.

Crystal Lake, the only natural lake in the San Gabriel Mounains. This turn-of-the-century view shows it the way nature made it: wild and beautiful, surrounded by hills of Jeffrey and sugar pine. – PETE GOODELL PHOTO

R.W. Dawson, around the year 1890, built the first cabin at Pine Flat, a sturdy stone structure located on the west edge of the flat. In 1897 Dawson was paid $5,000 by the Crystal Lake Irrigation and Power Company, incorporated for the purpose of piping water from the lake down to a pair of powerhouses in the lower North Fork. Dawson's stone cabin was used as a cookhouse by the construction crew working on a flume to bring water from the big spring at the foot of Mt. Hawkins to Crystal Lake, in the hope that the combined flow from the spring and the lake would be sufficient to run the power plants. The ambitious scheme fell through when it was belatedly discovered that Crystal Lake was fed by run-off water only and there was insufficient water to power a hydroelectric operation.

Two riders from Coldbrook Camp visit Crystal Lake, ca. 1914. The little body of water is fed by run-off only. – SEDLEY PECK COLLECTION

Shortly after 1900, a number of hunting and vacation cabins were erected at Pine Flat. George Bills used the boards from Dawson's old flume to build a stout lodge he called Pinehurst in 1907. The Negley sisters built a small cabin near the big spring. The Negleys were expert riflewomen and often had a buck hanging outside their cabin. Roger Dalton and

The Wawona Cabin on Pine Flat, near Crystal Lake, built by Occidental College students in 1908. This was the third cabin and the first resort building erected on Pine Flat.
– CORNELIUS SMITH PHOTO

his Azusa friends constructed a hunting lodge they called "Campo de Los Pinos" at the big spring. Students from Occidental College built their "Wawona Cabin" in 1909, the outgrowth of a happy camping party held at Pine Flat the summer before. Among those who built and enjoyed the cabin was Robert Glass Cleland, later to become one of California's leading historians. Ninety pack loads of lumber, cement and supplies were lugged up the old "heartbreak trail" from Coldbrook Camp to Pine Flat by the Oxy students. In those days the trip was a strenuous, zigzagging uphill journey, a far cry from the paved highway of today.

From about 1910 until well into the 1920s, parties from Coldbrook Camp rode horseback or sweated their way on foot up the steep heartbreak trail to picnic and camp at Pine Flat and Crystal Lake. The little lake became a popular swimming and boating spot for Coldbrook vacationers. An early Coldbrook Camp brochure includes a photograph of rowboats plying the lake.

One Coldbrook Camp visitor who took a particular liking to the forested high country above the resort was Jimmy Swinnerton, famed artist and cartoonist

Occidental College students and their pack mules at the Wawona Cabin, ca. 1909. College students camped there every summer. One of the cabin builders was Robert Glass Cleland, late historian.

"Little Jimmy" painted on a tree stump by cartoonist Jimmy Swinnerton in 1909. This 1914 photo shows the painting still intact. Since then, the campground and spring have been known as "Little Jimmy."
– HENRY RAYMOND NASH PHOTO (COURTESY RAY NASH, SON)

Jimmy Swinnerton (1875-1974), artist and famed cartoonist for the Hearst newspapers, ca. 1912. In the summer of 1909 Swinnerton hiked from Coldbrook Camp up to the shoulder of Mt. Islip and discovered what was then known as Gooseberry Spring. He camped there during the month of July 1909 and painted "Little Jimmy", his famous cartoon character, on a tree stump. Ever since the spring and campground have been known as "Little Jimmy."
– HAROLD DAVIDSON COLLECTION

for the Hearst newspapers. In the summer of 1909 Swinnerton puffed his way up the heartbreak trail and beyond, over Windy Gap, to a spring of icy-cold water and a nearby forested flat high on the slope of Mount Islip. He liked this sylvan retreat so much he spent the summer there, writing and painting. On a nearby tree stump he painted a life-size, color portrait of his popular comic character "Little Jimmy." Thereafter the little flat became known as Swinnerton Camp and the nearby waterhole, formerly called Gooseberry Spring for the gooseberry bushes around it, became known as Little Jimmy Spring.

In 1928 the Los Angeles County Board of Supervisors took out a lease from the Forest Service on 1,360 acres of the upper North Fork, including Crystal Lake and almost all of Pine Flat, for development as a county playground. Four years were required to build the county recreation area, complete with campground, picnic areas, boating and swimming facilities on the lake, a store, ranger station and a paved road up the North Fork. The 16-foot roadway, hewed out of sheer rock in one spot, followed a zigzag course up the steep headslope of the canyon, from Coldbrook Camp to Pine Flat. It was completed in the fall of 1931, and Pine Flat's long isolation came to an end.

Crystal Lake County Park was opened to the public in the spring of 1932. Almost immediately it became a popular weekend and holiday spot for picnickers and overnight campers. Over the July 4th and Labor Day weekends, the park was taxed to capacity, with over a thousand persons driving up from the valley. The 1938 flood severely damaged the North Fork highway, causing the county park to be closed temporarily, but within a year and a half the road was repaired and crowds once again thronged to the high mountain playground. The all-time record for attendance was reached in the month of August 1940, when 53,779 visitors enjoyed the county park.

World War II brought an end to Crystal Lake County Park. Wartime restrictions on driving and gasoline prevented all but a handful of campers from reaching the playground. In April 1943 the county supervisors voted to return the recreation area to the Forest Service, the reason being that it

Little Jimmy Campground as it looks today. Boy Scouts camp there almost every summer and fall weekend.

Los Angeles County campground at Pine Flat shortly after its opening in 1932. L.A. County operated the campground and resort facilities at Crystal Lake until 1943. – SEDLEY PECK COLLECTION

(left) The first ranger station at L.A. County Crystal Lake Park, 1937. The building is now a storehouse.

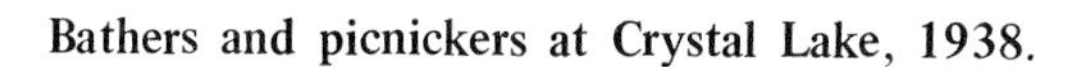

Bathers and picnickers at Crystal Lake, 1938.

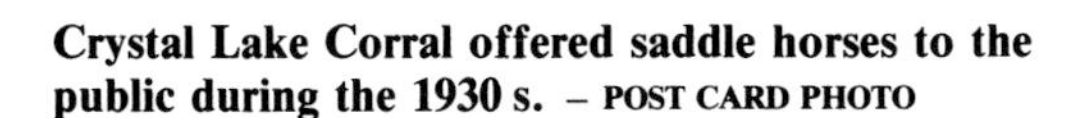

Crystal Lake Corral offered saddle horses to the public during the 1930 s. – POST CARD PHOTO

Crystal Lake Ranger Station, U.S. Forest Service (1979)

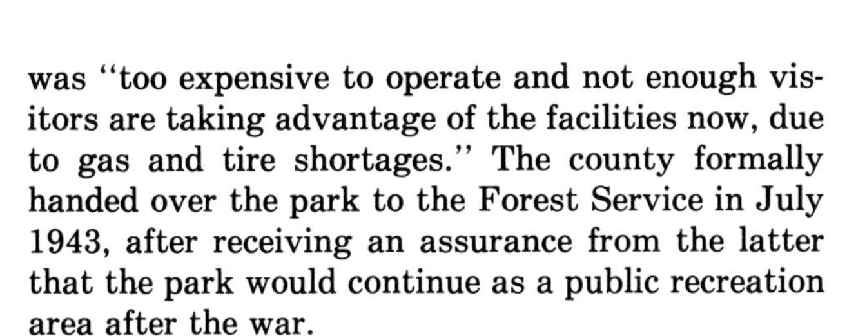

was "too expensive to operate and not enough visitors are taking advantage of the facilities now, due to gas and tire shortages." The county formally handed over the park to the Forest Service in July 1943, after receiving an assurance from the latter that the park would continue as a public recreation area after the war.

The Forest Service kept its promise. In 1946, the Crystal Lake Recreation Area was opened to the public and soon became a popular picnic and camping spot. Today, the 250 units of Crystal Lake Campground are filled to near capacity almost every summer weekend. The Forest Service operates a ranger station and visitor information service, and has constructed several nature trails. Crystal Lake itself, because of overuse no longer the scenic attraction it once was, sees picnickers and a few fishermen on weekends. The little store and food stand on the north shore closed down a few years ago.

Above Pine Flat and Crystal Lake loom a line of mountain peaks that are exceeded in elevation only by Mount Baldy and its nearby summits, in the San Gabriels. Their stories follow, listed generally west to east:

MT. WILLIAMSON (8248')

This massive triple-summited peak just northwest of Islip Saddle was named for Lieutenant (later Major) Robert Stockton Williamson (1824-1882), U.S. Army topographical engineer who made a reconnaissance of the north side of the San Gabriels for the Pacific Railroad Survey in 1853. He was looking for a railroad route across the mountains. Although he found no possible route in the Mt. Williamson area, he did locate two railway possibilities, one at each end of the San Gabriels — Soledad Canyon and Cajon Pass. The report Williamson submitted to Congress contained the first detailed description of the desert side of the range.

MT. ISLIP (8250')

This mountain directly above Pine Flat was named for George Islip, an early mountain pioneer from Canada who homesteaded in the San Gabriel Canyon during the 1880s. In 1909 students from Occidental College, led by Pete Goodell, built a huge rock and wood cabin with the name "Occidental" on top. For many years this "Occidental Monument" was a well-known landmark to hikers. In 1927 the Forest Service removed the old monument to make way for a steel fire lookout tower, which in turn was moved to South Hawkins Peak a decade later. Today, a dilapidated old stone cabin, sleeping quarters for the lookout, remains just below the summit as a lone reminder of those days when searching eyes guarded the high country.

MT. HAWKINS (8850')

This high peak directly east of Mt. Islip honors Miss Nellie Hawkins, beautiful and legendary waitress at the Squirrel Inn of Coldbrook Camp. Middle Hawkins (8505') and South Hawkins (7783'), the latter with a Forest Service lookout and fire road built in 1937, are take-offs from the same name.

THROOP PEAK (9138')

This mountain (pronounced "Troop") was originally called Dougherty Peak, after A.A. "Doc" Dougherty of Coldbrook Camp. In 1916 four college students arbitrarily placed the following notation in the summit register:

> To whom it may concern —
> I, the undersigned, on the 28th day of the seventh month in the year of our lord 1916, do hereby name this peak MOUNT THROOP after my Alma Mater, Throop College of Technology.
> signed: Samuel V. Broadwell
> witnesses: Alex W. Anderson
> Carroll Woodworth
> Philip A. Leighton

Throop Institute, founded in 1891 by Amos G. Throop (1811-1894), later became world famous as the California Institute of Technology. As the name "Dougherty Peak" was never made official, the U.S. Board on Geographic Names accepted the new designation, listing the name as "Throop Peak."

MT. BURNHAM (8997')

This forested bump on the ridge between Throop Peak and Mt. Baden-Powell was named in 1951 in honor of Major Frederick R. Burnham (1861-1947), a British army officer and explorer who later was active in the Boy Scout movement. He authored the Scout classic "Scouting on Two Continents." The Boy Scout's Silver Moccasin Trail crosses just below the summit.

MT. BADEN-POWELL (9399')

This second-highest peak in the San Gabriels, towering high above the headwaters of the East Fork, was long known as North Baldy. In 1931 the Forest Service and U.S. Board on Geographic Names sanctioned a request by C.J. Carlson, Western Regional Director of the Boy Scouts, to rename the peak Mt. Baden-Powell, in honor of Lord Robert Stevenson Smyth Baden-Powell (1847-1941), a British army officer who served in the Boer War and founded the Boy Scout movement in 1907. The official dedication of the new name took place on May 30, 1931, when a large party of Los Angeles area Boy Scouts erected a plaque and flagpole on the summit. Three years later, CCC workers constructed the present 4-mile zigzagging trail from Vincent Gap to the summit. For the next two and a half decades the peak was all but forgotten by the Scouts; the plaque disappeared and the flagstaff became bent and rusted. This sad situation was brought to the attention of Michael H. "Wally" Waldron, member of the executive board of the L.A. Area Council of the Boy Scouts. Under Waldron's inspiration, over 2,000 scouts took part in a nine-week project to erect a permanent bronze and cement monument on the summit. The official rededication took place on September 28, 1957.

Pete Goodell at the Occidental Monument on the summit of Mt. Islip. This monument was built by Occidental College students in 1909 and was a landmark on the summit for almost twenty years.
– CHARLES CLARK VERNON COLLECTION

Since then, the Scouts have made an annual "Silver Moccasin" pilgrimage across the San Gabriels to the peak. On the north summit ridge of the peak is a grove of ancient, weather-beaten Limber Pines, oldest living things in Southern California, discovered by Angeles Forest Supervisor Sim Jarvi in 1962. One of the largest specimens is named the "Waldron Tree" after the volunteer scout leader who organized the Boy Scout homage to the mountaintop.

NOTES

1 Henry Markham Page, *Pasadena: The Early Years* (Los Angeles, 1964), p. 161.

2 Ibid.

The fire lookout atop Mt. Islip, built in 1927 by the U.S. Forest Service and the L.A. County Forestry Department. In 1938 the lookout was removed to South Hawkins Peak, where it stands today.
– L.A. COUNTY FIRE DEPARTMENT

Weather-beaten limber pines near the summit of Mt. Baden Powell. These ancient forest monarchs are the old living things in Angeles National Forest.

The stone cabin on Mt. Islip, built in 1927 to house the fire lookout personnel. Only the lower walls remain today. – L.A. COUNTY FIRE DEPARTMENT

Sim Jarvi was Supervisor of Angeles National Forest from 1959 to 1964. Jarvi was an active supervisor, preferring the mountain trail to his desk at Angeles Forest Headquarters in Pasadena. Here he uses an increment borer to determine the age of one of the ancient Limber Pines he discovered near Mt. Baden-Powell in 1962. He died of a heart attack while hiking on an inspection trip near Mt Waterman, July 8, 1964.
– U.S. FOREST SERVICE

Mt. Baden-Powell from Blue Ridge. This 9399-foot peak was once known as North Baldy. The name was changed in 1931 to honor the founder of the Boy Scouts.

9
The Dalton And San Dimas Canyons

Wedged snugly between the lower reaches of San Gabriel and San Antonio canyons is a 32 square-mile rectangle of mountain country little known to most Southern Californians. Here, enclosed by lofty ridges on three sides, are the watersheds of Little Dalton, Big Dalton andd San Dimas canyons, a sinuous region of chaparral-coated hills, little forested flats, and delightful creeks luxuriant with live oak, alder, bay and sycamore.

Although Angeles National Forest as a whole received a total of 13,125,600 visits in 1979, only a small fraction of this multitude entered the Big Dalton and San Dimas watersheds. The reason for this paucity of visitors is that most of this superb mountain country is included within the boundaries of the San Dimas Experimental Forest, an extensive outdoor laboratory dedicated to learning about soil, vegetation, and erosion in mountain watersheds. The Experimental Forest has been closed to the general public since 1933.[1]

Long before the establishment of the Experimental Forest, this canyon country just above the foothill towns of Glendora, San Dimas and La Verne was heavily visited. As far back as the 1880s, valley residents enjoyed weekend hiking, horseback riding and camping in the sheltered folds of the Dalton and San Dimas watersheds. Trout fishing was fair to good in the streams and hunters searched the chaparral hills and forested flats for deer, bear and occasionally big horn sheep who would stray down from the higher ridges.

A few squatters and homesteaders ascended the canyons and found favorite spots to build their cabins. The names of many of these pioneer canyon settlers have been forgotten, but a few of them remained long enough to be remembered by today's old-timers. John Imbler came to Big Dalton in the early 1890s and fashioned a home at the junction of Bell and Volfe canyons. He ran a trap line and grew his own vegetables and fruits in a small orchard. For years, Imbler's place was the only cabin in the upper Big Dalton. Over in the shady West Fork of San Dimas Canyon, Harry Hynes fashioned a small ranch that was long the end-of-the-road gateway to the back country.

Trails were cut up the canyons and over the ridges. One of the earliest pathways was the Whitcomb Trail, named after and probably built by George D. Whitcomb, founder of Glendora. The trail went from Glendora north to the top of the ridge west of Little Dalton Canyon, and offered superb views of the valley below. The *Glendora Signal* of October 27, 1887 announced that the public had been granted use of the Whitcomb Trail: "Special attention will be given to conducting parties to the Summit of the Sierra Madre Mountains where a magnificent view can be had of the distant ranges, the valleys and the Pacific Ocean. This trail has been made at a large expense and is easy and perfectly safe so that invalids and nervous people can ascend without over fatigue or excitement." By the mid-1890s, there were well-beaten pathways up all the canyons and over the divide into San Gabriel and San Antonio canyons.

By the 1920s literally hundreds of valley residents picnicked, camped and fished in Big and Little Dalton and San Dimas canyons. Weekends and holidays saw citizens from the foothill communities pack up and drive into the canyons, set up temporary residence alongside the sparkling stream or under spreading oaks and sycamores, and enjoy a day or more away from urban worries. In 1928 alone, which apparently was the peak year, San Dimas Canyon saw 103,681 visitors by Forest Service count; Big and Little Dalton canyons were visited by 87,040.

Fraternal and youth organizations built camps in the canyons. The Loyal Order of Moose Lodge maintained "Moose Retreat" in San Dimas Canyon. The Moosemen are long gone, but the site of their weekend revelries is still known today as Moose Hill. The Boy Scouts, Girl Scouts, and YMCA all had camps in Big Dalton and San Dimas canyons, where young people partook in the delights of forest living and sleeping under the stars.

Old Baldy from Glendora, looking up Big Dalton Canyon. Telephoto taken by B. D. Jackson in 1907.
– HENRY E. HUNTINGTON LIBRARY

"Old Man" Jones at his cabin in Big Dalton Canyon, ca. 1910. Numerous squatters and homesteaders found mountain homes in the canyons of the San Gabriels.
– HENRY E. HUNTINGTON LIBRARY

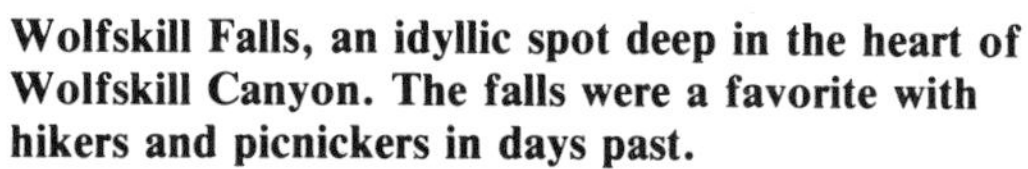

Wolfskill Falls, an idyllic spot deep in the heart of Wolfskill Canyon. The falls were a favorite with hikers and picnickers in days past.
– SAN DIMAS HISTORICAL SOCIETY

Albert and Maria Coulatti, proprietors of Wolfskill Falls Camp, a small tourist resort in Wolfskill Canyon. The camp catered to a small but select clientele from 1923 to 1934. – POMONA PUBLIC LIBRARY, SPECIAL COLLECTIONS

The interior of the pavilion, Wolfskill Falls Camp, 1928. Hikers could enjoy the warmth of the fireplace here, and enjoy a sandwich and drink. – POMONA PUBLIC LIBRARY, SPECIAL COLLECTIONS

To this writer, the most beautiful spot in any of these canyons is Wolfskill Falls, a half mile up Wolfskill Canyon from San Dimas Canyon. A silvery ribbon of water plunges sixty feet into a rock-ribbed sanctuary, verdant with live oak, willow and fern. A hundred yards down-canyon, above the stream to the south, is a delightful bench shaded by live oak trees. Here, in 1923, Albert Coulatti and his wife Maria fashioned one of the most idyllic resorts in the Angeles — Wolfskill Falls Camp. The little resort consisted of a lodge and several tent cabins for overnight guests, all in perpetual shade under the great oaks that towered above. The main attraction, Wolfskill Falls, was reached by a short walk up-canyon through a forest garden of ferns and other greenery. To reach the resort, guests originally were obliged to hike the half mile up from road's end in San Dimas Canyon. But the ingenious Coulatti, a welder by trade, soon devised easier access. He cut down the chassis of a Model T Ford, narrowed its wheelbase to four feet, and via this improvised contraption hauled people and supplies up Wolfskill Canyon to his resort. Wolfskill Falls Camp operated as a tourist resort until 1934. Today the buildings and tents are gone, and only a few remnants of resort days remain: some wood planks, a rusted refrigerator, an oversized oleander plant. Wilderness is reclaiming Wolfskill Canyon.

Whereas thousands of valley residents picnicked, camped and fished in the canyons, only the hardy few ventured up to the back-country flats. Perhaps the most delightful haunts in the Dalton-San Dimas watershed are these little forested flats, luxuriant with verdure, that are hidden high above the canyons.

Nestled snugly under Johnstone Peak, on the Big Dalton-San Dimas divide, with an all-encompassing panorama over the valley, is Sycamore Flat. There are no sycamores here; the name comes from Sycamore Canyon directly below the flat. Vegetable farming was done on the flat as early as the 1890s, and there were several unsuccessful attempts to turn the flat into a mountain resort community.

The largest of the back-country flats — which really isn't flat at all, but a gently rolling basin at the head of San Dimas Canyon — is Tanbark Flats. These flats are supposedly named for the tanbark oak, but strangely there are none here now and may never have been, according to Experimental Forester Charles Colver. In the early days, Tanbark Flats was dotted with live oak and watered by several springs and seepages. Hunters often camped here, and prospectors used it as a base for searching the surrounding hillsides. Tanbark Flats has undergone considerable change as the field headquarters of the San Dimas Experimental Forest, but this will be covered in the next chapter.

Tanbark Flats from south. These rolling, wooded flats were used by hunters and prospectors in years past. Today the flats are the field headquarters of the San Dimas Experimental Forest. – U.S. FOREST SERVICE PHOTO

The most isolated and idyllic of these back-country flats, and one of the beauty spots of the San Gabriel Mountains, is Browns Flat, a saucer-shaped meadow of about eighty acres that lies snugly against the San Dimas Canyon-San Antonio Canyon divide. Spotted with tall ponderosa pines, verdant in spring and early summer, with snow-capped Old Baldy as a backdrop, this little-known mountain bench offers a touch of the Sierra Nevada in Southern California. In times of abundant rainfall, a shallow lakelet forms in the center of the meadow, adding to the sublimity of the scene.

As early as the 1870s Browns Flat was a hunting outpost, rich in deer, bear and mountain lion. The origin of the name remains a mystery; perhaps one of its early-day campers was a hunter named Brown. In 1892 John Bradford Camp of Pomona began to use the flat as his hunting base. He applied for a homestead patent in 1898 and received title in 1902. Camp built a sturdy little log cabin on the southern edge and spent most of his summers there until 1915, when Angeles National Forest was made a game refuge and unrestricted hunting was no longer allowed. Camp planted apple trees on his flat and, according to historian Will Thrall, tried to make his property a hog ranch, "fattening the animals on acorns which were produced in great quantities in the thick oak forest around the rim, but this ended in failure because the mountain lions acquired such an appetite for acorn-fatted pork. It is said that they gathered in such numbers that killing

Browns Flat, a grassy meadow dotted with ponderosa pines, one of the beauty spots of the San Gabriel Mountains. The flat lies just below the San Dimas-San Antonio canyon divide.

lions for the bounty became the more profitable occupation."[2] Browns Flat later passed into the hands of John Bradford Camp's son, O.B. Camp. The younger Camp fancied turning the flat into a tourist resort. He sank wells to obtain a permanent water supply, but when this failed he considered pumping it up from nearby Fern Canyon. Some of his plans were rather grandiose, such as ferrying in tourists by airplane. He did clear a landing field and a small plane is said to have landed and taken off there. Camp sold out to William Gillette and Albert Stevens in 1937. Gillette and Stevens, La Verne developers, hoped to subdivide the flat for mountain home sites but were stymied by the Forest Service, which refused their request to build a paved highway up to their newly-acquired property. The Forest Service objection was based on the fact that Browns Flat was within the boundaries of San Dimas Experimental Forest. Gillette and Stevens repeatedly turned down Forest Service attempts to buy the flat. It was finally sold to Los Angeles County in the late 1940s, and the Forest Service acquired it at last in 1951. Two fires in recent years destroyed many of the ponderosa pines, including one mammoth tree over nine feet in diameter. Presently there are about eighty large ponderosas still

Browns Flat after abundant rainfall. A small lake forms in the center of the meadow, with snow-capped Old Baldy as a backdrop. – U.S. FOREST SERVICE PHOTO.

Log cabin on Browns Flat, built by John Bradford Camp about 1898. Camp homesteaded the flat as a hunter's camp in 1902. – JAMES B. MCNAIR PHOTO (1905)

John Bradford Camp cabin, Browns Flat ca. 1925.
– LLOYD COOPER PHOTO, POMONA PUBLIC LIBRARY

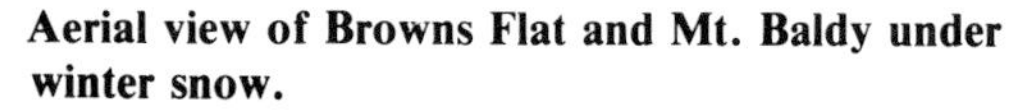

Aerial view of Browns Flat and Mt. Baldy under winter snow.
– LLOYD COOPER PHOTO, POMONA PUBLIC LIBRARY

alive, although air pollution is gradually killing them. All the young trees planted by the Experimental Forest were wiped out by the 1960 and 1975 fires. Even so, Browns Flat still retains beauty and charm.

Drivers today can get a good look over the Dalton and San Dimas watersheds by following the Glendora Mountain Road, a paved mountain highway climbing from Glendora to the top of the San Gabriel Canyon-Little Dalton Canyon divide, then dropping into the East Fork of the San Gabriel. The scenic mountain thoroughfare was the idea of Glendora businessman Sam Riser in 1907, but it was more than two decades later before the highway became reality. Los Angeles County prison labor hewed out the mountain road in the years 1926 to 1931, and in 1939 completed a continuation of the highway over Sunset Ridge to Mount Baldy village, the latter known as the Glendora Ridge Road. On clear days, when rainshowers have cleansed the atmosphere of smog and haze, the panorama from the mountain highway extends over a good part of Southern California, from Old Baldy to the sea.

Perhaps the most memorable "character" in the history of this part of the mountains was Miss Almyra Eckles, an eccentric and outspoken woman from a pioneer Glendora family with an abiding interest in her animals. Miss Eckles was an accomplished livestock handler and won many a prize with her horses and cattle at livestock fairs. What set her apart was her complete disregard for standard mores and customs. "Enjoying the unconventional, Miss Eckles took pleasure in shocking some of the conventional townsfolk. Her attire was a matter of local concern, for she invariably appeared wearing overalls, but for dress-up occasions she consented to slip a Mother Hubbard over them. She flirted with all the men in town and was universally liked by them for her masculine interest in livestock."[3] She had numerous brushes with the law and would defend herself, often successfully, in uproarious court trials. No man would cross her in personal encounter without risking a fist fight or wrestling match.

For many years Almyra Eckles lived with her animals on what became known as "Eckles Hill" at the east end of Glendora. Her problems with the Forest Service began after she leased eighty acres adjacent to Big Cienega Spring, located high on the ridge east of Big Dalton Canyon. Miss Eckles brought her large herd of goats up the mountainside, and the ravenous animals proceeded to devour the ground cover not only around Big Cienega Spring, but well back into the Big Dalton and San Dimas watersheds. It was at this time that Los Angeles County foresters were planting Coulter pine seedlings to replace trees burned in the 1919 fire, and, in some areas, Miss Eckles' goats were eating the seedlings as fast as they could be planted. Neither the County of Los Angeles nor the United States Forest Service could cope with Almyra Eckles. She literally gave them fits. She ignored repeated warnings to keep her goats off National Forest land. No sooner would rangers chase her hungry animals out of the forest than they would reappear at another location to devour more seedlings and ground cover. Legal proceedings were no more successful. Miss Eckles would sometimes ignore court summons, other times appear before the judge and defend herself. Nights in jail failed to dissuade her from her ways. Finally, Miss Eckles apparently grew tired of Forest Service harassment and withdrew her goats to Eckles Hill. But the battle was not completely over. The goats would occasionally cross the forest boundaries and nibble on seedlings and grass.

The old boy scout camp in lower Big Dalton Canyon. Hundreds of boys enjoyed a week or a weekend in the canyon vastness during the 1920s and '30s.

When Almyra Eckles died in 1939 she was deeply mourned not only by the citizens of Glendora but by forest rangers who had once been her nemesis. Her eccentricity has made her a folk hero.

NOTES

1 The San Dimas Experimental Forest includes all but the extreme lower portions of both Big Dalton and San Dimas watersheds. Little Dalton Canyon is not part of the Experimental Forest and can be visited by the public, subject only to the seasonal fire closure of the Angeles Forest "front country."

2 Will H. Thrall, "Browns Flat," *Trails Magazine* (Summer 1938), pp. 19-20.

3 Donald Pflueger, *Glendora: The Annals of A Southern California Community* (Claremont, 1951), p. 43.

The Glendora Mountain Road, shown here shortly after completion in 1931, was to have been the first link in a scenic highway across the San Gabriels from Glendora to Big Pines. The great flood of March 1938 wiped out the middle section through the East Fork, and the transmountain highway was never completed. – TOURING TOPICS

10
The San Dimas Experimental Forest

Western man has often attempted to improve his environment. Nowhere is this more evident than in the work of the San Dimas Experimental Forest. This extensive outdoor laboratory, dedicated to learning about the influences of geology, soil and vegetation on mountain watersheds, occupies almost all of the San Dimas and Big Dalton watersheds. The knowledge gained in almost a half century of forest research has benefited not only Southern California but the whole world.

The roots of scientific reforestation in the Dalton-San Dimas watersheds go back to 1919, a full fourteen years before the San Dimas Experimental Forest was born. Shortly after the great mountain fire of September 1919, Forester Stuart J. Flintham and a crew from the Los Angeles County Fire Department replanted thousands of trees on the burned slopes and canyons of the two watersheds. Most of the seedlings planted were Coulter pines, with a sprinkling of knobcone pine, digger pine, deodar cedar and big cone spruce. Flintham wanted the County to establish a scientific reforestation nursery at Tanbark Flats, but died before he could put his plan into effect.

Following Flintham's death in 1925, Spence D. Turner became Los Angeles County Forester and carried on the reforestation work of his predecessor. But he was distressed to find that most of the young trees planted on hillsides died. To discover why they failed to survive and to determine what forest trees were best suited to the Southern California mountains, Turner started a small reforestation nursery at Tanbark Flats in 1926.

After Los Angeles County established its main reforestation nursery at Henninger Flats above Altadena in 1928, the County's efforts in the San Dimas and Dalton watersheds tapered off. Plantings continued at Tanbark Flats until 1932, when Los Angeles County finally abandoned its efforts there. Today, the only legacies of the County efforts are groves of pines and cedars at Tanbark Flats, and the Flintham Memorial Plantation in the West Fork of San Dimas Canyon, honoring the county forester who started it all.

The reforestation efforts of Los Angeles County were watched with great interest by two leading citizens of San Dimas. Herbert S. Gilman, chief engineer of the San Dimas Water Company, and William A. Johnstone, fruit grower and banker who served several terms in the state assembly, were both aware of the value of the mountain watershed to the local water supply. Together, they were active members of the Angeles Forest Protective Association and the Conservation Association of Southern California, organizations that lobbied for forest protection. They received strong support from the Los Angeles Chamber of Commerce, a powerful organization in those days.

In 1926 Gilman and Johnstone were instrumental in drawing up a petition to the federal government, asking for a million dollar program of fire prevention and forest protection in Angeles National Forest. The petition was sent to Secretary of Agriculture William M. Jardine. Although Secretary Jardine made no promise of immediate action, he referred them to the newly-created California Forest Experiment Station in Berkeley, California.

The California Forest Experiment Station — a few years later its title was enlarged to The California Forest and Range Experiment Station — was established at the University of California, Berkeley, in 1926. Its purpose was to study the effects of fire and erosion on mountain watersheds and find better methods of protection. Under the guidance of Edward I. Kotok, one of the nation's premier silviculturists, field studies were undertaken in several northern California national forests in 1927.

Gilman and Johnstone were able to persuade Kotok to investigate the San Dimas and Big Dalton watersheds with an eye toward conducting forestry experiments there. During the next three years, numerous Berkeley foresters investigated not only

L.A. County reforestation nursery at Tanbark Flats, 1928. Seedlings were grown here to replace trees burned in mountain fires. The County nursery here was in operation from 1926 to 1932, when it was turned over to the U.S. Forest Service to become the field headquarters of the San Dimas Experimental Forest.
– LOS ANGELES COUNTY FIRE DEPARTMENT PHOTO

Stuart J. Flintham, Los Angeles County Forester from 1912 until his untimely death in 1925. Flintham pioneered the County efforts to reseed burned-over areas in the foothills and mountains. After the great mountain fire of 1919, thousands of pine, cedar and spruce seedlings were planted on slopes of the San Dimas watershed. The Flintham Memorial Plantation, a healthy growth of pines and cedars, in the West Fork of San Dimas Canyon, honors this reforestation pioneer today.
– LOS ANGELES COUNTY FIRE DEPARTMENT PHOTO

Spence D. Turner, Los Angeles County Forester from 1925 to 1952. Turner continued his predecessor's policy of replanting burned areas in the mountains, and established the reforestation nursery at Tanbark Flats in 1926.
– LOS ANGELES COUNTY FIRE DEPARTMENT PHOTO

William A. Johnstone (1869-1937), San Dimas fruit grower, banker and state assemblyman, active member of the Angeles Forest Protective Association, worked with Gilman toward the founding of the San Dimas Experimental Forest. Johnstone Peak, high on the divide between the Dalton and San Dimas watersheds, honors him today. – MRS. JEAN JOHNSTONE RIMPAU PHOTO

Herbert S. Gilman (1884-1941), chief engineer of the San Dimas Water Company, chairman of the Angeles Forest Protective Association, was instrumental in persuading the Dapartment of Agriculture to establish the San Dimas Experimental Forest.
– MRS. JOHN O. TILMAN PHOTO

the San Dimas-Big Dalton watersheds, but mountain areas all over Southern California for a proposed forest research station. In 1932, the California Forest Experiment Station made its decision: "After a thorough search . . . the proposed San Dimas Experimental Forest was found to meet the requirements more satisfactorily than any other area. Accordingly, it is selected as an Experimental Forest on which it is proposed to conduct a series of experiments applicable generally to the chaparral region of Southern California."[1]

The area initially set aside for experimentation was 13,000 acres surrounding the headwaters of San Dimas and Big Dalton canyons. Later the Experimental Forest was expanded to 17,153 acres. Tanbark Flats was chosen as field headquarters, with living and laboratory facilities for the research staff. Dr. Walter Lowdermilk, in initial charge of setting up the Experimental Forest, estimated the research program would take thirty years or more.

Why was the San Dimas-Big Dalton watershed chosen over the many other watersheds in Southern California? First of all, its vegetation pattern was typical of the Southern California mountains: chaparral in the lower and middle reaches, streamside woodland in the canyons, conifers on the higher ridges and flats. Moreover, the region is separated from the main mass of the San Gabriel Mountains by the deep canyons of San Gabriel and San Antonio, an isolation factor considered ideal for controlled study of water flow. Further, the two major drainages contain numerous small tributaries suitable for a variety of experiments. And lastly, both San Dimas and Big Dalton canyons were harnessed by dams, providing controls for measurement of water flow. No other similar-sized area in Southern California possessed all these advantages.

For Gilman and Johnson, a dream had finally been realized. Both were later honored for their pioneering efforts. In 1940 San Dimas Peak, a highpoint on the divide between Big Dalton and San Dimas canyons, was renamed Johnstone Peak. In 1943 a beautiful stand of deodar cedars at Tanbark Flats was dedicated as The Gilman Grove and a stone monument was erected in memory of the San Dimas conservationist.

J. Donald Sinclair, an enthusiastic, brilliant and knowledgeable young forester, was given the task of getting the San Dimas Experimental Forest underway in January 1933. He was destined to guide the Experimental Forest through its first twenty-five years. Aiding Sinclair was a skillful team of professional assistants: foresters Everett L. Hamilton, Harold G. Wilm, A.Z. Nelson, Jerome S. Horton, Wendel Davis; geologist Herbert C. Storey; and engineers John S. Cotton, C.D. Curry, O.D. Bramen

J. Donald Sinclair, manager of the San Dimas Experimental Forest from its founding in 1933 to 1958. With labor provided by the CCC and WPA, Sinclair was able to get the experimental forest underway in record time. – J.D. SINCLAIR PHOTO

and T.H. Moore. Among the second echelon of scientists who came to work in the Experimental Forest in the late 1930s and early 1940s, the names of foresters Edward A. Colman and Percy B. Rowe and soil expert Walter V. Garstka need to be mentioned. All of these men contributed greatly to the success of the Experimental Forest.

With the depression at its worst, the San Dimas Experimental Forest got off to a slow start. Franklin D. Roosevelt's New Deal came to the rescue. The Emergency Conservation Act of April 1933, one of a host of new federal programs designed to put the depression-ill country back on its feet, authorized the creation of a Civilian Conservation Corps to put unemployed young Americans to work. Most of this work would be directed toward protecting and improving the national forests. Thousands of Los Angeles County boys joined the federal work program during the years 1933 to 1942; many of them were assigned to camps in the national forests of Southern California.

In May 1933 Big Dalton Camp, located near the mouth of Big Dalton Canyon, was established, the first of nineteen CCC camps in the Angeles. The CCC boys of Dalton Company, under the guidance of the Forest Service, did a tremendous amount of work in the mountains — building new fire roads and trails and repairing old ones, carving fire breaks, stringing telephone lines, laying out campgrounds, constructing fire stations and bridges, planting trees, and, when called upon, fighting fires. Their most significant accomplishment in the Dalton-San Dimas watersheds was building, literally from the ground up, the facilities for the San Dimas Experimental Forest.

In the summer of 1933 a contingent of Dalton CCC Company was assigned to the Experimental Forest and moved to Tanbark Flats. Throughout the long, hot summer and into fall, the sturdy and tan-backed boys of the CCC labored eight hours a day, five days a week to build the laboratories, workshops, barracks and roads of the headquarters facility. Other crews constructed trails, dams, stream gauging stations and installed rain gauges. By year's end, a good start had been made on the Experimental Forest.

Work continued at a feverish pace for several years. The boys of the CCC were joined by laborers from the Works Projects Administration (WPA) and other relief agencies. In 1936, with the facilities almost complete, Sinclair paid a thankful tribute to the CCC lads and their fellow workers in the WPA: "Emergency funds and relief labor have permitted

Tanbark Flats, headquarters of the San Dimas Experimental Forest, 1938. The buildings were constructed by the CCC and WPA.
– U.S. FOREST SERVICE PHOTO

Headquarters building, Tanbark Flats, San Dimas Experimental Forest, shortly after completion in 1936.
– U.S. FOREST SERVICE PHOTO

rapid progress to be made in improving and equipping the experimental area . . . Under normal conditions this construction program would have required at least ten years and probably longer. The Experimental Forest is therefore an outstanding example of real and lasting public benefit accomplished with the aid of the emergency organizations."[2]

The San Dimas Experimental Forest was formally dedicated on June 15, 1935. Tanbark Flats was the scene of an impressive ceremony, attended by high officials of the California Forest and Range Experiment Station, the Forest Service, and Los Angeles County. A bronze plaque was presented by the Angeles Forest Protective Association and mounted on a boulder. Two members of the Association proudly attended the ceremony, their hearts filled with satisfaction over the accomplishment of what they had long sought — Herbert S. Gilman and William A. Johnstone.

When the CCC boys went to war in 1942, work in the Experimental Forest was carried on by conscientious objectors. The "C.O.s," as they were known, performed valuable service during the war years, maintaining roads and trails and providing the labor for experiments. Without their services, the Experimental Forest would have had to suspend operations for the duration of the conflict.

Over the years, a number of significant research studies have taken place in the San Dimas Experimental Forest, involving soil, vegetation, rainfall and erosion in mountain watersheds.

Watershed management research has been the most widespread and time-consuming project in the Experimental Forest. By the precise measurement of rainfall and runoff, along with climatic, vegetation and soil factors that influence these measurements, scientists are learning how to coax the maximum yield of water out of the mountain watershed for domestic, agricultural and industrial use.

To accurately measure rainfall throughout the experimental area, contour trails were built at 1000-foot intervals and precipitation gauges were installed along the trails roughly a half mile apart. Other rain gauges were placed at various points along roads. In all, some 400 gauges were distributed over the Forest, allowing precise long-term rainfall records to be accumulated for varying elevations. At Tanbark Flats (2,680 feet), the measured annual rainfall over 50 years of study has ranged from a low of 10.1 inches up to a maximum of 62.8 inches, with the yearly average being 26.8 inches.

To determine how much of this rain becomes runoff, the streams of the upper Big Dalton and San Dimas watersheds have been harnessed with dams, flumes, reservoirs and stream gauging stations. Ten major stations and seven secondary stations in smaller canyons, each capable of recording the precise amount of water flowing out of its respective watershed, are in the Forest. The Big Dalton and San Dimas dams have been fitted with gauges to measure the total runoff of the Experimental Forest.

Living Quarters at Tanbark Flats, S.D.E.F., shortly after completion 1936. – U.S. FOREST SERVICE PHOTO

Climatic station near Tanbark Flats, 1937. Stations like this, scattered over the experimental forest, measured rainfall, wind velocity and direction. – U.S. FOREST SERVICE PHOTO

Climatic factors such as air temperature, humidity, wind direction and velocity, evaporation, cloud cover and solar radiation have been measured and recorded at six climatological stations distributed at elevations ranging from 1500 to 5200 feet.

Detailed research on water runoff and erosion has been undertaken in the Bell and Fern canyon multiple watersheds, which vary in size from 35 to 100 acres. Observations have been made with a degree of refinement difficult to attain in the larger watersheds. After thoroughly studying the geology, soil and chaparral cover in each of the watersheds, experiments were conducted with various types of plants to determine which ones are best in protecting against erosion and producing more usable water.

Perhaps the most unusual project in the Experimental Forest involved the use of lysimeters — large rectangular "flower pots" — to determine the influence of different types of vegetation on water transpiration (water consumed in plants), evaporation, and percolation through the soil. The lysimeter installation at Tanbark Flats is the largest and most complete in existence. It consists of 26 concrete units, each 10½ by 21 feet in surface area and six feet deep, augmented by metal tanks and measuring gauges in tunnels underneath. Various species of trees, chaparral and grasses have been grown in the lysimeter units, and the water use of each has been measured.

In-depth studies of the Experimental Forest's vegetation, wildlife, geology and soils have been conducted to complete the picture of environmental influence on watersheds. Few other mountain areas of comparable size on earth have been as thoroughly and painstakingly examined as has the San Dimas Experimental Forest. There is, quite literally, no plant, no type of soil, no rock, no form of animal life that is unknown to the forest sleuths of Tanbark Flats!

What's more, the staff at Tanbark Flats seems to enjoy the forest research. "There is no greater satisfaction," wrote forester Edward Colman, "than

First fire truck stationed at Tanbark Flats, 1935. The fire truck suffered an accident on its first fire call; a young CCC boy riding on the truck was killed. – ORIE TROUT PHOTO

Rain gauges being checked in the experimental forest, 1953. – U.S. FOREST SERVICE PHOTO

Checking rain gauge, Bell Canyon, 1936. Over 500 rain gauges were placed in the experimental forest to measure rainfall at various elevations and topographic locations. – U.S. FOREST SERVICE PHOTO

Climatic station ruined by the Fern Canyon fire, Nov. 19, 1938. Lessons learned in these fires caused the S.D.E.F. to improve fire control methods. – U.S. FOREST SERVICE PHOTO

Stream gauging station in Bell Canyon during the great storm of March 1938. Many of these stations proved inadequate in times of high water flow and were later redesigned. – U.S. FOREST SERVICE PHOTO

Improved stream gauging station in Bell Canyon, 1941. – U.S. FOREST SERVICE PHOTO

Glendora Ranger Station, built by the CCC in 1940. Today it serves jointly as the headquarters of the Mt. Baldy District of Angeles National Forest, and headquarters of the San Dimas Experimental Forest.
– U.S. FOREST SERVICE PHOTO

to reach a gauging station in the small hours of a stormy morning and see a neat row of hour marks guiding the recorder chart safely through the ordeal."[3]

The fickle forces of nature have at times played havoc on the Experimental Forest, but more often than not, these setbacks have been turned to advantage. Studies of the causes and effects of fire and flood have resulted in better knowledge of these natural phenomena, and in better methods of coping with them.

The terrible flood of March 1-2, 1938 caused severe damage to roads, trails and installations in the Forest. In particular, the stream gauging stations were clogged with debris and failed to function accurately. As a result of the flood, the gauging stations and other installations were redesigned to operate in more adverse conditions. The San Dimas Flume, designed to measure high-velocity, debris-clogged streamflow during flood periods, was developed afterwards. Named for the San Dimas Experimental Forest where it was devised, it is now in world-wide use.

The worst fire in the history of the Experimental Forest was touched off by an electrical storm on July 20, 1960. The Johnstone Fire, as it became known because it started near Johnstone Peak, burned out of control for several days and spared none of the Forest's nineteen watersheds. Fire-fighting crews, working frantically, were able to save all but one building at Tanbark Flats even though surrounded by a ring of flame. When the final ember flickered out, 15,000 of the Experimental Forest's 17,163 acres lay in blackened ruin.

Once again, setback was turned to advantage. A major new program of post-fire research and experimentation was begun. Runoff and erosion on the denuded slopes were studied and compared with previous measurements made when the slopes had their full chaparral cover. Burned-over watersheds were sown with a variety of annual and perennial grasses to determine the best temporary cover. Various erosion control methods were tested, including contour trenches, channel check dams, and contour row planting. New and improved methods of fire control were developed, including broad fire breaks, chemical control of brush, and the use of fire-retardant or slow-burning plants. Just since the 1960 conflagration, a vast new reservoir of knowledge has been gained to help man combat brush fires and retard erosion.

Heavy precipitation in February 1969 caused the worst flood in the history of the Experimental Forest, with total damage in excess of one million dollars. (The 1938 flood was more severe, but there were fewer installations to be washed out.) Almost all the roads and trails in the Forest were cut by washouts. It required a number of years for the Experimental Forest to recover from its effects.

The San Dimas Experimental Forest continues to be a major research facility of the U.S. Forest Service. The name of its parent organization was changed from The California Forest and Range Experiment Station to The Pacific Southwest Forest and Range Experiment Station in 1959, to express the fact that experiments are conducted not only in California but also in Hawaii and other Pacific Islands. The field headquarters remain at

Charles G. Colver has been associated with the San Dimas Experimental Forest since 1946. He was supervising technician from 1962 to 1973, and has been the experimental forest manager since 1977.

Nels E. Peterson, District Ranger, Glendora, from 1929 to 1938. – HELEN TROUT PHOTO

Tanbark Flats, while the administrative headquarters are in the U.S. Forest Service office in Glendora. Research today is carried on in cooperation with Los Angeles County, the California Department of Forestry, and several educational institutions, most notably the University of California, California State University and Pomona College. San Dimas forester Lawrence W. Hill has writ ten: "We look to the day when we can write prescriptions for improving watershed management practices in southern California. Our aim is to develop a pilot model to guide the management of some of the most valuable watersheds in the country."[4] After a half century of research, this goal is within sight.

The San Dimas Peak fire lookout in 1935. District Ranger Nels Peterson above, Angeles National Forest Supervisor William V. Mendenhall below. In 1940 San Dimas Peak was renamed Johnstone Peak, in honor of William A. Johnstone, "co-father" of the San Dimas Experimental Forest. – ORIE TROUT PHOTO

1. "Report on the San Dimas Experimental Forest, Angeles National Forest, California," U.S. Forest Service, 1933. Typescript in SDEF records, Glendora.

2. J. D. Sinclair, "Watershed Management Research: The San Dimas Experimental Forest," *Trails Magazine* (Spring 1936), pp. 20-21.

3. Edward A. Colman, "The San Dimas Saga," U.S. Forest Service, 1938. Typescript in SDEF records, Glendora.

4. Lawrence W. Hill, *The San Dimas Experimental Forest* (Berkeley, 1963), pp. 1-2.

11

San Antonio Canyon

The broad, gravelly entrance to San Antonio Canyon offers a royal gateway into the high Mount Baldy country, summit of the San Gabriels. Unlike most major canyons on the south flank of the range, this one carves essentially a direct north-to-south path from the mountain crest to the plains, and in doing such presents a very obvious geographical feature when viewed from the valley below. The thousands of explorers, pioneers and settlers who passed the canyon's great portal must have readily noticed it.

One might assume that a canyon of this stature would have been utilized by the earliest settlers, and that its history would be well documented. Yet, for the years before 1880, such is not the case. Records of these early days in the canyon are very sketchy, and in some cases rely more on legend than fact.

The earliest story concerning the white man in San Antonio Canyon — to the effect that the padres of Mission San Gabriel obtained timber for the mission buildings from Icehouse Canyon, a major tributary of San Antonio Canyon — was written by canyon historians Fletcher Manker and Dan Alexander: "There is a story among the oldest settlers that the cedar beams of Mission San Gabriel were cut in the Ice House Canyon, brought by high-wheeled oxcarts over an old road, evidences of which were plentiful in the '80s, to the head of the falls at Hogsback, then floated in high water to a point where they could be picked up and taken to the Mission. The carts on which they were hauled over this road must have been packed over Hogsback in pieces and assembled above."[1]

Manker and Alexander offer no documentation for this story other than the statement that it came from "the oldest settlers." Historians of San Gabriel Mission fail to shed any light on the Manker and Alexander story, nor do they give any hint as to where the timber used in mission construction was obtained. Since pine and cedar trees do not grow naturally in the Southern California lowlands (with the exception of the Torrey pines near La Jolla), it is evident that the mission fathers obtained their lumber from somewhere in the nearby mountains. There are many canyons in the south front of the San Gabriel Mountains that are closer to Mission San Gabriel than San Antonio Canyon, and most of them have stands of pine and cedar in their upper reaches. Why would the mission padres have traveled so far — to San Antonio Canyon — when timber was readily available in San Gabriel, Sawpit, Monrovia and Santa Anita canyons, all much closer to the mission? It would appear that the Manker and Alexander story rests on a very shaky foundation.

It is very possible that the ancient road over the Hogsback noticed by the early canyon settlers was a remnant not of mission days, but of ice-procuring operations during the 1850s, carried on by two Los Angeles businessmen.

Many persons, including this writer, have long wondered how Icehouse Canyon received its name. Erwin G. Gudde, in his authoritative *California Place Names* (3rd edition, Berkeley, 1969), fails to mention Icehouse Canyon, nor do the several published histories of San Antonio Canyon account for its derivation.

In the course of this writer's research, a pamphlet advertising the merits of Camp Baldy, written by Dan Alexander about 1914, was found which included the statement that Icehouse Canyon was "so called because of the ice plant which was located there many years ago and supplied ice to Los Angeles."

Further research in the files of early Los Angeles newspapers brought to light information that not only supports Alexander's story but adds a heretofore unknown and colorful chapter to the canyon's early history. The citizens of Los Angeles, in 1858 and 1859, were supplied with ice cream made from blocks of ice cut from "the mountains of San Antonio." Although Icehouse Canyon is not men-

Lower San Antonio Creek, ca. 1880. Notice the snow on Old Baldy in the background. The canyon was a wilderness then, frequented only by prospectors, hunters and a few hardy fishermen. – POMONA PUBLIC LIBRARY, SPECIAL COLLECTIONS

tioned by name in the newspaper accounts, it is apparent from the descriptions of the ice-procuring operations that the ice came from there or from some other part of upper San Antonio Canyon.

The *Southern Vineyard* of April 17, 1858 gave first notice of this enterprise: "Mr. Marchessault and Beaudry arrived in town with the first consignment of ice from the mountains of San Antonio." In its issue of March 15, 1859, the *Southern Vineyard* elaborated on the ice-procuring operation: "The citizens of Los Angeles will, through the energy of Messrs. Beaudry and Marchessault, be enabled to refrigerate themselves with iced wine, cobblers and ice cream to their full satisfaction. They have made a large addition to their icehouse, which is now capable of containing one hundred and fifty tons of the cooling ingredient. They are now engaged in bringing the ice from the mountain of San Antonio, where they have in store enough to fill the house here and have a large surplus. The ice which they have made this season is equal to the best Sitka ice." The *Los Angeles Star* (March 12, 1859) described how the ice was brought down from the mountains: "Messrs. Beaudry and Marchessault have this week commenced filling their ice house in town, from their depot in the mountains, distant from the city about fifty miles. The ice this year is of excellent quality, and has been obtained in sufficient quantities to supply the demand of the city. The above named gentlemen have a train of thirty or forty mules packing ice down the canyon where it has been collected, to a point wagons can reach; it is there loaded on them and brought to town. The ice is cut in cubes, each of which is estimated to weigh one hundred pounds."

Piecing the story together from these contemporary newspaper accounts, it appears that Los Angeles businessmen Victor Beaudry and Damien Marchessault sent a team of ice-cutters into San Antonio Canyon – probably to Icehouse Canyon – as early as 1858. These workers cut the mountain ice into 100-pound cubes, loaded them on the backs of thirty or forty mules, and brought the heavy cargo down over the Hogsback to a point where they could be loaded onto wagons and shipped to Los Angeles. This mountain ice-procuring operation continued into 1859; how much longer it was carried on is unknown, since Los Angeles newspapers dropped mention of the venture after that date.

Another intriguing story of early San Antonio

Canyon concerns an old sawmill, allegedly located a short distance up-canyon from present Mt. Baldy Village. Manker and Alexander give the following account, based on information supplied by William B. Dewey, an early canyon resident: "W.B. Dewey states that an old sawmill was operating just above Camp Baldy long before the mining days; that part of the buildings were still standing, west of the stream and about 200 yards above the present store, in 1883, and were washed away when the stream changed its channel in the flood of 1884. He states that all of the larger trees were cut from that part of the canyon between Camp Baldy and Ice House and there were many big stumps and, until the flood, big logs scattered over this flat, a few logs remaining there as late as 1902."[2]

In a letter written to mountain historian Will Thrall, dated September 15, 1936, shortly before his death, Dewey referred to the buildings as "the old Russian sawmill" and stated that it had been abandoned for many years when he first saw it in 1882.

We have further corroboration of the existence of this sawmill from Belle J. Bidwell, who camped in San Antonio Canyon during the summer of 1887. Miss Bidwell wrote that "The sawmill is in ruins now," but that seventeen years before (1870) "a man could gallop his horse clear up to the sawmill."[3]

Who built this sawmill in San Antonio Canyon and when was it in use? Again, from the files of early Los Angeles newspapers we are provided with a possible solution to this mystery. The *Los Angeles Herald* of July 23, 1881 contains the story of a visit to San Antonio Canyon by one "J.A.G." Among his descriptions of camping, fishing and prospecting in the canyon, he describes an old wagon road up the canyon and over the Hogsback and states that it was "built by the late F.P.F. Temple, who constructed a sawmill 10 or 12 miles from the canyon mouth." He further states that "there is some pine timber there (at the sawmill) but not enough for successful milling purposes," and that the mill was destroyed by fire some years past.

Who was F.P.F. Temple? The answer to that question is readily available, for Francis Phiny Fisk Temple was a leading citizen and businessman of Los Angeles. Almost every major source of information about Los Angeles from the 1850s through the 1870s contains mention of Temple. From these sources we learn that he was born in Reading, Massachusetts in 1822, came to California around Cape Horn in 1841, and went into business in Los Angeles with his brother John Temple. In 1845 he married Antonia Margarita Workman, the daughter of William Workman, owner of the expansive Rancho La Puente. Soon thereafter Temple bought Rancho La Merced, immediately west of his father-in-law's vast holdings, where he resided most of the remaining years of his life. Here "Templito," as he was known to his many Spanish-speaking friends because of his short stature, tended his vineyards, raised cattle and bred fine horses. He lost everything in the Temple and Workman Bank failure in 1875, and died almost penniless in 1880.

In none of the accounts of Temple's activities by Los Angeles historians do we find any mention about a sawmill in San Antonio Canyon. However, we are provided with two possible clues.

Harris Newmark, in his *Sixty Years in Southern California*, writes that in 1860 "Temple, at a cost of about forty thousand dollars for lumber alone, fenced in a wide acreage, at the same time building large and substantial barns for his stock."[4] Did Temple obtain this lumber for his La Merced Ranch from San Antonio Canyon?

Another clue is contained in an advertisement that appeared in the *Los Angeles Semi-Weekly News* of September 24, 1867:

> NEW CUT-OFF TO SAN BERNARDINO
>
> The undersigned have made this road the most desirable one to San Bernardino, having built new bridges, etc., and straightened the road so that there is a saving of five miles to Cucamonga. Directions — New road from Los Angeles to Templito's, at sign post on Los Angeles river; from Templito's up by Workman's mill and Wm. Rubottom's to Cucamonga . . . . This road offers superior inducements for travelers and teamsters.
>
> signed: Wm. W. Rubottom
> F.P.F. Temple

In summation, we know that Temple had an extensive need for lumber on his La Merced Ranch and that, with Billy Rubottom, he built a road from Los Angeles to San Bernardino that passed just below the mouth of San Antonio Canyon. But we have only the word of "J.A.G." that Temple built the old sawmill in San Antonio Canyon. If Temple indeed built the sawmill, it must have been sometime before 1868, when he became totally engaged in the banking business in Los Angeles. Temple or someone else, possibly a Russian (according to W.B. Dewey), probably worked the sawmill for a number of years, for Dewey reported a large number of tree stumps between Camp Baldy and Icehouse Canyon in 1883. Sometime before 1881, when "J.A.G." visited San Antonio Canyon, the sawmill was destroyed by fire and its remains were washed away in the flood of 1884.

Then there was the mystery of the lone grave atop the Hogsback, marked by a weathered wooden post with the words "Jacob Shinner 1879." For years the grave and its marker were prominent landmarks along the road, known to thousands of canyon

Himon Pierce Ranch at the mouth of San Antonio Canyon, ca. 1900. Pierce arrived in 1888, built his ranch the following year and lived there until 1898. He was employed by the San Antonio Water Department to look after their canyon interests. – HENRY E. HUNTINGTON LIBRARY

The Kincaid Ranch in lower San Antonio Canyon, a half mile above the Pierce Ranch. Madison Moses Kincaid was the earliest known settler in the canyon, arriving in 1865. For years he was well known for his peach brandy, a product of his extensive peach orchard. He also raised sheep and cultivated bees.
– POMONA PUBLIC LIBRARY, SPECIAL COLLECTIONS

William H. Stoddard came to San Antonio Canyon in 1888 and founded Stoddard's Camp, first of the many canyon resorts. This picture was taken about 1902.

travelers for almost half a century. Who was Jacob Shinner and what were the circumstances of his death? The answer appears in a short column tucked on the back pages of the *San Bernardino Daily Times* for June 9, 1879. We learn that Shinner was a miner who was buried in a rockslide at his mine alongside the Hogsback. His two companions found him still alive, dug him out, but he expired soon afterwards. They buried him on the spot and erected the little marker that stood vigil over the grave for so many years.

The Hogsback, an imposing 400-foot high rock ridge, located five miles up from the canyon mouth, long posed a difficult barrier to canyon travel. For years, the old canyon wagon road ended abruptly at its foot. Prospectors, sportsmen and campers going into upper San Antonio Canyon were obliged to hike over the barrier via a steep and loose trail.

Settlement in lower San Antonio Canyon, below the Hogsback, began in the 1860s. As far as is known, the first to fashion a home in the canyon was Madison Moses Kincaid, who homesteaded 114 acres just inside the canyon mouth in 1865. Kincaid built an adobe home and planted fruit trees. In later years he regularly exhibited his prize-winning oranges at various citrus shows and county fairs. A.A. Dexter came into the canyon in 1875, filed on 160 acres just above Kincaid, built a stout ranch house, planted fruit trees and raised bees for a living. Also cultivating bees was Judge Evey, who settled in the canyon just above Dexter in the late 1870s. Evey Canyon honors his name today.

The first significant name in canyon history was William H. Stoddard, who fashioned the canyon's first resort at the mouth of the side canyon now named for him. Stoddard, brother-in-law of railroad magnate Collis P. Huntington, came from Connecticut to California in 1852, tried his hand at gold mining, then opened a store next to Huntington's in Sacramento. Lacking the business acumen of his brother-in-law, Stoddard suffered financial reverses and lost his health. To regain his health, he moved to Southern California, was told about the therapeutic benefits of San Antonio Canyon and decided to move there. In 1880 he settled in a shady grove of oaks and sycamores in a beautiful, waterfall-laced side canyon just east of the main canyon, about a mile above the entrance. Here he built a cabin and planted fruit trees. Around 1886 he decided to turn his canyon Eden into a resort. Stoddard constructed a frame dining room, several cottages and tent cabins, piped water down from a mountainside spring, and carved a scenic trail up to the waterfalls above camp. It was not long until scores of Pomona, Ontario and even San Bernardino citizens were enjoying summer weekends and holidays at Stoddard's Camp.

Stoddard's success encouraged others to cater to canyon visitors. Himon Pierce rented cabins and tents for a dollar a day at his camp at the mouth of Evey Canyon, "one of the most restful little nooks that one may find." A man named Kayne opened a store at the foot of Spring Hill, three miles up-canyon, so named because of the gushing springs of icy-cold water that emitted from its slopes.

Guests at Stoddard's Camp ca. 1888. William Stoddard stands with arms folded to right (above no. 1). The resort was popular with canyon visitors from its opening in 1886 until well into the 20th century. – HENRY E. HUNTINGTON LIBRARY

Hundreds came by wagon and camped in the canyon, under the magnificent overarching oaks and alders, alongside the sparkling waters of San Antonio Creek. Some stayed a few days, some remained for the whole summer. 1887 was a banner year for canyon campers. The *Pomona Progress* (June 2, 1887), after describing the camping craze, predicted, "San Antonio Canyon is destined to be a great summer resort. In the future there will undoubtedly be elegant hotels and residences. As a camping ground for Pomonians it is unexcelled."

Only a handful of this multitude of campers ever huffed and puffed their way over the Hogsback into the upper canyon. But for those who did, the rewards were well worth the effort. Upper San Antonio Canyon was a mountain paradise of trout-rich streams, waterfalls, and some of the tallest pines and cedars in Southern California. It was also abundant with wild game – deer, grizzly bear, mountain lion, and big horn sheep.

Up beyond the ruins of the old sawmill, almost at the canyon head, was a rustic stockherders' hut often used as an overnight stop by canyon travelers. Charles Knox of Upland remembered spending a night there in 1875, but being aroused by mountain lions threatening the horses. Next morning he noticed grizzly tracks "as large as a dinner plate."[5] A few years later, William B. Dewey, one of the real canyon pioneers, witnessed herds of big horn sheep in the upper canyon: "I have never seen mountain sheep so numerous . . . . They are big-horned fellows . . . Last Thursday morning I saw ten of the mountain sheep inside of three hours. You never saw such tempting shots for a sportsman."[6]

The falls in Stoddard Canyon, a popular short hike above Stoddard's Camp. – POST CARD VIEW

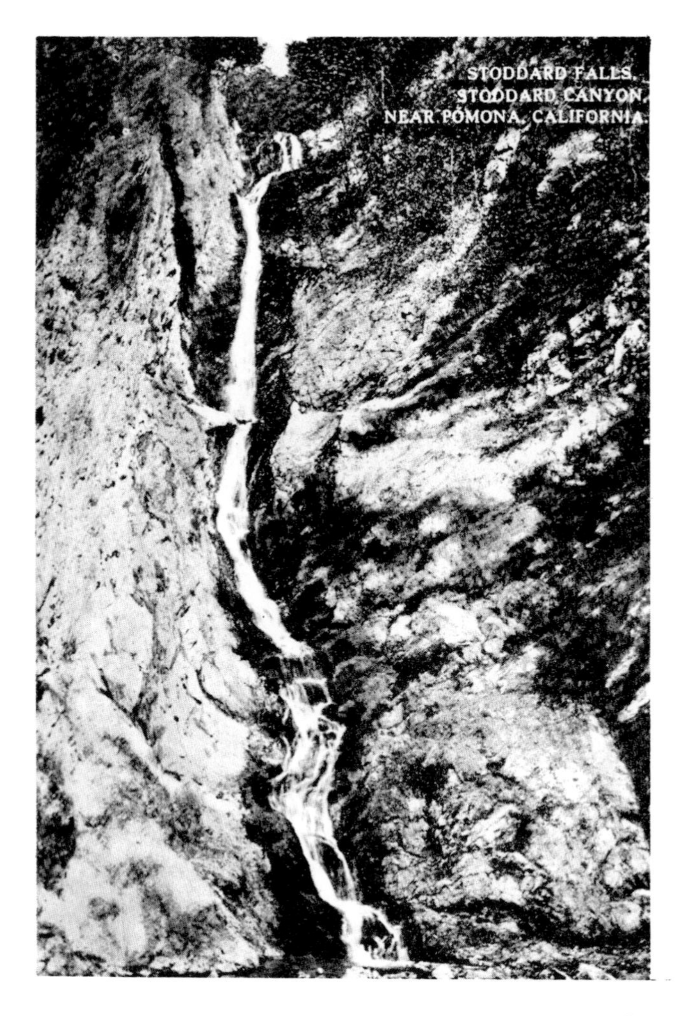

The "Old Falls" in San Antonio Canyon, ca. 1887. The falls were filled with rock and debris from the new road cut across the Hogsback in 1908.
– POMONA PUBLIC LIBRARY, SPECIAL COLLECTIONS

The old miners' pack trail up San Antonio Canyon ended right at the head of the canyon, on a little pine-shaded flat deep in the shadow of Old Baldy. Here, in the 1880s, Fletcher H. Manker of Upland built a cabin he utilized as a storehouse to supply the Baldy miners. Manker ran a weekly pack train from Upland to his little cabin, packing food, supplies and equipment for the gold mines. Since then, the spot has been known as Manker Flat.

One of those who ascended the old canyon pack trail was Fred Dell, a sportsman from Pomona. Dell particularly enjoyed hunting big horn sheep. In 1886 he filed on a forested flat just east and across the creek from today's Baldy Village. Here he built two stout log cabins and catered to the miners who passed by. In 1894 Dell leased his shady glen to Frank Keyes, who turned Dell's Camp into the first full-fledged resort in the upper canyon. Keyes spruced up the two cabins and added a number of tents for paying guests. Rates were $1.50 per day or $9 per week for room and board. For the thrifty-minded, tents were rented for $1.50 per week. By the late 1890s, Dell's Camp was the most popular resort in San Antonio Canyon, with as many as 100 guests on summer weekends. A camp guest wrote in the *Pomona Weekly Times* (June 12, 1895): "Dell's Camp is the cosiest rest-inviting mountain home that ever inspired the artist's brush or called up the latent poetry of the western novelist."

Getting there posed the main problem. Cyrus Baldwin's San Antonio Light and Power Company (see chapter *Water Struggles*) did improve the road in the lower canyon, but the hair-raising trail over the Hogsback was as bad as ever. "The only way was by a rough and steep trail over this shoulder of jagged rocks. It was bad going for even the sure-footed pack animals, and many a burro lost his pack which must be retrieved from among the rocks of nearly perpendicular slopes," wrote canyon historians Manker and Alexander.[7] Nevertheless, Frank Keyes did employ stage service between Pomona and Ontario and the camp, guests taking the stage to road's end, then transferring to horseback for the ride over Hogsback.

San Antonio Canyon campers were introduced to an ever-present danger when a brush fire, caused by careless campers, erupted in Stoddard Canyon on August 27, 1899. James Bradford, first ranger in San Antonio Canyon, appointed in 1898, rounded up a party of volunteers to fight the fire. He managed to save Stoddard's Camp, but the blaze continued to spread in lower Cucamonga Canyon. Forest supervisor W.A. Border and a forestry crew rushed over from Pasadena, and the combined crews were able to contain the blaze by September 1st. The *Pomona Weekly Times* (September 20, 1899) was lavish in its praise of Ranger Bradford and the forestry crew: "Too much praise cannot be given the men. No better crew ever fought a fire, they having worked under great difficulties, suffering greatly from heat and lack of water. Food had to be carried on the men's backs as no mule could follow where they went. Ranger Bradford showed that he is the right man in the right place. He worked day and night, taking very little rest. His work has been very satisfactory to Supervisor Border, who complimented him on his prompt action in getting men to the fire, and by so doing kept the fire from crossing San Antonio Creek, thereby saving the watershed."

The Stoddard Canyon fire that for a time threatened the San Antonio watershed, along with the increasing pollution of San Antonio Creek by campers, were viewed with apprehension by the San Antonio Water Company. Fearful of losing its precious irrigation and domestic water supplies, the company initiated a policy of discouraging public use of the canyon. The water company began by trying to buy up all usable land in San Antonio Canyon.

The first log cabin at Dells' Camp, built by Fred Dell in 1886. Dell first sold supplies and food to miners who passed by, later turned it into a tourist resort. The location in on the east side of San Antonio Creek across from today's Mt. Baldy Village. – HENRY E. HUNTINGTON LIBRARY

Dells' Camp, main hotel building, about 1895. The camp was founded by Fred Dell in 1886, turned into a full-fledged resort by Frank Keyes in 1894. – CHARLES CLARK VERNON COLLECTION

Baynham's Camp, ca. 1908. Charles Baynham, after his successful fight with the San Antonio Water Company, operated the resort camp for three years, 1907 to 1910. After Baynham left, the camp was enlarged and became known as Camp Baldy. – POMONA PUBLIC LIBRARY, SPECIAL COLLECTIONS

Dell's Camp was purchased in 1899 and closed to visitors. Little by little, the water company added to its canyon holdings, until by 1905 there was little prime land in the canyon it didn't control, either by outright ownership or government lease.

To further discourage visitors, the company, in 1901 and again in 1903, placed a locked gate across the road at the canyon entrance, claiming the right to do so because the road crossed its private property. Both times, however, the gate was removed by Los Angeles County officials who insisted the road was a public thoroughfare.

The San Antonio Water Company's brazen attempt to lock up San Antonio Canyon as its private domain was resented in the valley towns. Many sportsmen, campers and prospectors went into the canyon anyway, and James Bradford, who was hired as a water company guard at the same time he was being paid as a United States forestry ranger (we would call this conflict of interest today), was hardpressed to keep people from trespassing on water company property and polluting the creek. The Los Angeles County Board of Supervisors complained to the Department of Interior about the ranger's dual role, and Bradford was ordered off the water company's payroll. The company would have to hire its own guards.

Several citizens located land in the canyon not claimed by the water company. Hydroelectric tycoon William G. Kerckhoff, whose Pacific Light and Power Company bought out Baldwin's San Antonio Light and Power Company in 1901, filed on six acres above the Hogsback and built a 10-room vacation house in 1903. To give access to his place, Kerckhoff carved out the first wagon road over the Hogsback. But oh! what a road! It was too steep for an automobile and just barely negotiable by a four-horse wagon. The horses strained to the utmost to drag the slipping and sliding wagon over the loose rock to the top. Going down was a nightmare, and many a wagon ended up in pieces at the bottom of the Hogsback.

Another beautiful forested recess the water company had overlooked was Bear Canyon, located just west of today's Mt. Baldy Village. Here, in 1906, Dan Alexander secured from the Forest Service the first cabin lease in San Antonio Canyon. Other Bear Canyon cabin leases were immediately taken out by Wilfred Sanford and Phil Mulford, much to the chagrin of the water company.

It remained for Charles R. Baynham to finally break the San Antonio Water Company's stranglehold on the canyon. Baynham was an unlikely "David" to oppose the water company "Goliath." He was a young man from Claremont, just graduated from Pomona College, with no special legal training. He was a dedicated camper and fisherman, and on one of his fishing trips to the canyon he discovered a shady bench on the west bank of San Antonio Creek, directly across from the old Dell's Camp site. To his surprise, this section of the canyon had not been filed upon by the water company. On December 18, 1906, Baynham took out a Forest Service lease on forty acres for resort purposes. He made public his ambitious plans for his resort, to be named Camp Baynham: a large main building, numerous small cabins and tents, an improved road over the Hogsback, and regular stage service to his camp from Pomona and Ontario.

Sanborn's Camp, founded by Wilfred Sanborn in 1906, was a short-lived tourist resort in Bear Canyon, just behind the present Mt. Baldy ranger station.
– CHARLES CLARK VERNON COLLECTION

Water company officials, outfoxed by Baynham's government lease, were nevertheless determined to stop him. To prevent access to Camp Baynham and force the young resort host out of business, they locked the gate at the canyon mouth and stationed armed guards there to prevent entry. So began the year-long battle between Charles Baynham and the San Antonio Water Company that has been described in *Water Struggles*. The gate was ripped down and replaced several times, there were armed confrontations and legal battles that seesawed back and forth, and there was a near-war between Los Angeles and San Bernardino counties (the boundary between the two counties runs right through lower San Antonio Canyon). In the end, there was compromise that effectively terminated the San Antonio Water Company's near-monopoly of the canyon.

In conflicting court decisions, the San Antonio Water Company was adjudged owner of the road, but Baynham was given the right of access to his resort. Baynham wasted no time in improving the road over the Hogsback and extending it three miles to his camp. He initiated stage service late in 1907.

The final twist in the Baynham-water company struggle was totally unexpected: "An important deal was consummated on Saturday, December 21, 1907," reported the *Pomona Times* of December 23rd, "whereby Charles R. Baynham of Claremont sold his interest in Camp Baynham to the San Antonio Water Company of Ontario. The consideration was not made public, but it is believed to be in the neighborhood of $15,000. The purchase includes the hotel, cottages, forty saddle mules and burros, all tally-ho wagons and equipment. By the terms of the agreement the name of the camp will be retained and Baynham engaged as superintendent. Next week will begin wholesale improvements planned by the company to make San Antonio Canyon the finest resort in Southern California."

In a total about-face, the San Antonio Water Company decided to get into the resort business and allow the general public to use the canyon. Baynham, long the company's nemesis, was bought out, then hired to run the company's resort. Historian Will Thrall explained why: "The Water Company had not expected such dogged resistance from a college student and their resentment, changing to admiration of his pluck, resulted in an offer to buy his holdings. His success in the management of his affairs led to his being appointed manager of the new resort."[8]

To allow easy access to their newly-purchased resort, the water company repaired and improved the canyon road, put in a tollhouse and toll gate, and hired a gateman. Tolls were fixed at 50 cents per automobile and 25 cents per horseback rider. Hikers paid 10 cents. The water company's San Antonio Canyon Toll Road lasted for fourteen years, from 1908 until 1922.

The San Antonio Water Company was evidently unhappy to be in the resort business, for after only two years of operation, Camp Baynham was sold to Upland businessmen Arthur Neff and R.S. McMullen. The change of ownership took place on June 1, 1910. Baynham retired, and F.W. Palmer took his place as manager. At the same time, the name of the resort was changed to Camp Baldy.

Camp Baldy quickly became the premier resort in the San Antonio Canyon. A spacious main lodge was erected, with numerous housekeeping tents placed in forested coves nearby. A 1914 camp brochure proclaimed, "At the camp ample provision has been made both for those desiring hotel accommodations and those wishing tents for housekeeping. The splendid auto road from the city and the great variety of amusements and sports — among which are trout fishing, deer hunting, mountain quail and squirrel — attract many weekend parties. Camp Baldy is a center from which many interesting and beautiful trips may be made. The most popular of these is the excursion to the summit of Mount San Antonio or 'Old Baldy,' as it is more commonly called." About 1912 Dan Alexander opened Alexander's Studio at the resort, the first photographic studio in the eastern San Gabriels.

The Camp Baldy Auto Stage was inaugurated in 1912, providing easy access to the resort from Pomona and Ontario. Stage connections were made

Tollgate at the entrance to the San Antonio Water Company's canyon road, ca. 1908. The Water Company operated the toll road from 1908 until 1922, when Los Angeles and San Bernardino counties jointly purchased the road and opened it to free public use. Tolls collected were 50 cents per automobile, 25 cents per horseback rider, and 10 cents per hiker. – HENRY E. HUNTINGTON LIBRARY

with Santa Fe, Southern Pacific and Pacific Electric railroads. By the summer of 1914, hundreds were visiting the mountain resort every weekend.

F.W. Palmer remained as manager until 1919, when he was succeeded by A.E. Huntington for one year. Herbert McCullough took over in 1920 and stayed until 1928. McCullough improved and enlarged Camp Baldy, adding a swimming pool, open-air dance pavilion and more housekeeping tents. A grocery store provided for the needs of canyon campers.

The popularity of Camp Baldy and the improvement of the canyon road encouraged others to open tourist resorts in San Antonio Canyon.

Ann and Fred Courtney founded Bear Canyon Resort, just below Camp Baldy, in 1921. William Vernon took over in 1924 and ran the little resort until 1938.

Next door to Bear Canyon Resort was Eleven Oaks, founded in 1921 by R.D. Shiffer.

Clarence Roy Chapman started Icehouse Canyon Resort in 1919. Chapman and his bride had honeymooned in the canyon in 1901 and returned many times to visit. For several years he ran a citrus ranch near Ontario, but after his crop froze in unusually cold weather in 1920 he left the citrus business, and in 1913 built a cabin in Icehouse Canyon and moved there with his family. In 1919 he bought the land at the mouth of Icehouse Canyon from the Camp Baldy Company and began his resort. Originally, Ice House Canyon Resort was only a small general store, but in several years of work, Chapman himself constructed a number of cabins. He was an accomplished builder and over the years built over 100 cabins and 175 fireplaces in the San Antonio Canyon area. (Many of these cabins are still standing.) In 1929 Chapman sold his resort to George Allison in order to concentrate on his construction work, but he regained ownership in 1938 when Allison defaulted. He sold out for good to Gunner Bloomquist in 1944.

In 1930 Chapman bought twenty acres on the east bank of San Antonio Creek, between the mouth of Icehouse Canyon and the Camp Baldy bridge, from the San Antonio Water Company. Here he built the Chapman Ranch, complete with orchards, a sawmill

Camp Baldy, ca. 1915. This was the premier resort in San Antonio Canyon, from its founding by Charles Baynham in 1907 until its demise in the great flood of March 1938. The building to the right was the main lodge until Edmund and Ruth Curry Burns expanded the resort in the 1930s. The small building to the left was long the Mt. Baldy Post Office. – HENRY E. HUNTINGTON LIBRARY

The dining room at Camp Baldy, ca. 1919. 60 people could be served here at one time. – POST CARD PHOTO

The road to Camp Baldy, ca. 1912. The harrowing section over the Hogsback, completed in 1908, finally opened the upper canyon to automibles. Until the County improved it in 1922, the trip was not for the faint-hearted! – DAN ALEXANDER STUDIO

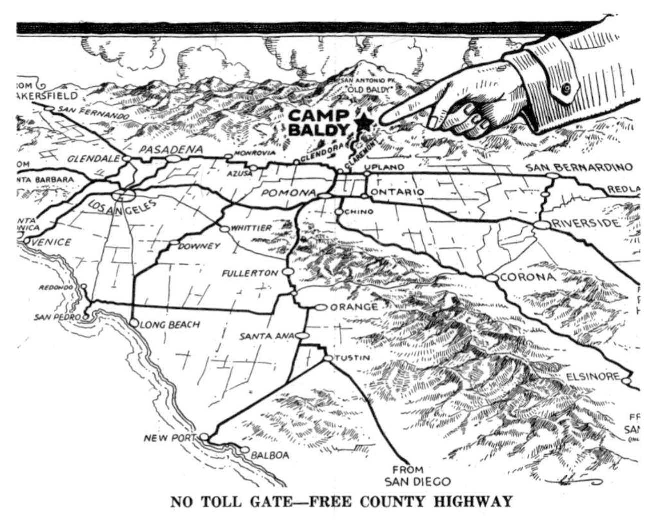

CAMP BALDY

IS ONLY thirteen miles from Upland, California, in the most picturesqu of San Antonio Canyon. The smooth canyon auto road of decom granite is of easy grade—easy on tires—with substantial bridges ove eams. Taking the Foothill Boulevard to Mountain Avenue, one mile we pland, turn north and follow automobile signs. A 2½ hours' automobile trip os Angeles to the camp.

Camp Baldy was one of the most widely advertised mountain resorts in California. Ads and brochures boosting the hostelry were distributed all over the state. The advertising paid off; thousands of visitors flocked in.

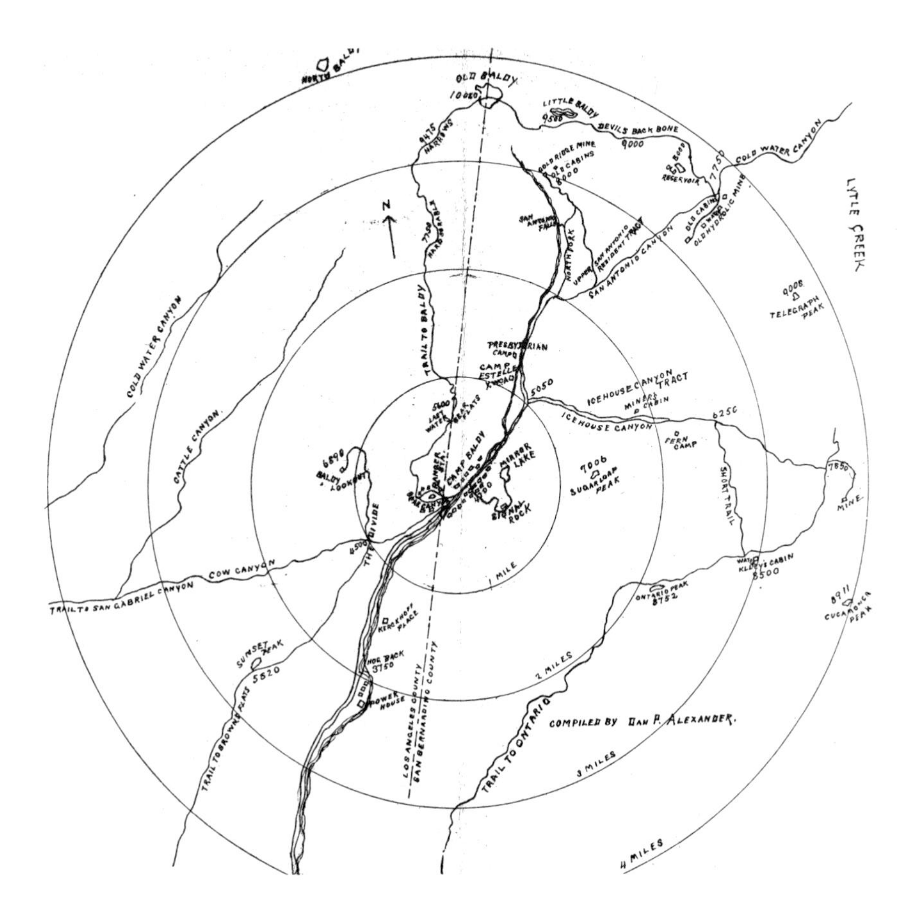

A tenthouse at Camp Baldy, ca. 1910. Tents, complete with beds, bedding, tables and stove, were rented to campers for $4 per week. – HENRY E. HUNTINGTON LIBRARY

Delivery burro and groceryman at Camp Baldy, ca. 1910. Sales were solicited among canyon campers in the morning, delivered by burro in the afternoon. – POST CARD PHOTO

San Antonio Theatre, Camp Baldy, ca. 1921. Feature Hollywood films were shown here every Friday and Saturday nights through most of the 1920s. Cost: 10 cents per person. – ROBERT CHAPMAN COLLECTION

Dan Alexander's first photographic studio at Camp Baldy, opened in 1912. Alexander ranged throughout the canyon and many times climbed Mt. Baldy, lugging heavy photographic equipment, taking hundreds of personal pictures and scenic views. Post cards bearing Alexander's name were produced by the thousands, and are still commonly found today.
– ROBERT CHAPMAN COLLECTION

Alexander's second, enlarged studio at Camp Baldy, ca. 1928. A visit to Camp Baldy was not complete without buying Alexander post cards and mailing them to friends from the Camp Baldy Post Office.
– ROBERT CHAPMAN COLLECTION

Dan Alexander at the Sierra Club Cabin, Baldy Notch, 1927. Alexander was a familiar figure in San Antonio Canyon from 1906, when he filed on a cabin lease in Bear Canyon, until he sold his Camp Baldy studio and moved to Tulare in 1935. Although best known for his photographs and post cards, he was a jack-of-all-trades, entertaining Camp Baldy visitors, guiding horseback and hiking parties, and helping new residents build cabins. – ROBERT CHAPMAN COLLECTION

Clarence Roy Chapman (shown with wife and two children, 1917) built a cabin in Icehouse Canyon in 1913. He started Icehouse Canyon Resort in 1919.
– ROBERT CHAPMAN COLLECTION

Chapman's Resort at the mouth of Icehouse Canyon, ca. 1922. Pictured is the general store. Chapman built a number of guest cabins in the lower canyon.
– HENRY E. HUNTINGTON LIBRARY

and forge. For a time he operated an amusement park on the lower end of the ranch, where the trout pond is today. Clarence Chapman died in 1954. Today his son Bob Chapman and family live on the ranch, the only one in San Antonio Canyon, and are almost totally self-sufficient, growing most of their own food, sawing their own lumber and using the forge to make nails, rods, wire and other implements.

Up near the head of San Antonio Canyon was Snow Crest Camp, founded by Mr. and Mrs. A.R. Collins in 1925. The Collins' built a main lodge, store and a dozen cabins. Snow Crest was popular in summer, but being located at an elevation of 6,300 feet, it was snowed in every winter.

Way up on the northwest slope on Ontario Peak, at 8,300 feet elevation, was Kelly's Camp. John Kelly located a gold mine here and built a little log cabin in 1905. The mine never turned a profit and Kelly left about 1912. In 1922 Henry Delker took out a resort lease with the Forest Service, built several more cabins, and opened Kelly's Camp to the public. The cozy little resort, nestled beside an icy-cold mountain spring under a forest of lodgepole pine and white fir, was a hit with hikers and wilderness lovers, but it was too high and too far from the road for most vacationers. Nevertheless, Delker hung on to his alpine camp until 1947, although it was all but deserted the last few years.

In 1922 Los Angeles and San Bernardino counties jointly purchased the San Antonio Canyon road from the San Antonio Water Company, thus ending

Icehouse Canyon Resort, ca. 1925. Horseback riding was a popular attraction.
– POMONA PUBLIC LIBRARY, SPECIAL COLLECTIONS

Bear Canyon Lodge, a popular canyon eatery, was located opposite the mouth of Bear Canyon just below Camp Baldy. The lodge was founded by Anna and Fred Courtney in 1921. William K. Vernon bought it in 1924 and was the genial host until the flood of March 1938. POMONA PUBLIC LIBRARY, SPECIAL COLLECTIONS

Eleven Oaks Camp, at the mouth of Bear Canyon just below Camp Baldy, was founded by R. D. Shiffer in 1921 and run by a succession of owners until the great flood of 1938. – POST CARD PHOTO

Snow Crest Resort was the highest of the San Antonio Canyon hostelries, located just below Manker Flats in the upper canyon. Founded by Mr. and Mrs. A. R. Collins in 1925, the resort was popular in summer but snowed in every winter. – POST CARD PHOTO

John Kelly and his log cabin high on the slopes of Ontario Peak, ca. 1910. Kelly located a gold mine here in 1905, but it never turned a profit and he left about 1912. Since then, the forested flat has been known as Kelly's Camp. – CHARLES CLARK VERNON COLLECTION

Kelly's Camp, elevation 8,500 feet, ca. 1936. Delker's resort was a hit with hikers, but it was too high and too far from the road for most vacationers.
– POST CARD PHOTO

Henry Delker standing in front of Kelly's original cabin at Kelly's Camp, ca. 1937. Delker took out a resort lease on the flat in 1922 and built a small lodge and several guest cabins. He operated the camp until 1947. – ROBERT CHAPMAN COLLECTION.

The well at Kelly's Camp. Icy-cold mountain water gushed forth. – ROBERT CHAPMAN COLLECTION

Kelly's Camp under winter snows, 1932.
– WILL THRALL PHOTOGRAPH

The Log'N Rock cabin in upper San Antonio Canyon, one of over 200 built by Clarence Chapman. Many of these cabins are still standing.
– ROBERT CHAPMAN COLLECTION

The Forest Service began leasing summer home sites in upper San Antonio Canyon in 1915. The lease fee was $15 to $25 per year. By 1930 there were over 250 cabins on national forest land in the canyon.

its toll status. County road crews immediately went to work, vastly improving the uphill stretch over the Hogsback, and extending the road farther up canyon. By 1925 it was paved to Camp Baldy, and a new well-graded dirt road extended past the mouth of Icehouse Canyon, zigzagged up to Manker Flat, and climbed to the old mining site at Baldy Notch. Here it joined the old mining road down the north side of the mountain to Stockton Flat and Lytle Creek. By the end of the 1920s anyone with a decent automobile could drive all the way up the canyon and over the divide to Lytle Creek — a far cry from the long years of abominable road conditions!

For those who desired summer homes in San Antonio Canyon, the Forest Service offered cabin lots for lease at very reasonable prices. The San Antonio Canyon tract was one of several in Angeles National Forest opened for public leasing in 1915. A Forest Service brochure read, "This beautiful canyon, one of the most picturesque in the Angeles Forest, is now open for residence purposes. The lots range in size from sixty to ninety feet in frontage, and rent from $15 to $25 per year . . . No lots are reserved. First come, first served. They may be rented for periods of from one year to fifteen. There are no land taxes, no filing fees. The few restrictions are reasonable, and there is no 'red tape.'"[9] Responding to this sales pitch were hundreds of valley residents. By 1930 there were over 250 cabins on national forest land in San Antonio Canyon. Most of them were clustered around Camp Baldy, with many others in Icehouse Canyon and below Manker Flat. So many people were now living in San Antonio Canyon that Camp Baldy School was opened in 1921, covering grades one through eight. High schoolers were bussed down to Upland.

For those who desired to own their land rather than lease it from the government, the San Antonio Water Company sold lots for summer cottages. The price for a mountain lot varied according to size and location: a 60 by 90-foot lot sold for about $800 in 1928. The water company constructed three small reservoirs in the canyon to supply water to cabin owners and permittees. Mirror Lake, the little body of water across the creek from Camp Baldy, was the largest of these.

The Forest Service was hardpressed to keep up with all this activity. A wood frame ranger station was built near the canyon mouth in 1917, replacing the old log structure in use since the turn of the century. In 1920 another, smaller ranger station was erected near the mouth of Bear Canyon, just below Camp Baldy. Rangers and fire guards regularly patrolled the canyon and nearby mountain trails, enforcing fire regulations and rescuing lost hikers.

In early 1928 Camp Baldy changed hands and the resort entered a new era — an era that was to make Camp Baldy one of the premier mountain resorts in Southern California. The new owners were Foster and Ruth Curry, of the famed inn-keeping family of Yosemite.

Foster Curry grew up at Camp Curry in Yosemite Valley, and after his father David Curry died in 1917, became manager of the famous camp. But

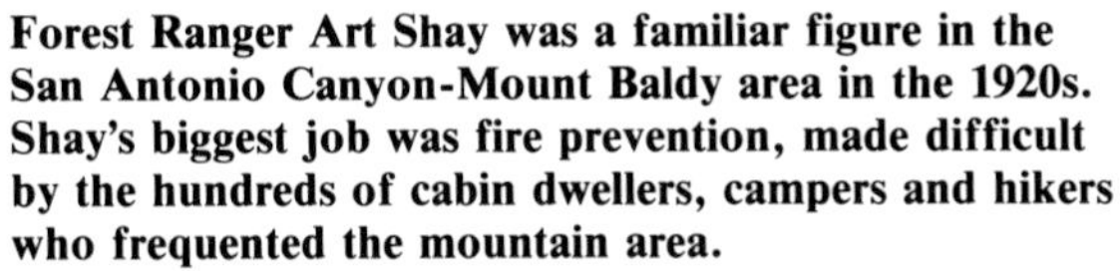

Forest Ranger Art Shay was a familiar figure in the San Antonio Canyon-Mount Baldy area in the 1920s. Shay's biggest job was fire prevention, made difficult by the hundreds of cabin dwellers, campers and hikers who frequented the mountain area.
– ROBERT CHAPMAN COLLECTION

In 1912, Angeles Forest Supervisor Rushton Charlton conceived of the idea of using herds of goats to maintain fire breaks. 200 of the animals from Warren Gale's goat ranch above Clarmont (pictured here) were drafted to crop the breaks above San Antonio Canyon, and 500 others were imported from Arizona. Unfortunately, the goats proved a failure at mountain lawn mowing. Many of the animals wandered off the fire breaks to greener pastures in the canyons, and some fell off precipices. The project was abandoned in 1915. – HENRY E. HUNTINGTON LIBRARY

San Antonio Canyon Ranger Station, 1926. Deputy Forest Supervisor Willian Mendenhall in front. The old station was located just inside the canyon mouth.
– WILLIAM MENDENHALL PHOTO

One of the early primitive cabins in upper San Antonio Canyon. Picture taken about 1924; cabin built much earlier. Will Thrall believed the cabin was built by Fletcher Manker and leased to a man named Bradley. – HENRY E. HUNTINGTON LIBRARY

The main lodge at Camp Baldy, 1930. Foster and Ruth Curry turned Camp Baldy into one of Southern California's top mountain resorts, patterned after the Yosemite Camp Curry where Foster grew up. Notice the "Foster Curry Will Greet You" sign on the tree, a take-off on David Curry's famous greetings in Yosemite.
– POMONA PUBLIC LIBRARY, SPECIAL COLLECTIONS

Birthday party for the Curry twins at Camp Baldy, 1932. Ruth and Foster Curry, proprietors of the resort, are standing. "Mother" Curry of Yosemite's Camp Curry sits to the left. Foster Curry died suddenly a few months later. – RUTH CURRY BURNS COLLECTION

The dining room at Camp Baldy, 1928. A good meal could be purchased here for $1.00.
– POMONA PUBLIC LIBRARY, SPECIAL COLLECTIONS

Camp Baldy's main lodge and dining room in 1935, before the Curry's began their expansion program.
– RUTH CURRY BURNS COLLECTION

things failed to work out well for Foster, and in 1921 he left Yosemite under less than pleasant circumstances, vowing never to set foot there again. Foster Curry was a resort manager by training and he was determined to stay in that line of work. In 1925 he married Ruth Woolsey Higgins, secretary to a Los Angeles law firm, and together they managed Lebec Lodge on the old Ridge Route and then a hotel in Ocean Park. When the opportunity came to buy Camp Baldy from Herbert McCullough, Foster and Ruth Curry jumped at the chance.

The Currys immediately set about to make Camp Baldy *the* top resort in the San Gabriels. The dining room was remodeled, the swimming pool enlarged, new buildings were erected and twenty new cabins were built. When they ran out of space on the Camp Baldy property, they leased land directly across San Antonio Creek from the water company and added a new open-air dance pavilion, an amusement park and more cabins. Camp Baldy was turned into a small mountain city, complete with U.S. post office and county lending library. By the early 1930s, the resort was jammed with people every weekend, with many a guest staying a week or longer in one of the cozy cabins.

The greatest asset of the new Camp Baldy, however, was Foster and Ruth Curry themselves. Foster patterned the resort after the Yosemite Camp Curry, using the genial "Welcome" and "Farewell" calls made famous by his father, and advertising it as "The Yosemite of the South." A bold sign outside the main lodge proclaimed "FOSTER CURRY GREETS YOU." A perfect counterpart for Foster's boisterous friendliness was Ruth Curry's quiet geniality and warmth. She also possessed a superb business head, tempering some of Foster Curry's grandiose ideas — particularly during the early depression years.

Tragedy struck the Currys on November 21, 1932 when Foster died of leukemia after a brief illness, leaving Ruth to manage the camp and care for their three young children. Foster Curry, during the last eleven years of his life, had stuck to his vow never to return to Yosemite, but on his deathbed he asked to be taken back. The following June a small plane approached Yosemite. Inside were Ruth Curry and the pilot. As the plane passed over Yosemite Valley, ashes swirled out. Foster Curry was at peace.

Ruth Curry continued to manage Camp Baldy, and the crowds continued to come. Among those visiting the resort in 1933 was Edmund Burns, a star of the silent screen who had played supporting roles with such Hollywood greats as John Barrymore, Gloria Swanson and Constance Talmadge. Burns fell in love with Ruth Curry. Actually what happened, Ruth related many years later, was that "Ed came up and fell in love with my three little kids, and then with me." They were married in September 1934, and Ruth had a partner to manage the camp.

Under Edmund and Ruth Curry Burns, Camp Baldy continued to expand. The casino was remodeled and more housekeeping cabins were put in. Camp Baldy became a favorite weekend retreat for many of Hollywood's greats and near-greats, friends of former actor Edmund Burns. John Barrymore was a frequent guest.

A setback occurred in July 1936, when the Camp

Edmund Burns, Hollywood actor, married the widowed Ruth Curry in 1934, and together they brought Camp Baldy to its peak of popularity.
– RUTH CURRY BURNS COLLECTION

Baldy Casino burned to the ground. Two were injured fighting the blaze, including William K. Vernon, manager of nearby Bear Canyon Resort. Fortunately, the strenuous efforts of Forest Service and state fire crews, aided by the timely arrival of units from the Upland Fire Department, confined the destruction to the casino.

The embers had hardly died out when Edmund and Ruth Burns began work on a new super casino, much more spacious than the original structure and extending out over the streambed of San Antonio Creek. By the summer of 1937, less than a year after the fire, the beautiful, rustic Wagon Wheel Casino was opened to the public. The heart of the casino was a 7,000-square foot dance pavilion, with a 32-foot high ceiling supported by enormous redwood beams. Great stone fireplaces stood at each end, and there was a large stage for orchestra and entertainers. The spacious dining room extended out over the stream and featured a 10-foot wagon wheel powered by the stream waters. The lighting fixtures were in the form of wagon wheels hanging from the ceiling. Walls were decorated with mounted heads of elk, moose, caribou and deer. Outside, overlooking the stream, was a terraced patio for outdoor dining. The Burnses brought in top-flight entertainment to perform at the Wagon Wheel Casino, and this in turn attracted even larger crowds. Camp Baldy reached its apogee of popularity and success. No mountain resort in Southern California was better known.

But the halcyon days at Camp Baldy and its new Wagon Wheel Casino lasted less than a year. Disaster struck on the night of March 1-2, 1938. That terrible night of flood is etched deeply in the memories of all who were in the San Gabriel Mountains at the time. Heavy rain started the afternoon of the 1st and continued all night. By morning creeks were raging far above their banks. The flood reached unbelievable proportions in San Antonio Canyon. A torrent of churning gray water 150 feet wide carried away everything in its path. Of the 588 privately-owned cabins in the canyon, 206 were completely demolished and 200 others were damaged. Camp Baldy was not spared. The new Wagon Wheel Casino was completely washed away, as were the new swimming pool and 68 of the 78 cabins. Half of the main lodge was destroyed.

Ruth Curry Burns recalled the disaster 40 years later: "We personally suffered a loss of $250,000 in property but fortunately only two lives were lost. Hundreds of private cabins and two other resorts were swept away. We had three acres of land left, with ten of our poorest cabins and part of our 49er Bar. The 42 acres that were claimed by the raging stream are still part of its rocky bed. I got in touch with my mother-in-law 'Mother Curry' of Yosemite. She promptly came down to survey our plight. Seeing the hopelessness of our situation, she advised us to leave the canyon, and go to Idyllwild, a resort in the San Jacinto mountains which we had heard could be leased.

Ruth Curry Burns with actor John Barrymore at Camp Baldy, ca. 1937. Many Hollywood greats and near-greats visited Camp Baldy during its heyday.
– RUTH CURRY BURNS COLLECTION

Wagon Wheel Casino at Camp Baldy, 1937. This beautiful mountain lodge was destined to last just one year, destroyed in the terrible flood of March 1938.
– POMONA PUBLIC LIBRARY, SPECIAL COLLECTIONS

Camp Baldy after winter storm, 1937. The open-air dance pavilion was across San Antonio Creek from the main camp.
– POMONA PUBLIC LIBRARY, SPECIAL COLLECTIONS

Twin Day at Camp Baldy, 1937. Ruth Curry Burns sits between her twins; behind are many other sets of twins who made the trip to Camp Baldy for the annual occasion during the 1930s.
– RUTH CURRY BURNS COLLECTION

Cabin row along San Antonio Creek, Camp Baldy, ca. 1932. There were 78 of these guest cabins before the 1938 flood. Only ten survived the disaster.
– RUTH CURRY BURNS COLLECTION

The great flood of March 2, 1938. In the foreground, nothing is left of the Wagon Wheel Casino; behind, half of the Camp Baldy Lodge is gone.
– POMONA PUBLIC LIBRARY, SPECIAL COLLECTIONS

After the flood of March 2, 1938. Looking east from Wagon Wheel Casino site across creek to what was left of Camp Baldy cabins and dance pavilion.
– WILL THRALL PHOTO

"After five months, we returned to the scene of the disaster. On more borrowed money, we rebuilt in a very small way our former resort. We refurbished the 49er Bar and ten small cabins that were left, and announced that we were back in business."[10]

The post-flood Camp Baldy bore little resemblance to its illustrious predecessor. The center of the Burns' refurbished resort was the 49er Bar, fashioned from the half of the old lodge that remained intact. This was supplemented by a small restaurant and the ten undamaged cabins. No attempt was made to rebuild the part of the resort in the floodpath — a wise decision, in light of subsequent floods that scoured the same area.

In 1948 Edmund and Ruth Curry Burns were at last ready to retire. They sold their small resort to Bill Sager. Sager dropped the historic name "Camp Baldy" and remodeled the 49er Bar, calling it the Buckhorn Restaurant. He still operates the restaurant today, the most popular eating spot in the canyon.

The 1938 flood badly damaged the San Antonio Canyon road. A half-mile stretch below the Hogsback was literally obliterated. Thanks to the young men of the Civilian Conservation Corps, stationed at the San Antonio Canyon C.C.C. Camp near the canyon mouth from 1933 to 1942, the road was repaired and reopened within a year of the disaster. But everyone in the canyon realized that the road was located too close to the creek and remained in acute danger of washout. What was needed was a "high line" route well above the flood-prone canyon bottom. World War II intervened before anything could be done. In 1950 the State of

Rebuilding a temporary bridge over San Antonio Creek after the great flood of March 1938. This view looks down-canyon from site of Camp Baldy.
– PHIL TOWNSEND HANNA PHOTO

California, Los Angeles County and the Forest Service jointly financed the construction of the much-needed high line road. The new highway, contouring high along the west slope of the canyon and utilizing two tunnels, was completed and opened for public use in 1955. The value of the highway was proved in 1969, when another severe flood again washed out the old canyon-bottom road. The old road was permanently abandoned, and today the mountainside highway remains the only direct route into the canyon.

The new highway proved a boon to canyon residents. It almost cut in half the time required to drive into the upper canyon. Made more accessible by the highway, the cluster of cabins around old Camp Baldy have grown into an unincorporated but viable community of almost 1,000 residents, many of whom commute daily to jobs in the valley. Many more spend weekends there. The community is officially known as "Mt. Baldy," but most know it as

The 49er Bar at Camp Baldy, ca. 1940. Camp Baldy was never the same after the great 1938 flood.
– POST CARD PHOTO

"Baldy Village." Besides the 300-plus cabins, the village contains an elementary school, general store, two restaurants, a church, post office, fire station and ranger station. In the San Gabriel Mountains, Baldy Village is second only to Wrightwood in population.

The Forest Service has its hands full managing and protecting San Antonio Canyon, particularly with the weekend crowds who often swarm into the area. Two campgrounds were opened by the Forest Service in 1969 — Glacier and Manker Flat, both in the upper canyon. The main Lower San Antonio Canyon Ranger Station, a mile inside the canyon mouth and just east of the creek, was rebuilt after the 1969 flood. The Mt. Baldy Ranger Station in Baldy Village, a quaint stone cabin built some fifty years ago, serves as a visitor center for canyon campers and hikers.

Bill Sager's Buckhorn Restaurant, formerly Camp Baldy, 1980. – AUTHOR PHOTO

The Sierra Club's Harwood Lodge shortly after completion, 1930. The spacious stone lodge just below Manker Flats in the upper canyon was built as a memorial to Aurelia Harwood, late Sierra Club director. – ROBERT CHAPMAN COLLECTION

Sierra Club's Harwood Lodge in wintertime. Many a congenial weekend have been enjoyed here by Sierra Clubbers over the past half century. – POST CARD PHOTO

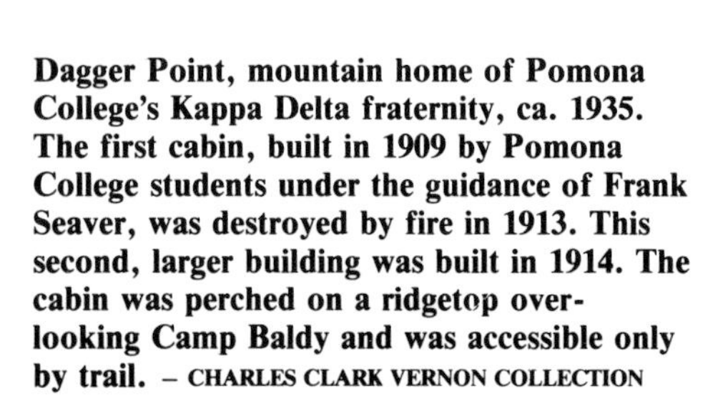

Dagger Point, mountain home of Pomona College's Kappa Delta fraternity, ca. 1935. The first cabin, built in 1909 by Pomona College students under the guidance of Frank Seaver, was destroyed by fire in 1913. This second, larger building was built in 1914. The cabin was perched on a ridgetop overlooking Camp Baldy and was accessible only by trail. – CHARLES CLARK VERNON COLLECTION

The Mount Baldy Village Ranger Station, 1980.
– AUTHOR PHOTO

Ice House Canyon Lodge, 1980. – AUTHOR PHOTO

Fire is an ever-present problem, and continues to be the Forest Service's major headache. The Baldy Village Fire of November 1975 burned several cabins and mountain terrain to the west until extinguished by a timely snowstorm. The village narrowly escaped disaster in the Thunder Fire of November 1980. The blaze erupted near the Mt. Baldy ski lift and, pushed by strong winds, quickly spread southward. Heroic work by Forest Service and state fire crews saved Baldy Village, even though the flames surrounded the village on three sides. The fire burned south as far as Barrett Canyon, westward to Lookout Mountain, north to the Devils Backbone, and eastward through Cedar and Icehouse canyons to Ontario Peak ridge and into the upper reaches of the Lytle Creek watershed, before finally being contained by exhausted fire crews and a fortunate abatement of the "devil winds." In all, some 12,000 acres of the San Antonio watershed were burned over, and 28 cabins were destroyed in the Thunder Fire (named for nearby Thunder Mountain).

Fire and flood will always be dangers that must be faced by mountain residents of Southern California. Baldy Village residents know this, yet few would leave their beloved canyon havens. The lure and delights of mountain living are in their blood.

NOTES

1 F.H. Manker and Dan Alexander, "At The Foot of Mt. San Antonio," *Trails Magazine* (Spring 1937), p. 9.
2 *Ibid.*
3 Belle J. Bidwell, "Our Camp in The Canon," *Overland Monthly* (August 1887), p. 148.
4 Harris Newmark, *Sixty Years in Southern California* (Los Angeles, 1970), p. 274.
5 Charles W. Knox letter, February 2, 1909, cited in Esther Boulton Black, *Stories of Old Upland* (Upland, 1979), pp. 6-7.
6 *Pomona Daily Review,* August 8, 1904.
7 Manker and Alexander, *op. cit.,* p. 11.
8 Will Thrall manuscripts, San Antonio Canyon folder, Henry E. Huntington Library, San Marino.
9 *Summer Home Sites in Angeles National Forest,* U.S. Forest Service, 1915 pamphlet in author's possession. It should be pointed out that Angeles National Forest encompassed all of San Bernardino National Forest from 1908 to 1925; today most of San Antonio Canyon is in the former.
10 Ruth Curry Burns, "Another Time," *Westways* (May 1978), p. 16.

Winter sunrise on Old Baldy, 1915. – B.D. JACKSON

Timberline on Old Baldy. – AUTHOR PHOTO

12

Old Baldy

St. Anthony of Padua, a 13th century Franciscan priest and worker of miracles, is well represented in Southern California. His name crowns the San Gabriel Mountains — Mount San Antonio. This massive peak, better known today as Mt. Baldy, is the grand climax of the fifty-mile backbone of the San Gabriels. No other peak in the range rises to challenge its 10,064-foot elevation. From its summit you look over a good part of Southern California — an expanse of mountain, desert and coastal lowland. On those rare days when haze does not muddy the atmosphere, the hiker on its boulder-strewn top can make out the tawny ramparts of the southern High Sierra, 150 miles to the north, and see ocean-ward as far as San Clemente Island.

Old Baldy is a huge mountain, by Southern California standards. Its sprawling gray bulk overwhelms lesser summits and makes up for any lack of sharp relief. Long descending ridges and broad slopes of disintegrating granitic rock drop far down into shadowy canyons. Among the folds of its granite robes are sylvan dells where sparkling streams and waterfalls rush downward, and ferns grow lush in the shade of pine and cedar. Its higher slopes are dotted with lodge-pole and limber pines. Some stand tall and erect, proud sentinels of the ridgetops; others, bent and gnarled by nature's high-altitude fury, form grotesque shapes. All contribute to the elegance, order and beauty of the alpine landscape.

Just when or how the peak was named "Mount San Antonio" is not known with certainty. Spanish padre Francisco Garces, traveling from Mexico to Monterey with Captain Juan Bautista de Anza in the most famous overland expedition in California history, wrote in his diary, March 21, 1774: "Going seven leagues to the northwest, we came to an arroyo called San Antonio. Here there are many bears and sycamores."[1] This is the earliest record of the place name "San Antonio" for the arroyo. A few years later, "San Antonio" was listed as an outlying cattle ranch in Mission San Gabriel documents. But there is no record of the mission fathers extending the name of the arroyo and cattle ranch to the mountain. (The Spanish settlers of early California showed little interest in mountain peaks.)

Phil Townsend Hanna, the late editor of *Westways* magazine and long a student of California place names, believed the name derived in the following fashion:

> SAN ANTONIO MT. Los Angeles Co. The origin of the name is uncertain. Legend has it that it was named for St. Anthony of Padua second-handed through Antonio Maria Lugo, grantee of nearby Santa Ana del Chino Rancho in 1841. Lugo was born at San Antonio de Padua Mission and christened there with St. Anthony's name by Father Junipero Serra. The explanation is plausible for Lugo was proud of his saint and when, in 1810, he was given a provisional grant of land in the vicinity of Compton it was recorded as San Antonio Rancho.[2]

Since there is no known Spanish or Mexican document or map that refers to the peak as "San Antonio," we can only assume that the name was carried over from the Spanish into the American period by word of mouth. The secret must have been well kept, for none of the early American visitors to Southern California called the mountain "San Antonio." The first Yankees to get a close look at the mountain must have been the Jedediah Smith party. Smith and his small band of trappers crossed near Cajon Pass enroute to Mission San Gabriel in November 1826, and recrossed the pass on their northward journey in February 1827. Their journals do not specifically mention the mountain peak, although mention was made of "high lofty mountains, handsomely timbered with pine and cedar," west of Cajon Pass.[3]

John C. Fremont, while exploring the Mojave Desert in April 1844, saw "a snowy peak to the southward [that] shone out high and sharply defined."[4] This may well have been Mt. San Antonio, for Fremont could hardly have missed sighting it.

Lieutenant Robert S. Williamson's Pacific Railroad Survey party examined both sides of the San Gabriel Mountains, looking for possible railroad routes, in 1853. William Blake, Williamson's geologist, called the knot of high peaks at the eastern end of the range "Qui-qual-mungo," after the Cucamonga Rancho in the valley to the south.[5] The "Cucamonga Mountains" was a term often used for the eastern end of the San Gabriels in the 1850s.

The earliest reference to the mountain peak as "San Antonio" found by this writer was in the *Southern Vineyard*, a Los Angeles newspaper. In the issue of April 17, 1858 was an announcement that Los Angeles businessmen Marchessault and Beaudry had arrived in town with "the first consignment of ice from the mountain of San Antonio." (See previous chapter.)

Josiah Dwight Whitney, director of the California Geological Survey, visited the southern fringes of the San Gabriel Mountains in 1861. In his final report on the geology of California, published in 1865, he made the first official mention of Mt. San Antonio:

> The highest point of the San Gabriel Mountains is known as San Antonio; it is towards the east end of the range, and is a conspicuous point from all the region to the south. We estimate it to be about 6500 feet high, although we were not near enough to give a very reliable guess at its altitude.[6]

Whitney was way off on the altitude. Later surveyors considerably heightened their estimate of Mt. San Antonio's elevation. In 1869 George Davidson of the U. S. Coast and Geodetic Survey, making triangulations from Dominquez Hill and other points south of Los Angeles, calculated that "The peaks lying between the great plains of Los Angeles and the Great Desert reach 9,940 feet above the sea."[7]. First to calculate that Mt. San Antonio topped 10,000 feet in elevation was A. W. Chase, also of the Coast and Geodetic Survey. Chase set up triangulation stations on the San Joaquin Hills (behind Laguna Beach) and reported the following:

> Observations were recorded for determining the positions and heights of the principal peaks of the Sierra Madre Mountains. The computed results give for the average height of the mountain chain from 8,000 to 9,000 feet, and for the highest peak, San Antonio Mountain, an elevation of 10,000 feet above the sea."[8]

The U. S. Army's Wheeler Survey ascended Mt. San Antonio in 1875 and calculated the height at 10,191 feet.

It was the gold miners, who scrambled over and dug into the slopes of Mt. San Antonio from the 1860s until the turn of the century, who first applied the name "Old Baldy." American miners of the 19th century excelled in vulgarizing place names; this is readily evident to anyone who studies western mining. The prospectors on Mt. San Antonio were no exception. To them, what better name for the barren, wind-swept summit of Mt. San Antonio than the earthy, descriptive title "Old Baldy." The name first appeared in the *Los Angeles Star* of October 24, 1871: ". . . a rich gold lode has been found in the neighborhood of the Old Baldy mountain by a party of prospectors from this city." Subsequently the name appeared with increasing frequency, particularly in regard to mining ventures on the mountain (see *A Century of Mining*).

Pomona newspapers of the 1880s and 1890s used "Old Baldy" or "Mt. Baldy" almost exclusively when referring to the mountain. The *Pomona Weekly Times* of October 14, 1882 described the mountain in glowing terms so prevalent in the Victorian era:

> Old Baldy stands pre-eminently head and shoulders above the mountains surrounding him. He is indeed monarch of the range. The first rays of the rising sun gild his bald and barren crown and its last golden tints are shed upon his summit . . . All summer long his rocky crown glistens in the sunshine, and in the winter season and sometimes far into spring, his lofty head is covered with snow.

Some resented the vulgar nickname. W. O. Goodyear, geologist for the California State Mining Bureau, writing in the *Los Angeles Times* of June 5, 1887, complained:

> When I was here, . . . in the employ of the old State Geological Survey under Prof. Whitney fifteen years ago [1872], I never heard of any other name for that peak than San Antonio. The change from San Antonio to Old Baldy is not only confusing to people who have known the mountain under its old name, but the name itself (Old Baldy) is not poetical. It is ridiculous and, if I may so express myself, it is hardly decent, however naked the towering peak may be.

Goodyear was also critical of the use of the name "Sierra Madre" for the San Gabriel Mountains: "The San Gabriel Range, the old name, is deserving.

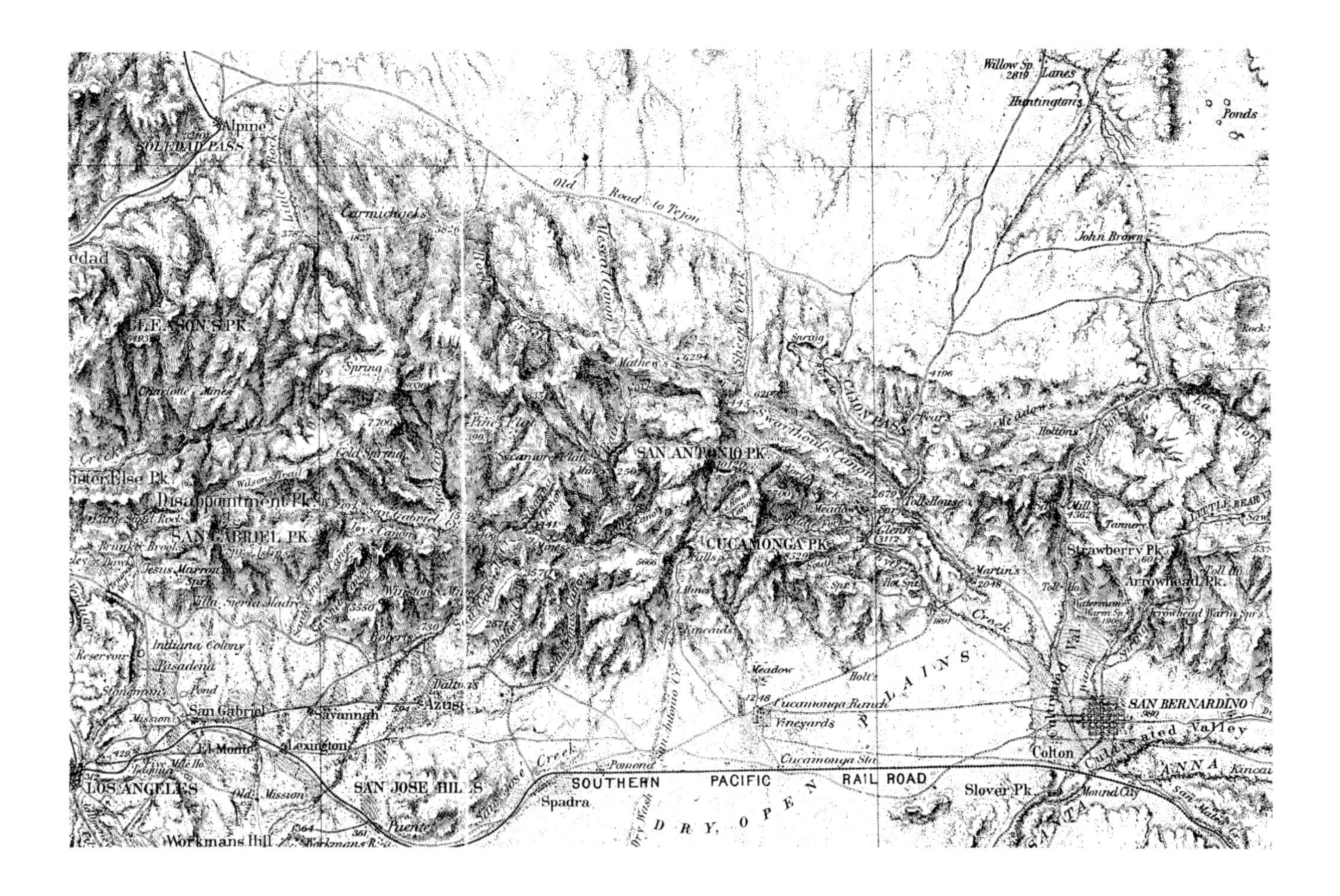

A section of the U.S. Army's Wheeler Survey Atlas Sheet No. 73, showing Mt. San Antonio and the eastern San Gabriel Mountains. The Wheeler Survey was an ambitious project to map the United States west of the 100th Meridian under the direction of Lt. George Montague Wheeler, undertaken between 1871 and 1878. On July 1, 1875 a Wheeler Survey party under Louis Nell, cheif topographer, made the first known ascent of Old Baldy, via Lytle Creek and the Devils Backbone. Cucamonga Peak was climbed at the same time by Lt. Eric Bergland and several soldiers. Old Baldy was climbed again in 1878 by Lt. Willard Young and a small party. The summit was used as a triangulation point in mapping the mountains.

But some 'genius' has changed it into 'Sierra Madre,' which is confusing and is an utter misnomer."

The protests of those who favored the original name of "Mount San Antonio" reached the U.S. Board on Geographic Names in Washington, D.C. In a decision reached on February 2, 1891, the Board ruled in favor of "Mount San Antonio — not Baldy, North Bald, nor Old Baldy." In recent years, the Board has reaffirmed that decision. Although Mount San Antonio is the legal name and has been for some ninety years, most Southern Californians don't call it that. "Mt. Baldy" is far and away the predominant name in use today. Even "Old Baldy" has fallen by the wayside.

The early-day prospectors and adventure-seekers who scrambled up the mountain found big game in abundance. Deer, big horn sheep, grizzly bear and mountain lion stalked the slopes. The grizzlies were particularly dangerous to man, and many an early prospector had a close brush with the beasts. Charles Tom Vincent, a prospector and hunter who lived hermit-style on the southeast slope of North Baldy (today's Mt. Baden-Powell), encountered three grizzlies at one time on Baldy's north side in 1888. As reported in the *Los Angeles Times* of October 6, 1888, Vincent and a companion named DeLancey were tracking big horn sheep on the north slope of Baldy when they suddenly encountered three angry bruins in the brush. The first grizzly charged DeLancey and was only a step away from the frightened hunter when Vincent managed to

This old cabin high in Vincent Gulch may have once been the home of Charles Tom Vincent (alias Charles Vincent Daughtery), the premier mountain man of the San Gabriels. From 1870 until just before his death in 1926, Vincent lived the solitary life of prospector and big game hunter in the extremely rugged high country between Mt. Baden-Powell and Old Baldy. Not until he was on his deathbed did he reveal his lifetime secret: he was a fugitive from the law after killing three men in Arizona in 1869. – DEE TRENT PHOTO

send a 50-calibre slug through the bear's head and neck, dropping it in its tracks. Immediately the two other grizzlies charged, one toward DeLancey and the other at Vincent. Vincent was able to down one of the bears with a shot through the chest just before it reached DeLancey. Upon turning around, the last grizzly jumped on Vincent, knocking him down. As man and beast grappled on the ground, Vincent pulled out his knife and plunged the blade into the bear's neck, just as DeLancey jammed his rifle against the bear's head and fired. The grizzly dropped dead atop Vincent, who was badly scratched but not seriously hurt. Afterwards, the hunters skinned the bears and carried the three hides, complete with claws and heads, to Vincent's cabin, where they hung as trophies for years.

Charles Tom Vincent had much in common with the mountain men of the early 19th century West. He was one of the most amazing characters ever to make a home in the San Gabriel Mountains. From 1870 until just before his death in 1926, he lived in a sturdy little cabin on a forested bench between Mine and Vincent gulches, high above the East Fork of the San Gabriel. He spent most of his time prospecting for gold and hunting wild game. His biggest discovery was the Big Horn Mine, which he located in 1894 and then sold. His cabin was a veritable trophy house, filled with the heads and skins of animals he had slain.

One of the few men Vincent trusted was Bob Pallett, a rancher from Valyermo, who brought the mountain hermit his mail now and then. Dorothy Evans Noble, postmistress of Valyermo who made the trip up to Vincent's cabin with Pallett in 1914, described him as "a thin old man in blue jeans and a faded blue shirt that barely covered his barrel chest, with piercing blue eyes that glared from under tufted white eyebrows and a little white beard under an aggressive chin."[9] He seemed to be overly suspicious of outsiders, chasing tresspassers off his land with a rifle and a volley of oaths.

Vincent almost never talked about his background, and refused to let anyone take his picture. He was a man of mystery, until just a few days before his death in a Los Angeles hospital on September 8, 1926. Then, knowing he had but a short time to live, he blurted out his life story to the attending doctor in the hope that he could be buried in the veterans' cemetery at Sawtelle.

Vincent revealed that his real name was Charles Vincent Dougherty, that he was born in Ohio in 1838, and that he had served in the 8th Ohio Infantry during the Civil War and had been wounded at Gettysburg. His war service would qualify him for burial in the veterans' cemetery, he hoped. Why did he change his name and live a hermit's life high in the mountains? the doctor asked. Vincent then told the dark secret he had guarded for sixty years. After the war, he and a friend had journeyed west to prospect. They located a claim in Arizona and built a cabin. One day, upon returning to their cabin, they found three men ransacking the place. They shot all three and buried them on the spot. The partners then split and Dougherty fled to California, changed his name, and sought a fugitive's hideout in the San Gabriel Mountains. The rest of his long life, he imagined that he was being hunted by the law.

Charles Vincent Dougherty, alias Charles Tom Vincent, died the next day. The old fugitive got his wish. He now lies with his fellow war veterans at Sawtelle — Section 9, Row G, Grave 22. In the San Gabriels, he is remembered by the names Vincent Gap, on the Angeles Crest Highway, and Vincent Gulch, a tributary of the San Gabriel's rugged East Fork.

Who made the first ascent of Mount San Antonio will probably never be known. Serrano Indians crossed the wind-swept ridges below the great mountain years before the arrival of the white man and may have walked the short distance to the top, although there is no evidence that Indians of that day had any interest in conquering mountain peaks. Perhaps an early prospector from the mines near Baldy Notch scrambled up the Devils Backbone to the summit.

The earliest climb of Mount San Antonio on record was made by Louis Nell, chief topographer of the U.S. Army's Wheeler Survey, and a small party of soldiers on July 1, 1875. Nell and his party made the three-day trip (June 30-July 2) via Lytle Creek, probably traversing the Devils Backbone, to "make necessary observations." Among these observations was the calculation of the mountain's elevation as 10,191.9 feet above sea level. (Today's U.S. Geological Survey topographical maps place the elevation at 10,064 feet.) On October 10, 1878 another party of the Wheeler Survey, led by Lieutenant Willard Young, Corps of Engineers, made the second known ascent of the mountain, also from Lytle Creek.

During the 1880s, ascents of Old Baldy were made by a number of energetic individuals from the valley towns to the south. William B. Dewey of Ontario, later famous as proprietor of Baldy Summit Inn, made the first of his 133 lifetime ascents in 1882. He reported seeing no human trail up the mountain, but bears were plentiful and many bear trails contoured the slopes. There were others who made the climb that year, too. The *Pomona Weekly Times* of October 14, 1882 remarked, "The ascent is rugged, and but few venture the task; but when once the journey is accomplished it is well worth the toll expended." In 1887 the *Pomona Progress* stationed a correspondent in the canyon all summer to report on doings there. He frequently reported ascents of "Old Baldy": July 14, 1887 — "Mr. Kingsley of Ontario, accompanied by his son and young Mr. Buffington, started on Saturday afternoon for a trip to Baldy, and a week's hunting in the mountains."; July 21, 1887 — "Mr. Thos. Dowse of Ontario has just returned from a trip to Old Baldy." Belle J. Bidwell, one of the canyon campers, described how the ascents were made that summer:

> The more sturdy and ambitious ones think the season not complete unless they climb 'Old Baldy' . . . Few women undertake it, for it is a very rough, hard climb. The men generally make a three-days trip of it, going the ten or twelve miles up the canon the first day, staying overnight at a mining camp at the foot of the mountain, making the ascent the second day, and returning to the camp at night; though some go to the summit the first day to have the pleasure of making a huge bonfire there at night, and of seeing the sun rise the next morning. Those who went in August could not stay long, for they could get no water; but in July there was still snow enough to quench their thirst and give them a chance at snowballing, too.[10]

Crossing "The Narrows" near the top of Old Baldy, ca. 1910.

Spending the night on the 2-mile high bare summit, as some parties did, was often a rather unpleasant experience. The *Pomona Progress* of August 1, 1889 reported such an episode:

> There is still a good deal of snow on top of Old Baldy, so we are informed by some young men who climbed there last week . . . . So cold was it up there one night last week that the party of young men built a great bonfire of the trunks and limbs of pine trees, and even then it was so cold that none of the party could sleep.

Mount San Antonio even managed to become involved in politics.

The *Glendora Signal* of September 10, 1888 reported, "The highest peak of Old Baldy now flies the most elevated Harrison and Morton flag in the United States, in plain view of Glendora with a good glass. The flag was made by a lady of Ontario and carried there by a gentleman of that place." (Harrison and Morton were the Republican candidates for President and Vice President that year, opposed by Democrats Cleveland and Thurman.)

These early ascents of Old Baldy were difficult and strenuous ventures, and only the sturdiest climbers were successful. The usual route of ascent was via the old miners' trail up the head of San Antonio Canyon to "Miners' Camp" — the small cabin settlement at the Banks Mine just south of Baldy Notch, then west over the Devil's Backbone — a precipitous knife-edge forming the east ridge of the mountain — to the summit. Those who climbed Baldy via the Devil's Backbone considered it a harrowing experience. George F. Leavens described it thusly in 1896:

> Had this been, in truth, the spinal column of His Satanic Majesty, we might well have quoted the ribald motto of Denys in 'The Cloister and the Hearth': 'Le Diablo est Mort!', for the dessicated skin was drawn tightly over his ribs, and the bleached vertebral processes protruded in numerous places. Metaphor aside, the sand and small rocks had been blown into ill-defined ridges by the fierce winds that sweep across the upper peaks, and the huge vertical vein or dyke of hard quartz — which is doubtless responsible for the extreme sharpness of the crest — stood out prominently on the steeper portions.
>
> We started rather timorously along the trail. On the north side we looked thousands of feet down into the abrupt-walled Lytle Creek canon . . . . On the south, we looked less abruptly into the San Antonio canon, and could trace its entire course to where its stream debouches into the valley, twelve miles away and 8,000 feet below. We soon came to a steeply-tilted section of the backbone, where we needed our hands to steady us in climbing over the jagged rock . . . .
>
> Before us loomed a rugged, brown-gray cliff, frowning desertward, and well toward a thousand feet in height. We were fearful our trail would lead us across the face of it; but, instead, it brought us around to the south, over a smooth, wind-swept slope of broken rock . . . .
>
> The main peak soon rounded into view, and then came much the longest, steepest and most tedious pull we had yet encountered. We felt keenly the effect of the tenuous atmosphere, and stopped every hundred feet or so to recover breath . . . .
>
> After repeated discouragements we reached the summit, crowned by a monument that has been built by increments from the angular blocks of granite scattered about.[11]

A second route up Old Baldy was forged in 1889 through the initiative and perseverance of two men — Fred Dell of Dell's Camp in San Antonio Canyon, and Dr. B.H. Fairchild of Fairview Ranch north of Claremont. Dell was a hunter when he was not running his camp, and in the course of his wanderings high on the mountain in search of big horn sheep and bear, he discovered a route up the south ridge, via Bear Flat, that he believed would cut the distance to the summit by four miles. This information he imparted to Dr. Fairchild. Fairchild was interested in Mount San Antonio for reasons other than hunting or recreation — he desired to see an astronomical observatory built on the summit. Harvard University astronomers had recently placed a temporary observatory on Mount Wilson and were searching Southern California for a permanent site for a 24-inch refracting telescope. In the spring of 1889 Dr. Fairchild wrote to Harvard

This is the earliest known photograph of Old Baldy's summit, 1889. Fred Dell (pointing) and his party from Dell's Camp built the first summit monument. — POMONA PUBLIC LIBRARY, SPECIAL COLLECTIONS

Harvard University, which had placed a telescope on Mt. Wilson early in 1889, considered placing another one on Mt. Baldy's summit. To inspect the mountain-top site, Harvard astronomer E.S. King (second from left) was escorted up the Fairchild Trail (today's Bear Flats Trail) by a party of Pomona Citizens, led by Fred Dell (sitting, far right). Bad weather hounded the party and discouraged Professor King, who recommended the telescope be placed elsewhere. This was the first horseback ascent of Old Baldy, November 20, 1889. — POMONA PUBLIC LIBRARY, SPECIAL COLLECTIONS

University and urged the university astronomers to look into the possibility of Mount San Antonio as an observatory site. Harvard showed interest in Fairchild's proposal and promised to send Professor E.S. King, then director of the Harvard Observatory on Mt. Wilson, to investigate. But first a horseback trail would have to be built to the summit.

Dr. Fairchild approached Fred Dell concerning the construction of a trail up the south ridge of Baldy to the top. Dell agreed to build the trail with Fairchild's financing. In the summer of 1889, Dell and a party of laborers completed the new horse pathway in remarkably short time. The new trail went from Dell's Camp up Bear Canyon to Bear Flats, then followed a zigzag course to the top of the south ridge, and followed the south ridge to the summit, seven miles in distance with 5,600 feet elevation gain — four miles shorter than the old Devil's Backbone route but much steeper.

In November 1889 Professor King arrived in Claremont and, in company with Dr. Fairchild, Dell and nine other interested valley citizens, set out on horseback for Dell's Camp and the summit of Old Baldy. The weather was clear at first, but as the party climbed high on the mountain, "The apparently insignificant clouds which were noticed about the horizon during the day previous and the early morning had gathered into an impenetrable mass many hundred feet below, completely obscuring the valley beneath; the canyons were enveloped with clouds and fog, and the fierce wind whistled through the trees, catching the fog in the canyons and twisting it into all sorts of fantastic shapes. Snow covered the ground to the depth of four to eight inches, and the bitter cold was anything but pleasant."[12] At 9,550 feet (according to Professor King's barometer) the party stopped and held a council of war. With the weather rapidly deteriorating, it was folly to go on. Two of the younger men made a dash to the summit and back amid snow flurries and gale-force winds, but Professor King had had enough. After making hurried meteorological observations, the party descended as quickly as possible to Dell's Camp, where they warmed themselves before a crackling fire. Next day they returned to Claremont. A few days later Professor King entrained for the East, promising that Harvard University would give proper consideration to Dr. Fairchild's request for an observatory on Old Baldy. An interesting and humorous sidelight to the expedition appeared in the *Pomona Progress* of November 21, 1889: "They say the party that started to accompany Prof. King to the top of Old Baldy had enough antidote for snake bites to last an army as big as Grant's for two months." Rattlesnakes, then as now, infested the lower slopes.

On the summit of Old Baldy, 1889. Notice the party is well equiped with firearms, necessary precaution in an era when grizzles still roamed the mountains.
— EVERETT HAGER COLLECTION

Subsequent Pomona newspapers contained no further mention of the Old Baldy observatory proposal. Needless to say, it was never built.

For many years, the Bear Flat trail was the main route used by parties to ascend Old Baldy, mainly because it was accessible by horseback while the Devil's Backbone route was not. Some climbers utilized both routes, going up one way and back the other. Although the Bear Flat trail was the shortest way to the top, it was exceedingly steep, gaining 5,600 feet of elevation in its seven miles. One particularly bad pitch of loose rock was known to climbers as "Hardscrabble;" another precipitous stretch where the trail crossed a knife-edge ridge was called "The Narrows." Willoughby Rodman of Los Angeles made the climb via Bear Flat in 1903 and described it as follows:

> At Fern (Bear) Flats the real climbing begins. The trail from there on is narrow, though distinct and well worn. For some distance it zigzags up the wall of the canon, coming out upon the southeast side of San Antonio, among large though scattered pines.
>
> Following the edge of the canon about half a mile, the trail reaches one of those very long, sharp ridges which form the approaches to the summit. The climbing was steep, but the view more than compensated for our labors.[13]

Although most parties ascending Old Baldy started from San Antonio Canyon and used either the Bear Flat or Devil's Backbone route, there were also other ways to climb the mountain. Some hikers

Party from Dell's Camp being photographed on the summit of Mt. Baldy, ca. 1894.
POMONA PUBLIC LIBRARY, SPECIAL COLLECTIONS

The mule train from Dell's Camp passing miners' cabins at Baldy Notch enroute to Old Baldy's summit, ca. 1895. Notice the ladies are riding sidesaddle, legacy of the prim and proper Victorian Era.
– EVERETT HAGER COLLECTION

took the northeast approach from Glenn Ranch, following the old miners' road up Lytle Creek to Baldy Notch, then up the Devil's Backbone to the top. From San Gabriel Canyon, Henry Roberts led parties up the peak via the East Fork and Prairie Fork as early as 1889. In the early years of the present century, a rough trail was built up the long southwest ridge of Baldy from Weber's Camp in Coldwater Canyon. With the demise of Weber's Camp in the late 1920s, the trail fell into disuse and disappeared.

Some men raced up Old Baldy. The *Pomona Daily Review* of August 1, 1904 reported: "Fred J. Vaile, a Pomona College football player, can do more than defend the pigskin on the gridiron. He has distinguished himself by taking eight minutes from the Old Baldy climbing record. On Friday morning he made the ascent from Bear Flats to the summit in one hour and forty-nine minutes. This bests Forest Ranger W.S. McFarland's record of one hour and fifty-seven minutes."

The years from approximately 1895 to 1938 were known in the San Gabriel Mountains as "the great hiking era." Every summer weekend saw thousands of hardy outdoor enthusiasts, young and old alike, crowd the mountain trails and resorts. Steep pathways throughout the range reverberated to the tramp of boots and the merry singing of hikers. To serve these high country ramblers, dozens of trail resorts sprang up along shady streams and on forested benches.

The most unusual and fantastic of these trail camps was William B. Dewey's "Baldy Summit Inn." Just when Dewey came up with his idea for a guest camp just eighty yards from the weather-battered summit of Old Baldy is not known, but in the spring of 1910 he took out a Forest Service lease on the top of the mountain and by June his resort was open for business. He first called it "Angel Camp," but soon changed the name to "Baldy Summit Inn," and by this latter designation it became well-known to Southern California hikers. The resort originally consisted of six tents securely anchored against a wind that sometimes reached gale force. Later, to protect food supplies from bear and mountain lion forays, two small stone storehouses were added. Dewey's wife Nannie served as camp chef. Saddle horses and burros brought up guests, supplies and mail from Camp Baldy three times a week, or more often when the traffic demanded. Many guests were mountain climbers who would hike up one afternoon, stay overnight to enjoy the magnificent sunset panorama, and descend on foot the next day. The resort was open for business from June 15th to October 1st during its three years of operation. Rates were a modest one dollar per meal and one dollar per bed. The curtain rang down on this mountaintop hostelry in June 1913, when a fire broke out in the cooking tent and razed most of the tents. Damage was so extensive that Dewey never rebuilt. Baldy Summit Inn soon became just a bygone memory, never forgotten by those select few who once made the trek to this refuge in the clouds.

Still the hikers came, lured into the mountains by the numerous canyon resorts throughout the San Gabriels, the multitude of hiking trails, and the publicity of the Pacific Electric Company. The "PE," organized by Henry Huntington in 1901, built a vast network of trolley lines over much of Southern California. The legendary "Big Red Cars" took hikers to the very foot of the mountains and in one case — the Mt. Lowe Railway — well into the high country. The branch line to San Antonio Heights, just east of the mouth of San Antonio Canyon, gave hikers easy access to Old Baldy. From line's end, they would take the Camp Baldy Stage into the heart of the canyon, then ramble up either the Bear Flats or Devils Backbone trail to the summit.

The ranks of hikers multiplied with the founding of the Angeles Chapter of the Sierra Club in 1911. Phil Bernays, Los Angeles art dealer, joined with Dean Clair Tappaan of the U.S.C. Law School, attorney Willoughby Rodman and attorney William Boland, to get the conservation and hiking organization under way. It was not long until large Sierra Club groups were climbing Old Baldy several times a summer. In 1923, with Forest Service sanction, the Club purchased one of the old miners' cabins at Baldy Notch and turned it into an overnight shelter. The "Baldy Cabin," as the old log shelter became known, was the scene of many weekend revelries, and the focus of early Sierra Club efforts to preserve what wilderness was left in the San Gabriels. Eventually the Baldy Cabin became too small for the

William B. Dewey built the most unusual resort in the San Gabriels on the summit of Old Baldy. His Baldy Summit Inn was open to the public from 1910 to 1913. Here, Dewey is about to set out from Camp Baldy to his mountaintop hostelry in 1911.
– HENRY E. HUNTINGTON PHOTO

Baldy Summit Inn, July 1910. The mountaintop resort camp was nestled among the stunted lodgepole pines, giving it some protection against the high altitude elements. The 10,000-foot summit of Baldy was only 100 yards away. – POST CARD PHOTO

The stone storehouse at Baldy Summit Inn. This was the only solid structure of the camp. – CHARLES CLARK VERNON COLLECTION

The remains of the storehouse at Baldy Summit Inn, 1950. – CHARLES CLARK VERNON PHOTO

William B. Dewey, founder and proprietor of Baldy Summit Inn, on his 133rd ascent of Mt. Baldy, October 14, 1936.

ever-growing Club. It was abandoned in 1928, and two years later, on November 15, 1930, the Aurelia S. Harwood Memorial Lodge was dedicated, in honor of a former Sierra Club president who died in 1928. Spacious Harwood Lodge, built on a five-acre tract leased from the Forest Service at Manker Flat, has ever since been the mountain home of the Sierra Club's Angeles Chapter.

The automobile brought an end to the halcyon days of hiking. A road was constructed to Manker Flats at the head of San Antonio Canyon in 1924-1925, and, from there, the Forest Service built a fire road up to Baldy Notch to join with the old miners' road down to Lytle Creek. In 1935-1936, the C.C.C. constructed the present fine trail across the Devil's Backbone to the summit, with guard rails along the precipitous section, finally taming this knife-edge that so long had frightened the faint-of-heart. Old Baldy was never again quite so isolated nor as wild. With the road to Baldy Notch and the new trail to the top, the old Bear Flat trail fell into disuse and was no longer maintained by the Forest Service. It is still there today, but seldom trod by hikers.

In 1929, a group of Los Angeles businessmen proposed a railroad from Camp Baldy to the summit and a hotel on top, to cost five million dollars. Part of their scheme was to persuade the Pacific Electric Company, whose "Big Red Cars" crisscrossed much of Southern California, to build a branch line to Camp Baldy. Mount Baldy would become another Mount Lowe, with a railroad and hotel complex that would be world famous. Fortunately, the depression

The last of the five log cabins at the Banks Mine, Baldy Notch, 1920. It was built in 1882 and burned in 1932. Pictured here are members of Will Thrall's San Antonio Hiking Club, who camped here the night of May 29, 1920 enroute to the summit of Mt. Baldy. – WILL THRALL PHOTO

Kasper Caspersen and D. D. Chalmers bringing up the stove to the Sierra Club cabin at Baldy Notch, 1927. The old miner's cabin, built in the 1880s was used by the Sierra Club from 1923 until it burned in 1930. NILES WERNER PHOTO

The summit of Mt. Baldy, ca. 1920. The metal sign and new summit register were placed there by the Sierra Club. Vandals removed them within a year.
– HENRY E. HUNTINGTON LIBRARY

The Baldy Lookout was not on Mt. Baldy itself, but 3 miles south on 6812-foot Lookout Peak. The wooden fire lookout was built in 1914-15 through the joint efforts of the San Antonio Water Company, the San Antonio Fruit Exchange and the Forest Service. A trail was built to the top from Camp Baldy via Bear Canyon, and a telephone line installed. The lookout was in operation from 1915 until 1927, when it was damaged by high winds and moved to Sunset Peak. – POMONA PUBLIC LIBRARY, SPECIAL COLLECTIONS

Sierra Club party atop Mt. Baldy, June 1918.

Sierra Club cabin, Baldy Notch 1925.
– POST CARD PHOTO

came along to end this grandiose scheme, and another similar plan to build a highway to the summit.

One of the most important scientific experiments of the 1920s took place on Lookout Mountain, a 6,812-foot high point on the south ridge of Mount Baldy. This was the experiment by Albert A. Michelson, America's first Nobel Prize winner, to determine the speed of light. In 1922, Dr. Michelson set up a rotating octagonal prism on Mt. Wilson, called "Station Michelson." On Lookout Mountain, 22 miles away, he installed a concave mirror two feet in diameter, called "Station Antonio." He then shot a beam of light through the rotating prism at Station Michelson to the mirror at Station Antonio; the light beam was reflected back to Mt. Wilson and the precise time measured. To insure the absolute accuracy of the experiment, it was vital to know the exact distance between the two stations. The distance was measured by the U.S. Coast and Geodetic Survey by triangulation from a 40-kilometer surveyed base line in the valley to the south. To quote William Bowie of the U.S.C.G.S., "It is believed that the length of this line has been determined with greater accuracy than that of any line of triangulation in this or any other country." The possible error in the 22-mile distance between Mt. Wilson and Lookout Mountain was less than one-fourth of an inch! Michelson conducted his experiments between the years 1922 and 1927, using various prism sizes and rotational speeds at Station Michelson. The importance of Dr. Michelson's work was aptly expressed by Albert Einstein during an address at Cal Tech in 1931:

"You, my honored Dr. Michelson, ... led the physicists into new paths, and through your marvelous experimental work paved the way for the development of the Theory of Relativity. Without your work this theory would today be scarcely more than an interesting speculation." Today, three in-line concrete piers, the tallest one 42 inches high with a metal tablet marked "ANTONIO 1922," stand alone amid the brush on Lookout Mountain. They are the sole reminders of one of the most significant scientific experiments of this century.

The most recent chapter in the Mount San Antonio story deals with winter sports. The numerous gentle slopes and natural bowls on the mountain and eastward around Baldy Notch make for superb downhill skiing — at least by Southern California standards. Mt. Baldy has become one of the half-dozen prime winter recreation areas south of the Tehachapis.

With the great popularity of skiing today, it is difficult to realize that in the 1930s — barely five decades ago — the sport was in its infancy in Southern California. Ethel Van Degrift, one of the pioneer local skiers, remembers how it was:

Horseback party on The Narrows, enroute to Baldy Summit, ca. 1916.

> There were so few of us that everyone knew everyone else. Skis were our introduction. We learned to ski by trial and error, cheered each other on, applauding every passable turn and every no-fall run, brushed the snow off each other after spills, coached one another as well as we could, gleaned our rudiments of technique largely from books and pictures. Occasionally we received instruction from an Austrian, Swiss or Norwegian who had learned to ski in Europe.[14]

The first of these transplanted Europeans who introduced skiing to Southern California was George O. Bauwens, a Bavarian who came to Los Angeles about 1920. Bauwens had long enjoyed skiing in his native land, and was surprised and perplexed when he could find no one in L.A. who really knew how to ski, much less join him on winter skiing trips. So he practiced his sport solo. On January 16, 1922 Bauwens drove to Camp Baldy with his long European skis, an object of curiosity to the local residents and resort visitors, and proceeded to make the first ski ascent of Old Baldy. From the summit, he enjoyed a long swish down the natural bowl into upper San Antonio Canyon.

Dr. Walter Mosauer, Austrian-born professor of zoology at U.C.L.A., founded the Ski Mountaineers of California in 1932. Two years later they became the Ski Mountaineers Section of the Sierra Club, Angeles Chapter. Dr. Mosauer, pictured here in 1932, introduced the "Arlberg Technique" of alpine skiing to southern California. – ROBERT C. FRAMPTON PHOTOGRAPH

The real "father" of Southern California skiing was Dr. Walter Mosauer, an Austrian professor of zoology at U.C.L.A. Dr. Mosauer, an enthusiastic and remarkable teacher and skier, began teaching alpine skiing techniques to a number of willing Southern California college students in 1931. By 1933 there was a nucleus of some twenty or thirty local alpine skiers — most of them from U.C.L.A. and Pomona College — who were disciples of Dr. Mosauer. They made frequent winter skiing excursions to the higher local mountains: Old Baldy, San Gorgonio, San Jacinto and the southern High Sierra.

On February 14, 1932 Dr. Mosauer, accompanied by Pomona College students Murray Kirkwood and Lloyd Cooper, made a ski ascent of Old Baldy. They were much impressed with the skiing delights of the natural bowl on the southeast slope of the mountain and foresaw the area becoming a prime winter resort center. Mosauer suggested the building of a ski hut near "Baldy Bowl," as they called it.

In the fall of 1934 Dr. Mosauer was instrumental in organizing the Ski Mountaineers Section of the Sierra Club. This athletic legion of young skiers turned to Baldy Bowl as one of their premier local skiing grounds. On many a winter and spring weekend during the mid-1930s they tested their fast improving skills on the smooth steep snow slopes of the mountain.

To provide overnight lodging adjacent to the ski area, the Sierra Club Ski Mountaineers, in 1935, took out a Forest Service permit and constructed the San Antonio Ski Hut. The steepled, wood-frame structure, perched on a forested ledge at 8,200 feet near the head of San Antonio Canyon, was erected through the volunteer work of Sierra Club members,

An early ski party atop Old Baldy, May 8, 1932. Left to Right: Murray Kirkwood, Robert Frampton, MacDonald Salter, Henry Ware (prone), all of Pomona College, and Walter Mosauer. All were members of Mosauer's Ski Mountaineers of California. – ROBERT C. FRAMPTON PHOTOGRAPH

Baldy Bowl, high on the southeast flank of Mt. Baldy, was a favorite target of the Sierra Club Ski Mountaineers in the 1930s. This photo was taken just above the Sierra Club Ski Hut, 1937. – ETHEL SEVERSON PHOTOGRAPH

most of them college students, each of whom carried daily loads of building materials and tools up from Manker Flat. George Bauwens designed the hut and supervised construction. A fire in 1936 destroyed the ski hut, but it was immediately rebuilt by the Sierra Club skiers.

In March 1935 the first annual Mt. Baldy downhill race was sponsored by the Sierra Club Ski Mountaineers. The course started on Baldy's summit and slalomed down through Baldy Bowl into upper San Antonio Canyon, a distance of two miles with a 1,500-foot drop. Scores of skillful young skiers and a handful of veterans climbed to the top, then raced with wild abandon down the two-mile course, tasting the thrill of victory or the agony of defeat. The winner of that first downhill race was German skier Otto Steiner, with a time of 2 minutes 51 seconds. The race was held every year before World War II, but Steiner's time was never bettered.

The years immediately after World War II witnessed a phenomenal increase in the sport of downhill skiing in Southern California. Thousands of enthusiasts, when winter snows were plentiful, crowded the developed ski resorts — Big Pines in the San Gabriel Mountains, Big Bear and Snow Valley in the San Bernardinos, Mammoth Mountain in the Sierra Nevada. This host of new skiers wanted it the easy way — ready access by paved highway, snack bars and hotels, rope tows and ski lifts. Few of them were of the hardy ski mountaineering breed. New ski resorts, catering to this new host, blossomed all over the Southern California mountains.

The Mt. Baldy area first bloomed as a commercial ski resort in 1944, when a rope tow was placed on what became known as Movie Slope, just above Manker Flats. (The name evolved from a Hollywood motion picture shot there in the 1940s.) Herb Leffler and Jim Chafee pioneered the skiing facilities in the upper canyon, and expanded their efforts until by

The upper half of the slalom course, under the pinnacles in the Big Bowl of Old Baldy, February 11, 1940. Jack Merritt of Pomona College took first place in the slalom. His father, Earle "Fuzz" Merritt, took first in the downhill. – ROBERT C. FRAMPTON, PHOTOGRAPH

Loyd Cooper (left), Claremont photographer, and Dr. Walter Mosauer, UCLA professor and founder of the Ski Mountaineers of California, pause at the spring below the Big Bowl on their unsuccessful attempt to make the first descent of the peak on skis, January 14, 1932. They were stopped by glare ice in the bowl. – ROBERT C. FRAMPTON PHOTOGRAPGH

1952 there were four rope tows, a snack bar and ski rentals. But lack of snow at the lower elevations during many winters made the venture a marginal success at best. Leffler had his eyes on the high divide that separates the San Antonio Canyon drainage from the North Fork of Lytle Creek — Baldy Notch. In June 1952, with a special permit from the Forest Service, work started on a double chair lift from the 6,500-foot canyon head to the 7,800-foot notch. Upon completion of this stage, a second chair lift was built up the northwest slope of Thunder Mountain, reaching an elevation of 8,600 feet. Restaurant and ski rental facilities were built at Baldy Notch. The new complex opened for business that December, and the Baldy region became one of the major winter sports centers in Southern California.

In the 1960s Leffler sold out to a new corporation, headed by former stock broker Charles W. Lewsadder, and named The Mt. Baldy Ski Lifts and Western Resorts, Inc. Under Lewsadder's guidance, the Baldy Notch ski facilities were expanded to include three double chair lifts and five rope tows, offering skiing access to new areas both east and west of the Notch — on Thunder Mountain and adjacent to the Devil's Backbone. The various runs that were opened up ranged from moderately easy to very difficult, sixteen in all. Some of the runs — Mullin's Mile, Bonanza, Blizzard Ridge, Devil's Backbone — rank with the best in Southern California. A new ski school offered expert instruction to beginners.

And there were ambitious plans for the future — too ambitious, in the eyes of conservationists. In

Mary Jane Edwards and Dick Jones carrying lumber up to build the Sierra Club ski hut on Mt. Baldy, 1935. – NELSON NIES PHOTOGRAPH

The original Sierra Club ski hut on Mt. San Antonio, designed by George Bauwens and built by the Ski Mountaineers in 1935. The hut was on a forested bench near the head of San Antonio Canyon, just below Baldy Bowl. This first hut burned in 1936.
– J. R. MINNICH PHOTOGRAPH

Original Sierra Club Mt. San Antonio ski hut, 1936.
– NILES WERNER PHOTOGRAPH

Second Sierra Club Mt. San Antonio ski hut, built in 1936 and still in use by Sierra Club ski and hiking parties.

The Mt. Baldy Ski Lifts, Inc., pioneered by Herb Leffler and Jim Chafee, brought popular skiing to the Mt. Baldy area in 1944. This 1952 photograph shows the lower station of the double chair lift, carrying skiers and sightseers from Manker Flats to Baldy Notch. – MT. BALDY SKI LIFTS, INC. PHOTO

Popular skiing on Movie Slope, 1952. – POST CARD PHOTOGRAPH

1970 Lewsadder came out with a proposal to extend skiing facilities to the summit of Old Baldy. The plan called for the construction of a lift (called 1-B) from the notch to the Devils Backbone, and another lift (1-A) from the Backbone to Stockton Flat at the head of Lytle Creek Canyon. Upon completion of these two projects, construction would start on the key phase of the development — a gondola climbing in two stages from Stockton Flat to a restaurant on the summit of Mt. Baldy seating 1,000 persons. Four chair lifts would provide access to ski runs from the summit down the north slope of the mountain.

These proposals immediately ran into a storm of objections from conservationists. Their main criticism was that the development would threaten the habitat of big horn sheep who make their home around the mountain. They also objected to the destruction of the unique alpine wilderness of Mt. Baldy.

In response to conservationist objections, San Bernardino National Forest supervisor Don R. Bauer refused — for the time being — Lewsadder's request for a permit to build the summit restaurant and gondola lift. But the supervisor did authorize the ski lifts from Baldy Notch to Stockton Flat and the development of lifts and ski runs on the lower north side of the mountain.

Nine years after Supervisor Bauer's decision, work has still not commenced on Stockton Flat-North Slope ski development. Conservationists, particularly the Sierra Club and those supporting the proposed Sheep Mountain Wilderness, are dead set against such a development.

What of the future? Is Old Baldy destined to become a sort of vertical Coney Island? Or will it remain a high alpine wilderness? The destiny of the mountain rests in the hands of the people of Southern California. They are the ultimate guardians of nature's handiwork.

Projecting eastward, then curving south from Old Baldy is the highest mountain backbone in the San

Winter on the Devils Backbone. – AUTHOR PHOTOGRAPH

Gabriels, the grand eastern climax of the range. The high points of this broken ridge all have interesting stories which follow:

MOUNT HARWOOD (9552')

This rounded hogback a mile east of Old Baldy was once known as Little Baldy. In the 1960s the U.S. Board on Geographic Names accepted a Sierra Club request to name it in honor of Aurelia S. Harwood, former president of the Club who died in 1928. Miss Harwood was a resident of Upland most of her life.

THUNDER MOUNTAIN (9598')

This summit between Baldy Notch and Telegraph Peak was unnamed for years. Then, in the early 1950s, two names were proposed almost simultaneously. The Sierra Club offered "Mount Harwood," while the Mt. Baldy Ski Lifts, Inc., which constructed a chair lift on the peak in 1952, suggested the more dramatic "Thunder Mountain." This contest between skiers and conservationists was won by the former, the U.S.B.G.N. deciding in favor of Thunder Mountain.

TELEGRAPH PEAK (9008')

There are two conflicting stories concerning the origin of the name for this high point between Baldy Notch and Icehouse Saddle. (1) In 1896 U.S. Army Signal Corps surveyors installed a heliograph on the peak and signaled to cohorts on Mt. Wilson, 24 beeline miles away. (2) Years ago, a murder was committed in a nearby canyon. A deputy spotted the killer escaping along the canyon rim and climbed the peak to signal the posse. The more accepted story is the first one; the latter tale was given to historian Will Thrall by an old-time San Antonio Canyon prospector.

BIG HORN MOUNTAIN (8441')

Years ago big horn sheep were numerous in the eastern San Gabriels, roaming at will over and around the high peaks. A few survivors can be occasionally observed today. This timbered rise at the north end of the Ontario ridge was named in honor of these hardy dwellers of the lofty crags.

Wind and ice-tortured lodgepole pines near summit of Old Baldy.
– AUTHOR PHOTOGRAPH

ONTARIO PEAK (8693′)

This summit of the long Ontario ridge was named for the horticultural colony established on part of the old Cucamonga Rancho by George and William Chaffey in 1882. The Chaffeys, former residents of Canada, named the colony after their native province of Ontario.

CUCAMONGA PEAK (8859′)

This lofty summit, two miles east of Ontario Peak, guards the eastern terminus of the San Gabriels. Its name is derived from the great Rancho Cucamonga, established in 1839 on the plain to the south, which in turn was named for the old Indian rancheria of Kukil-Mongo. The word is a Shoshonean place name, the meaning of which is obscure. Anthropologists have come up with three possible derivations: (1)sandy place, (2) place of many springs, and (3) lewd woman — from a legend that an Indian chief sent his wayward daughter to live on the peak.

ETIWANDA PEAK (8662′)

This bump on the ridge northeast of Cucamonga Peak was named after the agricultural colony established on Cucamonga Rancho lands in 1881 by the Chaffeys. "Etiwanda" was an old Indian chief who lived near Lake Michigan, and was friend of the Chaffey family.

NOTES

1 Herbert Eugene Bolton, *Anza's California Expeditions,* Vol. II (Berkeley, 1930), p. 346.
2 Phil Townsend Hanna, *The Dictionary of California Place Names (Los Angeles, 1951),* pp. 266-267.
3 Alson J. Smith, *Men Against The Mountains: Jedediah Smith and The Great Southwest Expedition of 1826-29* (New York, 1965), p. 103.
4 John C. Fremont, *Narratives of Exploration and Adventure,* edited by Allan Nevins (New York, 1956), p. 399.
5 Lt. R.S. Williamson, *Report of Explorations in California for Railroad Routes, 1853* (Washington, 1855) Part II (Geological Report), p. 80.
6 J.D. Whitney, *Geological Survey of California* (Sacramento, 1865), Vol. I (Geology), p. 173.
7 *U.S. Coast and Geodetic Survey Report, 1869-1870* (Washington, 1870), p. 39.
8 *U.S. Coast and Geodetic Survey Report, 1873-1874* (Washington, 1874), p. 36.
9 Dorothy Evans Noble, "Old Man Vincent," typescript in U.S. Forest Service Big Pines Ranger Station, cited by Pearl Comfort Fisher, *The Mountaineers* (San Bernardino, 1972), pp. 51-52.
10 Belle J. Bidwell, "Our Camp in The Canon," *Overland Monthly,* X (Second Series) (August 1887), p. 150.
11 George F. Leavens, "By Way of The Devil's Backbone," *Land of Sunshine* (August 1896), pp. 96-98.
12 *Pomona Daily Times,* November 25, 1889
13 Willoughby Rodman, "The Ascent of San Antonio," *Sierra Club Bulletin,* V, 2 (June 1904), pp. 126-128.
14 Ethel Van Degrift, "The Way It Was," *Westways* (February 1965).

13

Wilderness

For me, and for thousands with similar inclination, the most important passion in life is the overpowering desire to escape periodically from the clutches of a mechanistic civilization. To us the enjoyment of solitude, complete independence, and the beauty of undefiled panorama is absolutely essential to happiness.

Robert Marshall (1901-1939)

Robert Marshall — forester, conservationist and pioneer wilderness defender — wrote these words some forty-five years ago, but for many people the same passion holds true today. To these individuals, the enjoyment of wilderness is the most satisfying form of recreation. To spend a weekend in the forest primeval, away from highways, resorts and noisy public campgrounds, with only the natural sounds of earth — the wind rustling pine needles, the stream dancing over boulder and cascade, the soft antiphony of Clark's nutcracker, the deer darting through the forest — is pure pleasure for the wilderness buff. More and more urban Americans are discovering that the nourishment afforded by wilderness is a redeeming and enriching experience.

True wilderness is hard to find in Southern California. The desert, once a stronghold of undisturbed nature, is being overrun with off-road vehicles and gun enthusiasts. Fortunately, the local mountains contain isolated, difficult-of-access areas that still possess wilderness values. The federal government has seen fit to set aside some of this mountain country for preservation. In the San Gabriels there are two such wilderness areas, with a third in the process of being set aside.

The San Gabriel Wilderness encompasses the twin watersheds of Devils and Bear canyons, deep in the heart of the mountains, 36,000 acres of ridge and canyon terrain blanketed by chaparral. Only three trails penetrate the wilderness, giving access to the delightful watery haunts of Devils and Bear creeks. Although civilization is just over the ridge, this primitive sanctuary remains as wild as ever, guarded by nearly-impenetrable chaparral.

In contrast, the Cucamonga Wilderness at the eastern end of the range is a high sub-alpine region, bounded by 8,000-foot peaks, pine-forested, precipitous and view-encompassing. This lofty primitive country, administered by San Bernardino National Forest, extends from the Telegraph-Ontario Peak ridge eastward some three miles to Cucamonga Peak, and includes the rugged headwaters of Lytle Creek's Middle Fork, some 5,000 acres in all.

In both of these wilderness areas the works of man are kept to a minimum: a few trails and primitive campgrounds. Entry is by wilderness permit only.

It would be nice to report that the San Gabriel and Cucamonga wilderness areas were set aside through the initiative and wise foresight of local forest officials, but such was not the case. Both Rushton Charleton and S.A. Nash-Boulden, supervisors of Angeles and San Bernardino National Forests respectively in the 1920s, were Gifford Pinchot conservation-for-use disciples and saw little need for wilderness preservation. The impetus for this preservation came on the national level.

On the national scene, the Forest Service, in the 1920s, had several enlightened spokesmen who preached the value of wilderness preservation. Foremost among these men was Aldo Leopold, brilliant graduate of Yale Forestry School and at the time a forester stationed in Albuquerque, New Mex-

High on the Ontario Ridge, Cucamonga Wilderness. Old Baldy is framed between two weather-beaten lodgepole pines. – BETTY DESSERT PHOTOGRAPH

ico. Leopold proclaimed that undeveloped sections of the national forests were as much an asset as the timber, water, forage and minerals — a revolutionary concept among foresters at the time. Through Leopold's efforts, the Gila Primitive Area in Arizona was established in 1924 — the first national forest wilderness in the United States.

Aldo Leopold's persistence, along with that of a young and upcoming forester named Robert Marshall, finally caused the Forest Service leadership to consider wilderness preservation as a worthy goal. William B. Greeley, Chief Forester of the United States, and his deputy L.F. Kneipp were converts. The two initiated a survey of wilderness lands under Forest Service jurisdiction. In late 1926, Greeley asked all the national forest regions in the U.S. to submit a list of suitable forest lands for wilderness protection.

Paul G. Redington, regional forester based in San Francisco, requested all of the California national forests under his jurisdiction to submit such a list. Angeles and San Bernardino National Forest officials delayed almost a year before answering. Supervisor Nash-Boulden finally recommended three areas in San Bernardino National Forest for wilderness preservation — San Gorgonio Mountain, San Jacinto Peak, and Cucamonga Peak. George Cecil, who had replaced Charleton as Angeles National Forest supervisor, recommended only the Devils Canyon-Bear Canyon area.

In July 1929 Chief U.S. Forester Greeley issued Forest Service Regulation L-20 — a landmark in conservation history — providing for the establishment of Primitive Areas "within which will be maintained primitive conditions of environment, transportation, habitation, and subsistence, with a view to conserving the value of such areas for purposes of public education, inspiration, and recreation."

In accordance with Regulation L-20, Chief Forester Greeley proclaimed 14 million acres of national forest land in the United States as "primitive areas" on April 23, 1931. Among these were two in the San Gabriel Mountains: The Devils Canyon-Bear Canyon Primitive Area, and the Cucamonga Primitive Area. Protection for these

Big horn sheep in the East Fork of San Gabriel Canyon, within the proposed Sheep Mountain Wilderness.
– GLEN OWENS PHOTOGRAPH

two pristine sanctuaries finally came about, thanks to enlightened Forest Service leadership.

In the mid-1930s, the two primitive areas were made more accessible through the work of the Civilian Conservation Corps (C.C.C.), a New Deal federal work relief program for unemployed young men. C.C.C. boys hacked out trails into Devils and Bear canyons, and from Icehouse Saddle to Cucamonga Peak. Trail camps were built in Devils and Bear canyons.

The old "primitive area" designation was changed to "wild area" in 1941, to better express the wilderness purpose of the protected sanctuaries. It was now the Devils Canyon-Bear Canyon Wild Area, and the Cucamonga Wild Area.

The final major administrative change came with the passage of the Wilderness Act in 1964, its purpose "to secure for the American people of present and future generations the benefits of an enduring resource of wilderness." Wilderness was defined as "an area where the earth and its community of life are untrammeled by man, where man himself is a visitor who does not remain." Secure, permanent protection was extended to millions of acres of American wilderness; only an act of Congress could alter this protection. In accordance with the new act, the Devils Canyon-Bear Canyon Wild Area was renamed the San Gabriel Wilderness, and the Cucamonga Wild Area became the Cucamonga Wilderness.

The precipitous mountain country around the head of the San Gabriel River's East Fork is presently in the process of gaining wilderness status, although its exact boundaries have yet to be agreed upon. This upper East Fork region and its surrounding peaks — 9,399-foot Mt. Baden-Powell on one side, 10,064-foot Old Baldy on the other — is the summer home of one of the largest herds of Nelson big horn sheep in the state. To protect these "statuesque masters of the lofty crags," and to preserve some of the wildest mountain country left in Southern California, the Sheep Mountain Wilderness has been proposed and accepted by the Forest Service. The new wilderness needs only the approval of Congress to become reality.

The Sheep Mountain Wilderness has been a long

High in the Cucamonga Wilderness. – AUTHOR PHOTOGRAPH

time in reaching fulfillment. The first proposal to preserve the East Fork headwaters was voiced by the Azusa Chamber of Commerce in 1935. The "San Gabriel Gorge Primitive Area" proposal was supported by the Sierra Club and several hiking organizations, but it never got beyond the talking stage.

The idea lay dormant for some thirty years, until the Sierra Club renewed its support of the wilderness proposal in the late 1960s. A group of concerned conservation-minded citizens formed the Sheep Mountain Task Force in 1972, and began working energetically to get a wilderness designation for the area. Their efforts were rewarded in 1976, when President Ford signed a bill creating the Sheep Mountain Wilderness Study Area. This was followed by three years of scientific study, public hearings and voluminous correspondence. The major dispute among wilderness supporters and opponents was over the size of the proposed wilderness. Conservationists asked for 52,000 acres, while mining and skiing interests wanted less than 25,000 acres set aside. The Forest Service proposed a 30,400-acre enclave surrounding the East Fork headwaters, from Mount Baden-Powell east to Mt. Baldy's summit.

Although the Sheep Mountain Wilderness seems assured, its size, as of this writing, has not been determined. In November 1979 Congressman Jim Lloyd of the 35th District, encompassing the Claremont-Pomona area, introduced a Sheep Mountain Wilderness bill to set aside 45,000 acres. It remains to be seen whether Congress will support a bill such as Lloyd's or opt for a more modest proposal as urged by developers and miners.

In the continuing struggle between those who would develop and those who would preserve the mountains, the question arises as to just where the balance should lie. How much should be made accessible by highways and ski lifts, built upon, mined? If we choose wholesale development over preservation, the decision is irrevocable. You do not open up a wilderness; you either keep it wild, or you lose it. Wallace Stegner has written: "... it has never been man's gift to make wildernesses. But he can make deserts, and has."

Looking east over the San Gabriel Wilderness. Old Baldy in distance. – CHARLES KASSLER PHOTOGRAPH

14

Lytle Creek

Three-pronged Lytle Creek drains the far eastern end of the San Gabriel Mountains. The three canyons that become one were formed in prehistoric times by torrents that gushed down from glaciers and snowfields high on the back-side of Old Baldy, Telegraph and Cucamonga peaks, then flowed southeastward along the deeply-grooved lines of the San Jacinto Fault Zone, finally to empty into the San Bernardino Valley. Today the North Fork, the largest branch of Lytle Creek, rises from springs in the Happy Jack area; only in time of flood does it flow all the way from its head under Old Baldy. The Middle and South forks are both fed by icy springs high in the mountains. Most of the main canyon is a broad boulder wash,the result of periodic flooding. Located here and there — particularly around the great double bend of the North Fork — are beautiful streamside benches, lush green with foliage.

In ancient times Lytle Creek Canyon was the home of the San Sevaine Indians, a small subgroup of the Serranos who inhabited the San Bernardino Valley and adjacent mountains. Archaeological research indicates that there were aboriginal villages at the present site of the ranger station, on the little flat at the confluence of the North and South forks, and on the big mesa now occupied by Glenn Ranch. There was probably an Indian summer camp amid the white oaks on San Sevaine Flats, high on the ridge south of the canyon. Evidence of these ancient habitations is in the form of mortars, manos (hand stones) and other primitive implements found by early canyon settlers.

In Spanish and Mexican days Lytle Creek was known as "Arroyo de los Negros" (Creek of the Blacks). The derivation of this name is unknown. The lower section of the creek was within the Muscupiabe land grant given by Mexican Governor Micheltorena to Michael White, a transplanted Englishman, in 1843. Three years later Pio Pico, last Mexican governor of California, granted three square leagues adjacent to Muscupiabe, including part of lower Lytle Creek Canyon, to Ignacio Coronel. (This grant was later disallowed by the U.S. Land Office.) There is no evidence that White, Coronel, or any Mexican *Californio,* showed any interest in the canyon, other than utilizing the water that flowed from it into the San Bernardino Valley.

It was the Mormons who first showed an interest in Lytle Creek. In 1851 Brigham Young dispatched three companies of his Latter Day Saints to found a colony in the San Bernardino Valley. Commanding one of these companies was Captain Andrew Lytle. After a difficult journey across the desert from Utah, Lytle and his men crossed Cajon Pass and on June 20, 1851 set up camp in a beautiful grove of sycamores at the mouth of "an imposing and dark canyon." From this camp they explored the valley as far west as Cucamonga Creek, looking for a favorable site for the colony. Lytle's company fished and hunted along the abundant creek that flowed past their camp, and when the decision was finally made to establish the colony at San Bernardino, a few of the men decided to stay. They would make their home along "Lytle's Creek," as the stream and canyon became known. (Captain Andrew Lytle left for San Bernardino and, as far as is known, was never again associated with the creek named for him.)

The first Mormon settler to claim land in Lytle Creek Canyon was probably Almon Clyde, although the evidence is inconclusive. Legend has it that the first canyon dweller arrived with a wagon so badly wrecked that he could not get out, so he remained,

Looking up the North Fork of Lytle Creek. Glenn Ranch in foreground.

– C.W. MCLAUGHLIN PHOTO

built a crude log cabin on the lush flat where Glenn Ranch now stands, and a year later traded his property rights for a new wagon. Whether or not this story is true, it is known that Clyde crossed the ridge into Lone Pine Canyon and homesteaded the ranch that still bears his name.

Nathan Wixom and his sons David and Willard were the next to settle on the verdant flat where the North Fork makes its first big bend. The Wixoms built a cabin, cleared the land, and planted a little orchard of apples and pears. They were just settling down to enjoy the fruits of their labor when Brigham Young, in 1857, ordered all the Mormon faithful back to Salt Lake. An invasion by the U.S. Army was thought to be imminent. The Wixoms reluctantly returned to Utah but didn't stay long. They found themselves in disagreement with church authorities over plural marriages and, eluding forcible detention, set out for Southern California during the night. (This was a time of rift in the Mormon Church; the Wixoms adhered to the Reorganized branch which opposed polygamy.) David and Willard Wixom returned to their Lytle Creek ranch but didn't stay long, leaving sometime around 1860. The next owner of the flat was W.W. Maxey, who acquired the land by possessory claim in 1862.

Several other Mormon families, their names unknown, also found homes in Lytle Creek Canyon around this time. They were industrious workers and it was not long until most of the little verdant benches in the lower canyon were under cultivation. Apples grown in the canyon found a ready market in San Bernardino.

It is said that two participants in the Mountain Meadows Massacre in southern Utah in 1857 fled to Lytle Creek and hid in the upper reaches of the canyon. Later they supposedly climbed over the ridge and built the first cabin in Prairie Fork.

Big game was plentiful in the upper reaches of Lytle Creek. The *Los Angeles Star* of April 19, 1862 reported, "Messrs. Warren Hall, W. Runk and two other gentlemen went out on a hunting expedition, from which they returned this week, bringing three bears and two deer. The range visited was in the mountains of Lytle Creek. So abundant was the game that the party sighted nine bears at one time. They killed four of them, but were compelled to stop the hunt for want of means to pack out the carcasses."

The pastoral calm of Lytle Creek was rudely shaken when gold was discovered in the creek gravels in early 1864 (See *A Century of Mining*). Several hundred prospectors and hopefuls hurried into the canyon, tore up the streambed and squatted on ranch property, causing some friction with the Mormon settlers. At least two deaths occurred in disputes involving the miners: John Abbott shot Robert Kier, whom he accused of claim jumping, in 1864; and Fabien Abadie was murdered after trying to repair the five-mile flume of the Texas Point hydraulic mine in 1873. The long flume was a point of contention during seasons of low water in the creek, as it diverted precious water needed by other canyon miners and settlers.

There is some evidence that horsethieves used upper Lytle Creek as a refuge for stolen animals. The *Los Angles News* of October 28, 1865 alleged that the notorious Mason and Henry gang of horsethieves had a hideout "near the source of Litel [sic] creek," where they managed to elude posses sent to apprehend them by disappearing over the ridges behind Old Baldy. San Sevaine Flats was also reputed to have been a hideout for stolen horses. Horsethievery was of epidemic proportions in the San Bernardino, Pomona and San Gabriel valleys during the 1850s and '60s.

Renegade desert Indians were also a problem. With federal troops withdrawn to fight the Civil War, Mojave and Paiute warriors became bolder in stealing horses and harassing desert travelers. Several Lytle Creek settlers and miners joined San Bernardino residents in forming an Indian-fighting posse. David Wixom was one of twenty who surprised and defeated 150 Paiutes in the decisive "Battle of the Mojave River" in 1866. Never again were desert Indians a serious threat to the valley ranchers.

The year 1865 saw the arrival of Silas Glenn and his large family, the most famous name in the long history of Lytle Creek. Silas Glenn, his wife Mourning, and their five children left Texas in 1860 and accompanied a wagon train over the Butterfield Trail to Southern California. The Glenns settled first in El Monte, but a short time later moved to the San Bernardino area. Sometime before 1865 they relocated on twenty acres near Cajon Pass, naming their new home the Cajon Rancho. On one of his hunting trips, Silas Glenn climbed over the ridge and looked down upon the enchanting green bench where the North Fork of Lytle Creek makes its first big bend. He purchased a portion of the flat from W.W. Maxey and moved his family over the ridge. He sold his Cajon Ranch to two San Bernardino men named Keene and Bailey, who renamed the ranch Keenbrook, a name preserved in the Keenbrook Station on the Santa Fe Railroad.

Glenn Ranch quickly became the garden spot of the canyon. Silas Glenn and his sons expanded the area under cultivation, doubled the size of the orchard, built a barn and other buildings, and raised a large herd of cattle. In 1873 he filed a possessory claim to 160 acres of the North Fork. No other ranch in the San Gabriel Mountains was as large nor as profitable.

Silas Glenn died in 1878, and his aging widow turned the management of the ranch over to her daughter and her husband, Mr. and Mrs. James Applewhite. In the 1880s, the Applewhites turned Glenn Ranch into a resort, complete with guest cabins, a dining room, and stable horses. Guests were brought over the ridge via stage from the Keenbrook Station of the Santa Fe Railroad. At the ranch, they could enjoy trout fishing, ride the canyon trails, or bathe in the warm mineral springs a mile down-canyon. Glenn Ranch became one of the premier mountain resorts in Southern California, and remained so for over seventy years.

Mother Glenn, the grand old lady of Lytle Creek, came into the canyon in 1865 with her husband Silas and founded Glenn Ranch. She reigned over the quarrelsome Glenn family until her death in 1905.
– ARDA M. HAENSZEL PHOTOGRAPH

Meanwhile, Lytle Creek attracted other settlers. John H. Miller filed on land now occupied by the ranger station. On the hillside immediately above were the warm springs, long a popular canyon attraction. Miller put in a bath house and tubs and charged a small fee for their use. Most of his customers were guests from Glenn Ranch. In 1895 he lost his patent through some irregularity and was obliged to leave.

Harvey Bradshaw, a Civil War veteran, settled on the little flat near the confluence of the North and South forks and grew vegetables he sold to Glenn Ranch. Later this verdant spot became the Green Mountain Ranch, and still later, Green Mountain Inn.

Guests at Glenn Ranch, 1895. Second and third from the left are James M. Applewhite and wife. Standing first on left is James Oliver Applewhite. Douglas Champion is the barefoot boy in the tree. – WILL THRALL COLLECTION

The Lytle Creek road, ca. 1912. The road needed repair every spring, thanks to high water in the creek. – POST CARD PHOTO

Just downstream from Glenn Ranch, Charles B. Hughes filed on a quarter section in 1894 and planted vegetables and a fruit orchard. The Scotts, later owners, subdivided the land for cabin lots. The cluster of cabins and stores then became known as Scotland.

Across the creek and upstream from Glenn Ranch was the home of "Happy Jack" Pollard. Happy Jack, whose real name was Joseph, came to Lytle Creek as a gold miner in 1888. He left, then returned in 1905 and built his ranch. It wasn't long until Happy Jack was known and loved by almost all the canyon dwellers for his geniality and humor.

Near the headwaters of Lytle Creek, a number of timber claims were filed in the late 1880s. Joseph Crosland took out a patent on the heavy growth of big cone spruce in Grizzly Gulch, a branch of the North Fork about four miles upstream from Glenn Ranch. William H. Stockton, one of the early San Bernardino pioneers, filed on the sloping, pine-covered bench way up at the head of the North Fork, known today as Stockton Flat. As far as is known, Stockton did no cutting and the flat later reverted to the Forest Service.

Also in the 1880s, a rough wagon road was carved all the way up the North Fork of Lytle Creek to its head at Baldy Notch, the site of the James Banks gold mine. The road was used to bring supplies and equipment, including heavy mining machinery, to the notch and haul gold-bearing ore out. The final stretch of the road was exceedingly steep and rocky, and many a wagon broke loose and was shattered on the rocks.

High on the ridge south of Lytle Creek is a charming mountain flat nourished by a cold spring and shaded by oak, spruce, cedar and pine. As early as the 1860s, cattle were driven up the mountainside from the mouth of Lytle Creek to fatten themselves on the lush grasses of the flat. Mountain lions were a constant menace. To protect the cattle from the big cats, rifle-toting cowboys patrolled the flat night and day. The first name associated with the flat was that of George Foote, who gained a possessory claim and built a small cabin there sometime in the early 1870s. San Bernardino County records reveal that Foote sold the flat to Michael Sainsevain in 1878. Sainsevain, previously, had bought the land at the foot of the mountains west of Lytle Creek from Thomas Hawker in 1874.

The Sainsevain family of French winemakers was well known in the San Bernardino Vally in the 1870s. The brothers Jean-Louis and Pierre Sainsevain arrived in Los Angeles in the 1840s and quickly established themselves as premier winemakers.

Stockton Flat, at the head of Lytle Creek's North Fork, was filed upon by William H. Stockton in 1888. His purpose was timber cutting, but as far as is known he cut down no trees. – C. W. MCLAUGHLIN PHOTOGRAPH

Old miner's cabin at Stockton Flat, ca. 1890.

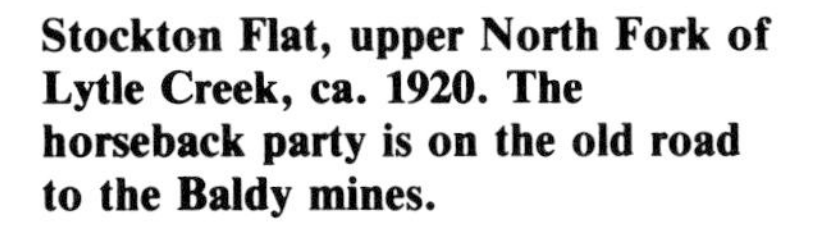

Stockton Flat, upper North Fork of Lytle Creek, ca. 1920. The horseback party is on the old road to the Baldy mines.

About 1865 the brothers were contracted to operate the winery and vineyards of Rancho Cucamonga, which they proceeded to develop into one of the major winemaking enterprises in Southern California. Another family member, Paul Sainsevain, had a winery in San Bernardino.

The Sainsevain brothers' vineyard was located in the northeastern part of Rancho Cucamonga, right at the foot of the mountains. Water was first obtained from San Sevaine and Cucamonga canyons. When these sources proved inadequate, Pierre Sainsevain built an elaborate flume system to tap several springs high on the mountain. His most ambitious project was to dig a well on the flat atop the mountain ridge and connect it with his vineyards far below by a network of ditches and wooden flumes. The ambitious enterprise proved a failure, probably because of the technical problems involved in transporting water so far down the mountain. It seems also likely that the water supply on the flat was inadequate except in seasons of heavy rainfall. Today, this fascinating but short-lived venture is remembered in the name San Sevaine Flats (the name corrupted from French to Spanish by an unknowing and careless government map-maker around the turn of the century), a verdant glen atop the eastern crest of the San Gabriels.

Two miles west of San Sevaine Flats, on the crest above the South Fork of Lytle Creek, is a grove of unusually large sugar pines. One of these, 7′ 6″ in diameter, is believed to be the largest conifer in Southern California. It is named the Joe Elliot Tree, in honor of the supervisor of San Bernardino National Forest from 1929 to 1935. To commemorate Elliot's efforts in forest conservation, the County of San Bernardino and San Bernardino National Forest dedicated this memorial in his honor on October 12, 1935.

No account of Lytle Creek history would be complete without reference to the "Battle of Glenn Ranch," in which two sons of Silas Glenn were slain in the blazing climax of a bitter family feud. The feud pitted James Applewhite and his son Oliver against John and Silas Glenn, Jr., both of whom had departed the ranch and were living in Bloomington, a small town west of San Bernardino, in the early 1890s. The Glenn boys, although no longer residing at the ranch, considered it their property and thought of James and Oliver Applewhite, husband and son of the elder Glenn's daughter who now managed the ranch, as interlopers. The bitter feelings were further inflamed by personality differences and marital difficulties which the Glenn boys blamed on Oliver Applewhite.

On Friday, June 23, 1893, John and Silas Glenn, Jr. went up to the ranch with the avowed intention of having it out with James Applewhite and his son. Finding that the Applewhites were gone, the boys went back down the road to the lower ranch gate to await the formers' return. Old Mother Glenn was extremely disturbed by the smoldering feud between her two sons and her son-in-law and grandson. When Oliver arrived that night, over the ridge from Keenbrook instead of by the canyon road, she warned him to stay out of sight.

Historian Will Thrall, who was in the canyon at the time and later studied court records, tells what happened next:

> About 10 A.M. the next day, Saturday, June 24, John and Silas returned to the house and asked for Oliver, stating that they knew he was somewhere about and, on being told that he was not there, started a quarrel with his father. Both were armed and threatening what they would do, while their mother and sister did their best to calm them down and avert a tragedy.
>
> Fearing the trouble was about to start, Oliver, also armed with a revolver, came up from the barn where he had been hiding to stand by his father. John, catching sight of him, exclaimed, 'take that damn you' and shot as he spoke. But those few words and the seconds they took cost him his life for, though the shots sounded as one, the sixteen year old boy was a split-second first and his Uncle died with a bullet through the heart.
>
> In these few seconds the father ducked into the house, picked up a handy shotgun, and coming through the front door downed Silas with a charge of buckshot. He died from his several wounds two days later, on June 26.[1]

An inquest was held at Glenn Ranch later that month. Evidence was brought forth that the Glenn boys had many times threatened to "get" the Applewhites, and that they had lain in wait all night at the ranch gate with loaded revolvers. The killing of John and Silas Jr. was judged to be self-defense, and James and Oliver Applewhite were exonerated by the judge. But no verdict could have pleased everyone in the canyon, and the "Battle of Glenn Ranch" was argued back and forth for years afterward.

Despite the tragedy, Glenn Ranch continued as a popular guest resort, managed by James Applewhite. In fact, the shooting was publicized all over Southern California and for a while appeared to increase attendance. Advertisements offered room and board for $1.50 per day, or $9.50 per week. "Guests will be met at Keenbrook Station on the Santa Fe Railroad, two miles from the ranch, when notice is received two days in advance," the ad stated.

Mother Glenn passed away in 1905, as did James Applewhite a year later. Mrs. Applewhite attempted to manage the ranch herself but the job was too big. In 1908 she leased Glenn Ranch to Douglas and

Glenn Ranch, founded by Silas and Mourning Glenn in 1865, long was famous as a tourist resort. This scene, looking northeast, dates from about 1923.

The rustic, farm-like atmosphere of Glenn Ranch, ca. 1938. POST CARD PHOTO

The barn at Glenn Ranch. – POST CARD PHOTO

Glenn Ranch brochures, dating from 1915 to 1952. The resort was well advertised in southern California.

Thomas Champion. Douglas Champion had been raised on the ranch by Mother Glenn and considered almost part of the family. When Mrs. Applewhite died in 1912, her will gave a half-interest in the ranch to Douglas Champion, the other half to her nephew Theodore Harper. The resort was run by Champion and Harper until 1921 when it was sold to Seymour and Barbara Tally.

Under the gracious Tallys, Glenn Ranch reached its apogee as a popular resort. A swimming pool and tennis courts were added, as were facilities for croquet, badminton and shuffleboard. Moonlight dances were staged in the patio of the spacious new lodge built by the Tallys. A stable of saddle horses provided opportunities for mountain trail riding. Trout fishing in Lytle Creek was ever popular. By the late 1920s, Glenn Ranch was crowded with happy guests the year around. Reservations were required well in advance, and on holiday weekends the waiting list was long.

The halcyon days could not last forever. In the 1930s several factors combined that started beautiful Glenn Ranch on the downward path. The depression took its toll, sharply cutting the number of guests in the early '30s. The age of the automobile and high speed highways cut attendance at almost all the mountain resorts; people could drive up and back in a day and there was no need to stay overnight. The terrible flood of March 2, 1938, although doing minimal damage to the ranch situated well away from the creek, wreaked havoc on most of Lytle Creek Canyon, destroying scores of cabins and almost obliterating the village of Scotland. The canyon road was almost impassable for months. Hardly had the road been repaired than World War II broke out, and resorts everywhere were closed for the duration.

Still, the Tallys hung on. After the war there was a revival, and verdant Glenn Ranch again echoed to the merry chatter and songs of contented guests. Although there was a nucleus of people who returned time and again, the crowds who thronged the ranch in the 1920s never returned. The resort, during the late 1940s, was a marginal operation at best.

In 1952 Seymour and Barbara Tally, after thirty-one years of "Glenn Ranching," sold the resort to Lloyd A. Frederick, Sr. and Jr. of Beverly Hills. The Fredericks continued the Tally tradition of "good food, fun and friendship" through the 1950s, and even expanded the accommodations, but the crowds of yesteryear never returned. The Fredericks finally subdivided portions of the original two quarter sec-

Glenn Ranch in winter, ca. 1938. – POST CARD PHOTO

Off for a horseback ride at Glenn Ranch.

tions of Glenn Ranch. They sold the portion that included the Glenn Ranch buildings, but continued to operate the remaining southern half of the ranch as a resort, less a small area that was subdivided for residential properties. The Fredericks dredged a swampy area and put in two small lakes for fishing, swimming and boating. It was first called Sportsmans' Park, and later Lloyd's Lakes.

The northern portion of the ranch that included the old resort buildings has had a series of owners, the most recent being Bob Burlingame. Burlingame bought the ranch in 1979 and immediately began restoring as many of the old buildings as possible. Some were termite-ridden and beyond redemption. The old Glenn residence with the bullet hole in the door was lost.

In 1980 Burlingame purchased the recreational area from the Fredericks, so that except for the small residential subdivision, the old Glenn Ranch property is once again under single ownership. Burlingame is presently retaining the old buildings' section for his own use, and has renamed Lloyd's Lakes "Mountain Lakes" and turned it into a membership recreational vehicle park.

Today, some five hundred people live the year around in Lytle Creek Canyon. The major population center is Happy Jack. The Post Office was moved here from Glenn Ranch in the early 1950s.

Lloyd's Lakes at Glenn Ranch, dredged from a swampy area by Lloyd A. Frederick. – POST CARD PHOTO

Happy Jack, main population center of Lytle Creek. The post office was moved here from Glenn Ranch in the early 1930s. – POST CARD PHOTO

San Sevaine Flats, high on the ridge south of Lytle Creek, was named for French winemaker Pierre Sainsevain, who operated a Ranch Cucamonga winery and tapped the springs here for his vineyards in the valley below in the 1870s.

The Joe Elliot Tree, a mammoth sugar pine 7 feet, 6 inches in diameter, believed to be the largest conifer in southern California. The tree, located two miles west of San Sevaine Flats, is named in honor of the supervisor of San Bernardino National Forest from 1929 to 1935. – ROBERT C. FRAMPTON PHOTOGRAPH

Big Horn Lodge, a small tourist camp on the Middle Fork of Lytle Creek, catered to hikers in the 1920s. Today the site is known as Stonehouse Trail Camp. – NILES WERNER PHOTO

The Lytle Creek Ranger Station, San Bernardino National Forest

Bonita Falls, beautiful double falls in a side-canyon of Lytle Creek's South Fork. – C. W. MCLAUGHLIN PHOTOGRAPH

The second largest community is Scotland. There are two stores here: Scotland, a local landmark of many years, serves fast foods and has a small grocery section; and Dale's Market, of recent origin, offers meals, cocktails and groceries. On the point of land between the confluence of the Middle and South forks is Bonita "village." Bonita Campground, which adjoins the village, is a privately-managed recreational vehicle campground on government lease land. A large Forest Service public campground occupied the site before the great flood of 1938. Across the South Fork from Bonita is Green Mountain Inn, boasting a restaurant and a trout pond.

San Bernardino National Forest has a spacious ranger station just below the canyon's first big bend, below the old warm springs. There are two Forest Service public campgrounds in Lytle Creek Canyon: Applewhite, located on the North Fork just upstream from Glenn Ranch, and Big Horn, at Stockton Flats near the North Fork's head.

A popular hike is from Bonita village to Bonita Falls, a beautiful double waterfall located in a small side-canyon of the South Fork. Unfortunately, the idyllic spot holds danger; several hikers have been killed in past years trying to climb the upper falls. Another popular trail goes up the Middle Fork from road's end into the scenic Cucamonga Wilderness, entry by permit only.

Lytle Creek remains an enchanting and delightful enclave at the eastern end of the San Gabriel Mountains.

1. Will Thrall, "Lytle Creek Canyon from the Indian Days to 1900," *Historical Society of Southern California Quarterly,* XXXII, 3 (September 1950), p. 247.

15
Wrightwood And Big Pines

The great San Andreas Rift Zone cuts a bee-line swath along the desert side of the San Gabriels, forming a series of parallel mountain valleys. Deepest and most scenic of these fault-carved depressions is the Swarthout Valley, the location of the mountain communities of Wrightwood and Big Pines. The country here is clothed in tall Jeffrey pines and white fir, with a scattering of juniper and pinon pine on the lower slopes. Aromatic desert sage provides much of the ground cover. The cool, dry air, along with the rich blend of mountain and desert environment, have attracted many to this delightful valley on the north slope of the San Gabriels.

As far as is known, the first to settle in this mountain valley were the Mormon brothers Nathan and Truman Swarthout. The brothers left the main Mormon settlement of San Bernardino shortly after its founding in 1851 and homesteaded in Lone Pine Canyon, a long, straight valley wedged between Lytle Creek and Cajon Canyon. A few months later they crossed the divide to the northwest into the beautiful forested basin named for them. Here the Swarthouts fashioned a wilderness home, building a small cabin, growing vegetables and herding cattle. When Brigham Young summoned his faithful back to Salt Lake in 1857, the devout brothers heeded the call and abandoned their homestead. One son, George Swarthout, remained, herding cattle in Swarthout Valley until his death in 1872.

In 1863 Almon Clyde crossed the ridge from Lytle Creek and filed a claim on the old Swarthout homestead in Lone Pine Canyon. Clyde built a ranch house next to a lone pine tree in mid-canyon (from whence the name Lone Pine Canyon is derived) and planted apple trees. It was not long until apples from the Clyde Ranch were in great demand in San Bernardino and other valley communities. Clyde also herded cattle. When the grasses of Lone Pine Canyon were devoured by his herds, he drove them over the divide into Swarthout Valley and on up over Blue Ridge to Prairie Fork. By 1875 the Clyde Ranch sprawled over almost all of Lone Pine Canyon and into the eastern end of Swarthout Valley.

Good friends of Almon Clyde were Wyatt and Virgil Earp, legendary frontier lawmen and part-time outlaws of Tombstone fame. Virgil built a cabin on the Clyde Ranch, and Wyatt spent considerable time there between his hair-raising episodes. The little Earp cabin is still standing and is used as a storage building. Wyatt Earp died in Colton in 1929, in his 90s, just about the only gunman of the Old West to die a natural death.

Grizzly bears were a constant menace around Swarthout Valley in the early years. Slover Canyon, a small tributary near the southeast end of the valley, is named for Isaac Slover, early San Bernardino Valley pioneer, who was killed by a grizzly here in 1854. As late as 1879, the *San Bernardino Daily Times* (May 29) warned, "Bears are somewhat too numerous for comfort near the Forks, in Cajon Pass. The other night five of them prospected around the premises of Mr. Clyde and frightened his horses badly. Mr. Clusker struck bear tracks suggestively thick the other day in Swarthout Canyon. People visiting that section should go equipped as walking arsenals."

Despite the menace of grizzlies, Almon Clyde and others continued to herd cattle through Swarthout Valley. In 1886 Harry Heath homesteaded the eastern part of the valley and built a corral for his cattle. The dry and cool climate was just right for growing apples and pears, and it was not long until Heath had a fair-sized orchard, irrigated by water from Heath and Sheep canyons.

Also in the late 1880s, an eccentric Scotch prospector known as "Guffy" McGuffey built a stone

The lone pine in Lone Pine Canyon. This canyon at the northeast edge of the San Gabriels lies smack on the San Andreas Fault.

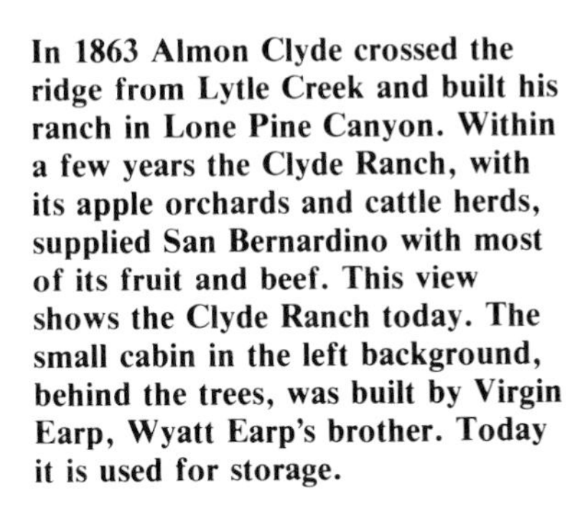

In 1863 Almon Clyde crossed the ridge from Lytle Creek and built his ranch in Lone Pine Canyon. Within a few years the Clyde Ranch, with its apple orchards and cattle herds, supplied San Bernardino with most of its fruit and beef. This view shows the Clyde Ranch today. The small cabin in the left background, behind the trees, was built by Virgin Earp, Wyatt Earp's brother. Today it is used for storage.

cabin alongside a small lake in the center of the valley, and used this as a base to search the surrounding hills for minerals.

Next on the scene was the pioneer whose name is most closely associated with the history of Swarthout Valley — Sumner Banks Wright. Born in Ohio in 1866, Wright came west to the Santa Cruz Mountains as a small boy. The elder Wright was a minister who spent more time cattle ranching and fruit growing than spreading the gospel. Young Sumner Wright left the ranch in his early 20s and came south to Colton, where he married, settled down, and set up a title claim business. The Wright Abstract Company was incorporated in 1888. Wright spent much of his time surveying land and fixing boundaries, and in the course of this work he visited Swarthout Valley. He was captivated by the mountain valley, as much for its potential as a cattle spread and apple orchard as by its beauty. In 1890 he bought forty acres from old McGuffey and took over the little stone cabin beside the lakelet, which soon became known as Wright Lake.

Sumner Wright spent more and more of his time in Swarthout Valley, leaving his Colton abstract business in the capable hands of associates. By 1895 he owned 3,300 acres in the valley, was growing apples and herding several thousand head of cattle. Apples were Wright's main interest; his orchards produced not only Wagner baking apples but also varieties of Snow and Delicious apples. Wright's cowboys ran his cattle to summer pasture on Blue Ridge, high on the crest of the San Gabriels, and down into the Prairie Fork headwaters.

Sumner Banks Wright (1866-1943), father of Wrightwood. Wright came to the Swarthout Valley in 1890, bought most of the valley and developed it as a cattle ranch and apple orchard. In 1924 he subdivided much of his property, giving birth to the community of Wrightwood. This 1916 photograph shows him alongside one of his apple trees in full bloom.
– PEARL COMFORT FISHER COLLECTION.

Twin Lakes, Wrightwood. – POST CARD PHOTO

In 1906 Wright bought the Heath Ranch, thereby gaining control of almost all of the Swarthout Valley. He developed an intricate irrigation system for his orchards, allowing for a plentiful supply of water in dry seasons as well as wet ones. He constructed a spacious frame home under great black oak trees on a knoll above Wright Lake, where he entertained numerous visitors, including the governor of California. He maintained a stable of fine riding horses. By 1910 Sumner Banks Wright was the patron of a mountain estate befitting a Southern plantation owner of the pre-Civil War period.

To allow more time to oversee his apple orchards and his Colton title abstract business, Wright turned over the management of his cattle to his nephew Buford Wright and his wife's nephew Bob Smith. In 1910 they organized the Circle Mountain Cattle Company, with corrals and feed yards in the east end of the valley. The Circle Mountain brand — a big C within a circle — became familiar to everyone in the eastern San Gabriels, from Big Rock Creek to Cajon Pass, as the Wright herds ranged over miles of mountain and hill country.

Good times could not last forever. By 1919 the market for cattle was down, and the ever-increasing number of settlers in adjacent valleys fenced their lands and prohibited grazing. Buford Wright was obliged to sell the Circle Mountain Ranch to Ivy and Emory Kid, who continued to operate it until the depression days of 1930.

Sumner Wright suffered financial hardships, too. To recoup his fortunes, he decided to subdivide his Swarthout Valley property for home sites. With the backing of Los Angeles real estate interests, the eastern half of the mountain valley was divided into lots and criss-crossed with streets. The proposed new community was named "Wrightwood." The sales campaign got underway in 1924. Los Angeles realtor C.C.C. Tatum distributed a brochure extolling the virtues of leisure living "in the Kingdom of Four Seasons at Wrightwood Mountains, California." The sales force was headed by Warren Sears, a tall, persuasive Canadian, who escorted prospects up to Wrightwood and dined them. Advertisements appeared in all the Los Angeles newspapers.

Thousands came to see, and scores bought lots. By 1930 Wrightwood was a viable, thriving mountain community, biggest in the San Gabriel Mountains. George Richardson built a general store, cafe and gas station. He joined with Lloyd Nix and George Preston to form the Wrightwood Commercial Corporation, which served a dual role as chamber of commerce and construction firm. The Corporation built the Tradin' Post store and res-

Wrightwood in its early days as a real estate development, 1930. To recover his losses in cattle ranching, Sumner Wright joined Los Angeles real estate interests to subdivide his property in Swarthout Valley in 1924. Within a decade Wrightwood was a thriving mountain community.
– POMONA PUBLIC LIBRARY, SPECIAL COLLECTIONS

Stoner Lodge, Wrightwood, lasted only three years. Built in 1930 by John Andrew Stoner, it burned in 1933. Only the massive rock ruins remain today. – POST CARD VIEW

Wrightwood today, a vibrant mountain village with a summer population of around 5,000, making it the largest community in the San Gabriel Mountains.

taurant and the post office. The Wrightwood Lodge, Twin Lakes Lodge and a recreation hall were all erected during this period. William Bristol, originator of the "Sunkist" trademark and citrus grower, built the spacious Acorn Lodge, complete with art gallery, mammoth fireplace and pipe organ chimes. Behind the lodge was a treehouse called "Honeymoon House" because it was rented only to newlyweds. Bristol himself fashioned the furniture out of local oak trees.

For years, the only automobile access to Wrightwood was via the long dirt road through Lone Pine Canyon. In the late 1920s San Bernardino County constructed a new two-lane paved highway to the mountain resort town from Cajon Canyon, still the main access today.

Sumner Wright, who made it all possible, did not stay to witness the rapid growth of the community named for him. He sold his home at Wright Lake and retired to Colton, where he lived until his death at the age of 77 in 1943.

Wrightwood has gone through good times and bad. The depression years of the 1930s slowed growth, as did World War II. Stoner Lodge, a magnificent steep-roofed stone and wood resort known as "The Gables," succumbed to fire two years after it was completed. An earthquake on May 7, 1941 (Wrightwood lies smack on the San Andreas Fault) caused numerous mud slides in which four houses and a sawmill were buried. More mud and land slides, sweeping down from the steep south wall of Swarthout Valley, hit Wrightwood in 1965, 1969 and 1977. An ominous warning of massive slides that might be triggered by a future quake was made by Forest Service geologist Eugene Kojan in 1978, much to the disgust and disagreement of Wrightwood real estate interests.

Still, Wrightwood continues to grow. The completion of the Angeles Crest Highway in 1956 was a great boost, providing a through paved route across the San Gabriel Mountains. Today, Wrightwood supports a population of from 2,400 to 5,000 people, depending on the season. The community is made up of more than a thousand homes and an assortment of small shops, businesses, cafes, motels and real estate offices. Real estate continues to be the premier economic enterprise. Russ Leadabrand called Wrightwood "a curious amalgam of real estate salesmen's enthusiasm and the passivity of old-time residents who silently wish that the salesmen weren't quite so zealous."[1] Many of the retired folks who live here would be satisfied to see the town remain the small, pleasant mountain community it is, sans the congestion and confusion inherent to real estate booms.

Three miles west of Wrightwood, at the upper end of Swarthout Valley, is the mountain playground of Big Pines. This is the center for the largest recreational complex in the Angeles National Forest — eleven campgrounds, five picnic areas, and three major ski areas, all within a radius of five miles.

It was R.F. McClellan, chairman of the Los Angeles County Board of Supervisors, who first envisioned Big Pines as a family recreation center.

Davidson Arch, Big Pines County Park in February 1938. This Los Angeles County playground was a popular winter resort from its development in 1923 until the County gave it up in 1940. William Davidson designed the twin stone towers and arch in 1922. The twin towers contained prison cells in which drunks and rowdies could be confined until the sheriff arrived. – LOS ANGELES COUNTY DEPT. OF RECREATION

In the early 1920s he persuaded his fellow supervisors to purchase 760 acres from Harry Heath and other land owners. The reported price for this prime forest land at the head of Swarthout Valley was $60,000. In 1923 the County began construction of the recreational facilities, many of which are still there today. An administration building, recreation hall and coffee shop, main lodge and employee residences were all erected in remarkably short time. Campgrounds and picnic areas were laid out. Trails were built. The most unusual structure was Davidson Arch, a pedestrian overpass supported by twin towers built of native stone, designed by William Davidson in 1922. Davidson presented it to the County upon completion. The twin towers contained barred cells in which drunks and rowdies could be confined until the sheriff arrived.

Big Pines County Park became popular at once, and overcrowding was a problem by 1925. To expand the recreational facilities, the supervisors attempted to gain title to 3,500 acres of adjacent forest land. This request was denied by the Forest Service, which felt it would be setting a dangerous precedent to give national forest lands to local governments. Instead, the Forest Service granted the County a special use permit for 3,560 acres, extending westward to Jackson Lake and South to Prairie Fork in the San Gabriel River's East Fork headwaters.

Between 1923 and 1933 the Los Angeles County Department of Parks and Recreation spent four million dollars in developing Big Pines County Park into a first-class recreational facility. By 1930 the park boasted a swimming pool, ice skating rink, tennis courts, children's playground, numerous public and organizational campgrounds, and a beginning of ski and toboggan facilities.

Downhill skiing, long popular in Europe, was just gaining acceptance in Southern California in the late 1920s. The slopes of Blue Ridge above Big Pines were well suited to this new sport, and it was not long until Southern California ski enthusiasts were swishing down the snow-covered slopes almost every winter weekend. To promote skiing in the

Swarthout Lodge, headquarters of Big Pines Los Angeles County Park, shortly after construction in 1925. L.A. County spent over four million dollars to develop Big Pines Park, only to give it all to the Forest Service in 1940. – POMONA PUBLIC LIBRARY, SPECIAL COLLECTIONS

Crowds of skiers utilized Big Pines County Park during the winter months in the 1930s. This 1938 scene shows skiers arriving at Swarthout Lodge. The cabins in the background were rented for $4 per night. – HENRY E. HUNTINGTON LIBRARY

Tobogganing at Big Pines County Playground, 1928. Winter sports was in its infancy in Southern California; a few hundred enthusiasts from Los Angeles drove up on weekends to indulge in these new snow activities. – POMONA PUBLIC LIBRARY, SPECIAL COLLECTIONS

area, the Big Pines Ski Club was organized on January 2, 1932. The charter members included many of the big names in local skiing — Will Vaughan, Virgil Dahl, Harlow Dormer, W.A. Readwell, Lester LaVelle, Glen and Muir Dawson.

The Big Pines Ski Club quickly grew into one of the major skiing organizations in the West. A spacious ski lodge was built, and, with C.C.C. help, ski runs were cleared on the slopes of Blue Ridge and Table Mountain. Four ski jump courses were hewed out of the steep mountainside below Blue Ridge.

The ski club received a big boost when Big Pines was selected as the site for the 1932 Olympic Winter Games ski jump competition. But, as so often happens in Southern California, poor snow conditions that winter caused the competition to be moved to Lake Placid, New York. The Blue Ridge chair lift, built for the Olympics that were not held there, was only the third such facility in California, the fifth in the United States. L.A. County footed most of the bill.

By the winter of 1935-1936 a Big Pines winter sports program was in full swing. Competition was staged in downhill and slalom, cross-country skiing, and exhibition skating. Participants came from all over the country, and some from Europe. A famous Norwegian skier, Birger Rund, set the local ski jump record at Blue Ridge in 1938.

Commercial ski developments, geared to the general skiing public rather than to the competitive few, commenced in the Big Pines area in 1937. In that year Harlow Dormer and Craig Wilson secured a Forest Service lease on Table Mountain and began building facilities and clearing ski runs. Soon afterwards, Frank Springer and Tom Triol took over management of the Blue Ridge ski area and developed a series of varied downhill runs to suit the desires of beginner and advanced skier alike.

Although the new sport of skiing blossomed into popularity during the 1930s, Big Pines County Park did not. The years of depression took their toll on the finances of L.A. County. The County simply could not afford the $80,000 required annually to maintain the park. The supervisors had second thoughts. Prairie Fork, where the County had constructed facilities but never completed the access

Winter fun at Big Pines, 1928. – POMONA PUBLIC LIBRARY, SPECIAL COLLECTIONS

The slalom course at Big Pines, 1935. A handful of young enthusiasts formed the Big Pines Ski Club and gradually developed into alpine skiers of the first rank. – HENRY E. HUNTINGTON LIBRARY

Ski jump competition at the Los Angeles Junior Chamber of Commerce winter carnival, Big Pines, January 31, 1931. – ROBERT FRAMPTON PHOTOGRAPH

Ice skating at Jackson Lake, L.A. Jr. Chamber of Commerce Winter Carnival, Big Pines, January, 31, 1931. – ROBERT FRAMPTON PHOTOGRAPH

Ice skating at the outdoor rink, Big Pines, 1938. Thousands enjoyed the winter recreation facilities provided by Los Angeles County in the late 1930s.
– HENRY E. HUNTINGTON LIBRARY

The Swarthout Lodge today (1980), now occupied by the Forest Service. Crowds of winter guests no longer haunt its halls.

road, was returned to the Forest Service in 1934. In 1934 and again in 1937, hints by the supervisors that Big Pines might be turned over to the Forest Service were met by loud public outcries, and the politically-conscious supervisors delayed action they knew would eventually come to pass. The Forest Service, too, was unhappy over the County's practice of charging fees for campground use (something the Forest Service itself would do twenty years later), a violation of the lease agreement, they alleged. L.A. County and the Forest Service began negotiations in 1938 aimed toward altering the lease agreement and bringing financial relief to the County. Final agreement was reached on August 31, 1940. Big Pines Park was turned over to the Forest Service with the understanding that the latter would continue to operate Big Pines as a recreational center.

Forest Service efforts to maintain Big Pines as a recreational center were complicated by the fact that L.A. County, upon leaving, removed everything that could be carried out — picnic tables, stoves, furniture, even the plumbing from the outdoor skating rink. Then World War II intervened, and Big Pines went into wartime "hibernation." With the conflict over, the Forest Service — which had been woefully short of personnel during the war years — gave first priority to long-neglected fire control measures. Big Pines would have to wait.

In 1950 Davidson Arch was removed to allow the highway to be widened. Only the north stone tower remains today, a lone reminder of an era long gone.

The completion of the Angeles Crest Highway in 1956 brought new life to Big Pines. Recreation was given a higher priority by the Forest Service in the late 1950s. Old campgrounds were improved and new ones built. New trails were hewed, access roads were cut through. The old site of the Big Pines post office and general store became the Big Pines Ranger Station and Information Center. Today, the Big Pines area — which includes Jackson Lake, Table Mountain and Blue Ridge — is one of the most heavily used in the Angeles, winter as well as summer.

Winter recreation is highlighted by three well-developed ski areas — Holiday Hill, Mountain High and Ski Sunrise.

Holiday Hill was developed by John Steinman, starting in 1950. Its feature is a mile-long double chair lift with a vertical rise of 1,700 feet from Swarthout Valley to the top of Blue Ridge. There are three other chairlifts, and a beginners' area known as Little Holiday Hill. Heinz Steinman, son of John Steinman, managed it until he retired a couple of years ago, but he and his family still hold financial control.

The Ford Observatory on Table Mountain has done pioneering work on variable steller systems.

Mountain High is the new name for the Blue Ridge ski area that was developed by Frank Springer with two chairlifts and runs for expert, intermediate and beginning skiers. Dick Woodworth bought Springer out in 1975 and changed the name to Mountain High.

Ski Sunrise on Table Mountain is reputed to be the only upside-down ski run in the country, with the parking area on top of the mountain and lifts to bring the skier back up after his downhill run. It was developed by Howard Moore in 1944, later expanded by Dave Ward who changed the name to Ski Sunrise.*

All three of the ski areas are serviced by new snowmaking machines, which manufacture custom snow and allow skiing from November to April, whether or not natural snow falls.

*The first road up Table Mountain was built in 1918 to give access to a lumber mill for the Socialist colony of Llano. In 1926 the Smithsonian Observatory for solar observation was built atop the mountain. Today the observatory, with expanded facilities, is operated by Cal Tech's Jet Propulsion Laboratory. The Ford Observatory on East Table Mountain has done some pioneering work on variable stars.

NOTES

1 Russ Leadabrand, "Crossing The Cajon Country," *Westways* (September 1971), p. 13.

16

The Literary San Gabriels

As Franklin Walker points out in his superb *Literary History of Southern California*, one can gain considerable insight into a region's background and development by examining its literary heritage. In the case of the San Gabriels, this literary heritage is rather sparse and, with a couple of exceptions, not well known. These chaparral-clad hills can claim no master laureate similar to Carmel's Robinson Jeffers, the Sierra Nevada's John Muir, or the desert's Mary Austin. Yet, a good number of writers have made the San Gabriels the locale for a paragraph, a page or a chapter of their literary efforts.

More often than not, the manner in which the mountains are portrayed reflects the prevailing attitudes of the era. To the Spanish padres the San Gabriels were largely *tierra incognita* — unknown, uninviting and untrod. Father Juan Crespi, diarist for the 1769 Portola party referred to "a high and dark range" north of the San Gabriel Valley. Another diarist, Pedro Fages, described "high, barren hills, very difficult for beasts of burden" while crossing San Fernando Pass at the western end of the range. Succeeding Spanish mission fathers and Mexican rancheros generally ignored the mountains. Mission records, voluminous on lowland matters, scarcely mention the "high and dark" range on the northern skyline.

Anglo writers gave the mountains much more attention, particularly after the discovery of gold in San Gabriel Canyon in 1854. Los Angeles newspapers ran columns of news about the San Gabriel mines, very little of it of literary merit. However, the perspective of the mountains was changing. With prospectors combing the hills, no longer were the San Gabriels unknown and foreboding. Some began to see beauty in the mountains, as exemplified by this piece that appeared in the *Los Angeles Star* of November 23, 1861:

> The range of mountains on our northeast boundary is at all seasons an object of admiration. Rearing its peaks three or four thousand feet high, they are subject to most fitful changes . . . Sometimes enveloped in clouds, dark and threatening, the base is clothed in sunshine; and again the more lofty peaks lift themselves above the clouds which envelop their base, and stand out in bold relief, as if suspended between earth and sky. Now that the winter season has set in, the mountains are clothed in their seasonal garb, and their snowtops are seen glittering in the bright sun, objects of beauty and admiration.

The first literary figure to visit and write about the San Gabriels was naturalist John Muir. The young and footloose Scotchman, a resident of Yosemite since 1868, came south in 1877 to visit a friend from his University of Wisconsin days, Dr. O.H. Congar. From the Congar home in Pasadena, Muir gazed up at the olive-green rampart of the San Gabriel Mountains, directly to the north. He took leave of his host and, in his own words, "made a fine shaggy little five days' excursion" into these hills so close at hand. He ventured alone, as was his custom in his early mountaineering years, toting only three loaves of Mrs. Congar's bread and a half pound of tea.

Muir's excursion into the chaparral-smothered mountains was a real challenge to him. Never before had he struggled through such a foreboding thicket of interlaced brush. A few weeks after his return he penned a vivid description of his adventure for the *San Francisco Evening Bulletin* (September 11, 1877): "In the mountains of San Gabriel, overlooking the lowland vines and fruit groves, Mother Nature is most ruggedly, thornily savage. Not even in the Sierra have I ever made the acquaintance of mountains more rigidly inaccessible." But all was not toil and hardship. Muir rejoiced in the hidden beauty of the canyons he found deep within the chaparral hills: "But in the very heart of this thorny wilderness, down in the dells, you may find gardens filled with the fairest flowers, that any child would love, and unapproachable linns lined with lilies and ferns, where the ouzel builds its mossy hut and sings in chorus with the white falling water." Muir was most impressed with the falls of Eaton Canyon, which he described as "a charming little thing, with a low, sweet voice, singing like a bird, as it pours from a notch in a short ledge, some thirty-five or forty feet into a round mirror-pool." He called it the "Yosemite of the San Gabriel."

John Muir enlarged and refined his description of his San Gabriels jaunt in the chapter "The Bee Pastures" in *The Mountains of California*, his best known book, published in 1894.

John Muir (1832-1914) visited the San Gabriels in 1877 and rejoiced in the hidden beauty of the sylvan canyons. He was particularly impressed with Eaton Falls, which he called "a charming little thing, with a low, sweet voice, singing like a bird."
– BANCROFT LIBRARY

The last three decades of the 19th century witnessed remarkable growth in Southern California. Los Angeles quadrupled in population, and dozens of new communities dotted the surrounding landscape as thousands were attracted to "The Land of Sunshine." A great deal of credit for this spectacular growth went to the resident boosters of California's golden southland who sang the praises of this sun-drenched country in songs, poems, magazine articles and books. Most of this literature of boosterism was written in the florid, overblown prose so popular during the Victorian era.

The San Gabriel Mountains received their fair share of attention among the scores of books and articles boosting Southern California during this period. One of the earliest boosters to proclaim the glories of the region was Major Ben C. Truman, Rhode Island-born school teacher, Civil War correspondent and printer. Truman came to Los Angeles in 1867 and immediately fell in love with the area. During the ensuing years, as a Los Angeles resident, he edited several newspapers, served as a publicist for the Southern Pacific Railroad, and authored several books. In *Semi-Tropical California* (1874), a booster book about Los Angeles County, Truman vividly portrayed the San Gabriels as "the ruggedest of mountains, majestically lifting their hoary heads to sky's azure dome, or enveloping themselves in wanton clouds of the most bewitching colors and exquisite pencilings." He went on to describe the gold and silver prospects in the mountains.

Ben Truman's purple prose was echoed by other late-19th century writers. Theodore S. Van Dyke, member of a prominent New Jersey family and brother of desert author John Van Dyke, came to Southern California in 1875 to regain his health. He spent much of his time in the healthful outdoors, hunting and fishing. In *Flirtation Camp* (1881), a frivolous Victorian novel in which two young people — Laura and Bellville — prance through the Southern California mountains on a romantic chase, Van Dyke vividly describes a trip up Lytle Creek to Glenn Ranch amid clouds and wind. His young lovers continue their coy adventure, climbing over hill and ridge, pausing here and there to fish and hunt. Van Dyke's best known work is *Southern California: Its Valleys, Hills and Streams; Its Animals, Birds and Fishes; Its Gardens, Farms and Climate* (1886). In the preface he writes, "In an age when the study of Nature has become the most popular of all subjects, no apology seems needed for a book treating of a land where the leading features of animate and inanimate nature are quite unknown to the great majority" of Southern Californians. "The Sierra Madre," as Van Dyke called them, "rise with a sudden sweep much higher above the valley than most

George Wharton James (1858-1923) leads a party of tourists through the San Gabriels back country, ca. 1895. Although much of his writing was pedestrian and colored with purple prose, James could write beautifully about nature, particularly about the California mountains and deserts. – CALIFORNIA HISTORICAL SOCIETY

of the great mountains of our country rise above the land at their feet, lifting one at once into a different climate and to a country where primeval wilderness still reigns supreme. Few parts of the United States are less known and less traversed than these great hills; yet they look down upon the very garden of all California."

Van Dyke's portrayal of wild and untrodden mountains changed rather dramatically within a few years. The Mount Lowe Railroad, the Mount Wilson Toll Road, and numerous mountain resorts that sprang up in the 1890s brought people by the hundreds into the San Gabriels. The boosters of these tourist attractions proclaimed the Sierra Madre "The Alps of America," equal to the great mountain ranges of the world.

Florid, grandiose prose reached ridiculous heights. Kate Sanborn, in *A Truthful Woman in Southern California* (1894), described a Pasadena lecture on the glories of the Sierra Madre that almost caused her to swoon:

> I listened to a lecture lately where a man was struggling to do this, and it was positively painful. The flowery verbiage, the accumulated adjectives, the poetical quotations were overpowering. I seemed actually sinking into luscious mellifluousness. I shook it off my fingers, as if it were maple syrup. Then, as he climbed higher and higher, never getting away from the richest verdure and the sweetest flowers, scenes for an artist to paint with rapture, and a poet to sing in ecstacy, I found myself pushing up my forehead to improvise a mansard roof for my brain to swell in sympathy. And when he reached the summit and the panorama burst upon his enraptured vision, it was too much for my strained emotions, and I quietly slipped out.

Trumpeting the delights of Professor Thaddeus Lowe's mountain railroad was George Wharton James, an English-born, defrocked Methodist minister who spent the last three decades of his life traveling around western America and writing prolifically about his adventures. Hired by Lowe to publicize his unique railway, James set up residence on Echo Mountain and commenced turning out pamphlets, press releases and magazine articles singing the praises of the project. Tourists, flocking to his clarion call, rode the aery incline cable car up to Echo Mountain House, and on to Ye Alpine Tavern on the forested slope of Mount Lowe. James used the typical Victorian prose to extoll the mountain atmosphere: "Mind and eye absorb the surrounding scene; the nostrils inhale the indescribable mingled fragrance, and the heart is insensibly lifted in adoration for this marvelous creation of the Almighty Lord." In *California, Romantic and Beautiful* (1914), James describes a camping trip to Mount Wilson and the glories of mountain life: "There is no sweetener of human life more reliable and sure than the mountains. Flee to them. Help comes to body, mind and soul. The trees wave you a hearty welcome and afford shade and shelter. The brook sings its joyful message of the beauty of life and work, and at night soothes you with the assurance that 'something attempted, something done' has earned a night's repose."

Reading George Wharton James today is a tedious and sometimes painful experience. Yet, in the words of Franklin Walker, "There is something about James that makes one like him even though much of his work is shoddy and his manner is constantly that of a salesman." His *Wonders of The Colorado Desert* (1906) is considered a classic by no less an authority than Lawrence Clark Powell. Despite his literary excesses, James found adventure, mystery and beauty in nature and expressed these traits with a sublimity rarely achieved by western writers.

Writers of the 1800s and 90s seized upon the term "Sierra Madre" almost to the exclusion of "San Gabriels." There was something majestically warm and maternal in "Mother Range," and no one expressed this more fervently than Charles Fletcher Lummis, the brilliant, cantankerous, slightly eccentric editor of *Land of Sunshine,* Southern California's first literary journal. Lummis had tramped across the continent in 1885 to become city editor of the *Los Angeles Times.* He suffered a stroke after only a few months on the job and went to New Mexico to recover, where he became fascinated with the Indian and Spanish cultures and authored the best known of his many books, *The Land of Poco Tiempo* (1893). Returning to Los Angeles, he took over *Land of Sunshine* and made it into an instant success. Lummis fell in love with the Sierra Madre and ran numerous articles proclaiming its attractions. In "The Mother Mountains" (*Land of Sunshine,* August 1895), he extolled: "There is wonderful significance in the name Sierra Madre; a poetry which the self-satisfied race would be none the worse for capacity to feel; an aptness upon which science at a latter century's end cannot improve. It means more than the shaping of an infinite brood of foothills; more than a synonym for 'the tallest range.' It is not Mother of Mountains, but Mother Mountains; whose offspring is — Southern California." Lummis spent his last years in El Alisal, the home he built with stream boulders amid the sycamores of the Arroyo Seco, not far from the Mother Mountains he cherished.

Lummis' *Land of Sunshine* (renamed *Out West* in 1902) was graced by a good number of essays and stories by a budding young writer from the Owens Valley. Mary Hunter Austin held a metaphysical, almost mystical view of nature and its effect on mankind. In her autobiography *Earth Horizon* (1932) she revealed how, early in life, she determined "that I would write imaginatively, not only of people, but of the scene, the totality which is called Nature, and that I would give myself intransigently to the quality of experience called Folk, and to the frame of behavior known as Mystical." This philosophy she evoked in her first and best book, *The Land of Little Rain* (1903), a moving tribute to the landscape and lore of the desert country east of the Sierra Nevada.

Following the success of *The Land of Little Rain,* Mary Austin traveled widely through California, the Southwest, and as far as England, singing the praises of the semi-arid lands in numerous books and stories. In 1913, while residing briefly in London, she was asked to provide the text for a book containing Sutton Palmer's watercolor paintings of California scenes. This she did beautifully in *California: Land of The Sun* (1914), a volume described by Lawrence Clark Powell as "a lyrical hymn to California, its contours and configurations of seacoast, valleys, and mountains." The chapter in the book entitled "Mothering Mountains" describes the Sierra Madre and contains some of the best prose so far written about the range. "The heads of the Sierra Madre are rounded, the contours of great dignity," writes Mary Austin; "Its charms, and it has many, of forested slope, leaping waters, and lilied meadows, do not offer themselves to the casual glance . . . Entering the canons of the San Gabriel, one is struck with the endearing quality of their charm. In a country which disdains every sort of prettiness, and dares even to use monotony as an element of beauty, as California does, it is surprising to find . . . little dells all laced with fern and saxifrage, and wind-swung, frail, flowery bells. Little streams come dashing down the runways with an elfin movement, with here and there a miniature fall 'singing like a bird,' as Muir described it, between moss-encrusted banks."

Like Charles Lummis, Mary Austin was intrigued with the universal, mystical connotation of "Mother Mountains." "Was there ever a name at once so absolute, so understanding as Sierra Madre, Mother Mountain? . . . Never again for me will the Sierra Madre be a mere geographical term, a feature of the landscape . . . Shall not the Mother of the land do what she will with it?"

California: Land of The Sun was published in Britain at the onset of World War I. It was unavailable to most Southern California readers until 1927, when it was at last published in the United States under the title *The Lands of The Sun*, without Sutton Palmer's magnificent watercolors. The original illustrated edition is a scarce collector's item today.

Abbott Kinney — tobacco heir, land developer, creator of Venice (California), conservationist, chairman of California's first Board of Forestry — was a businessman and engineer rather than a literary figure. Yet he produced a treatise which, though essentially technical, is also full of lively perception and vigorous prose about the Southern California mountains. Kinney's *Forest and Water* (1900) is an urgent plea for the preservation of the mountain watersheds, wise forest management, fire prevention, reforestation and reclamation. He calls for the creation of an efficient forest protection force and gives details on the personal qualifications of prospective rangers, including the following bad news for bachelors: "Marriage is one essential of a life in harmony with natural law. Every man in the forestry force should be married by thirty. This is not only in consonance with the highest statesmanship to preserve the population in its reproductive power, but also for the highest responsibility and vital strength of the forestry force." Kinney was well acquainted with the San Gabriels; his home from 1885 until his death in 1920 was his beloved Kinneloa Ranch in the foothills above Altadena. He pleads, "We hold in Southern California something in climate as near perfection as humanity can hope for on earth. Not only do we offer cities of refuge from the relentless frost king to the winter frozen world, but we also offer the unique condition of delightful refuges from the fiery breath of the desert and the long fatiguing heats of the interior . . . For beauty alone and beauty considered only as a commercial asset, we must put an end to the folly of forest fires."

Charles Frederick Holder, author of *Life in The Open* (1906), was an avid sportman-author of a dozen hunting and fishing books. He loved to fish in San Gabriel Canyon and hunt big horn sheep in the Mt. Baldy region.

Charles Frederick Holder was probably the most avid sportsman-writer in Southern California history. Whether deep sea fishing off Catalina, angling for trout in San Gabriel Canyon, or big game hunting high in the mountains, Holder was actively involved in his chosen avocation. He was founder of the Valley Hunt Club in Pasadena and the Tuna Club in Avalon. Scores of his sporting articles appeared in such nationally-renowned periodicals as *McClure's Magazine, The Century,*

Outing and *Scientific American.* His dozen books included *The Log of A Sea Angler, The Channel Islands of California,* and *Life in The Open: Sport With Rod, Gun, Horse and Hound in Southern California* (1906). It is this latter book, probably Holder's best, that contains within its covers much about the San Gabriels: fishing the canyon streams, hunting with hounds in the foothills, stalking big horn sheep, deer and mountain lion in the back country. Holder knew the mountains well. A native of Massachusetts, he came to California in 1885 and found a home in Pasadena. He lived for a time on "Las Casitas," a sloping foothill bench just outside the mouth of the Arroyo Seco, *Life in The Open* is written in vigorous, straight-forward fashion; its chapters abound with enthusiasm, vivid description and triumph. Holder also sees great beauty in the mountains. In a horseback trip up the Arroyo Seco into the heart of the range, he writes, "There is something in the smiling face of the mountains that takes strong hold of the fancy and imagination. There is an impulse to stop and bare the head before the works of the Infinite Designer of all these mountains, hills, and valleys." Listen to how he describes a storm in the back country: "The rainstorms in the mountains fill the streams with melody and the forest thrills with ten thousand vibrant notes. The roar and cadence of the greater falls, the ripple over rocky beds, the wild sweep and surge of rain against granite cliffs, and the wail of the wind as it rises and gives rein to its fancy, sweeping over the ridges, rushing down into the canons, through the chaparral, . . . are all features in the splendid setting of the forest stage." Today's preservationists and nature lovers tend to look with a frowning eye on Holder because of his passion for hunting animals — particularly the endangered big horn sheep. Nevertheless, this disciple of the sporting life wrote superbly about the mountain and hill country he loved.

More to the liking of conservationists was Francis M. Fultz, a midwestern school superintendent who moved to Los Angeles, ostensibly to retire, in 1916. Instead of leading a sedate life in retirement, Fultz, in his 60s, joined the new Los Angeles chapter of the Sierra Club and developed a new passion — exploring the local mountains and studying their plant life. The academic botany he learned in the Midwest now became an avocation; he was fascinated with chaparral — what he called the "elfin forest" — and set about to learn all he could about this uniquely Southern Californian type of ground cover. Out of this study came a series of articles for the *Los Angeles Times Illustrated Magazine.* These articles became the basis for a delightful book, *The Elfin Forest* (1923). "Striking and impressive as the

Francis M. Fultz, midwestern educator, came to southern California to retire in 1916. Instead, he roamed the mountains and authored the classic book on chaparral, *The Elfin Forest* (1923).
– LOUISE WERNER PHOTOGRAPH.

mountains of Southern California are in their physical features, yet the most wonderful and marvelous thing about them is the forest of elfin trees which clothes them as with a garment," writes Fultz. "To stand on some high vantage point, where I can gaze out over the limitless sea of chaparral is to me a delight; to follow it with my eye, as it runs over ridges and dips down into canyons, then up another ridge and on again, is an inspiration; to see it extend on and on, until it disappears in the horizon or drops behind some distant range, and realize the part it plays in the Creator's plan of Conservation, is an exaltation." Fultz proceeds to describe each species of the Elfin Forest, writing with clarity and accuracy to please the layman as well as the professional botanist. Indeed, the strength of *The Elfin Forest* is that it combines scientific knowledge with easy-flowing, enthusiastic prose — something seldom seen in technological monographs. The book is as valuable today as when Fultz wrote it over a half century ago.

Charles Francis Saunders (1859-1941), a Pennsylvania Quaker and self-taught botanist, wrote the classic *Southern Sierras of California* in 1923. In the book, Saunders tramps throughout the San Gabriels and other southern California ranges, vividly describing the beauty and the flora of the mountains.
– HENRY E. HUNTINGTON LIBRARY

Saunders busy writing in his Yosemite Valley camp, 1910. He was a prolific writer on such subjects as outdoor travel, flora, the Spanish missions, and Southwest Indians. – HENRY E. HUNTINGTON LIBRARY

If any book on the San Gabriels and the other Southern California mountain ranges might be termed a literary classic, it would have to be Charles Francis Saunders' *The Southern Sierras of California* (1923). What makes a book a classic? When it possesses the quality of excellence that causes it to transcend time and be read beyond the author's own generation, says Lawrence Clark Powell. *The Southern Sierras* is such a book. Within its pages, Saunders does for the Southern California mountains what John Muir does for the Sierra Nevada. He, like Muir, is able to evoke the spell of wilderness and make the mountains come alive in timeless, vibrant prose. Literature and landscape blend in perfect harmony.

Saunders was at his best when describing the mountain flora, for he was an accomplished botanist. He seemed particularly intrigued with the chaparral. Here is how he describes it in a tramp through the upper Big Tujunga: "Once the mind is cleared of its conventional views as to woodlands, this Tom Thumb forest appeals to the eye as very lovely, leafy the year through, rounded and dimpling as it compliantly conforms like a garment to the moulding of the mountain to which it clings, yet with a decided will of its own as you will find if you step from the trail and attempt to pass through its midst . . . . For all its littleness it is infinitely harder to travel than the great forests of the Sierra Nevada, where the trees stand apart at liberal distances, while these puny arboreal folk of the chaparral, linking arms, could halt an army."

Saunders did not confine his rambles to the trails; he was equally adept at climbing the peaks. Take, for example, his scramble to the summit of Strawberry Peak: "So I started up once more, clutching carefully at every projecting hold and keeping steadfastly an upward look, until finally, after fifteen minutes' tedious creeping, I scrambled out on the top, and lo! the kingdoms of the earth. Twenty-five miles eastward, 'Old Baldy,' genial giant of the Sierra Madre, blocked the view; but over one shoulder San Gorgonio peeped, revealing an arc of his smooth back outlined with a fringe of snow. Still farther on, San Jacinto's summit, lifted above a sea of vapor, floated like an island of the air. To the north beyond the range, a yellow smudge marked the desert's whereabouts; and nearer, almost at my feet, the great gray basin of the Big Tujunga lay in clear-cut relief. Oceanward the sierra sank gradually till its feet were sunk in a thin white fog that hid the great plain of San Gabriel; and beyond that, in the light of the evening sun, the sea gleamed like a shining platter, bearing twin-peaked Santa Catalina in its golden midst."

Who was this writer who used the English language like an artist's brush? Charles Francis Saunders was born in Warminster, Pennsylvania in 1859 and educated in Quaker schools in Philadelphia. Until he was well into his 30s, he led an uneventful life as a clerk for a Philadelphia import-export firm. It appeared he was destined for obscurity until, on his way home from work one night, he chanced to drop in on a public lecture on botany. The talk revealed to Saunders a world of beauty and interest of which he had previously been unaware. His life now had renewed purpose. Several years of intense study and field work made him one of the premier botany students in the East. Weekends and holidays he spent walking through the hills and mountains from Vermont to North Carolina, studying the flora. In 1897 he began his literary career by writing a series of articles on flowers and plants for a Philadelphia newspaper.

1902 was a watershed year in Saunders' life. At the age of 43, he married for the first time and paid his initial visit to California.

His union with Elisabeth Hallowell was felicitous, but tragically short-lived. She was an accomplished artist and shared her husband's interest in nature. Whenever her fragile health would allow, she accompanied him on his outings, toting paintbrush and colors to illustrate landscapes, flowers and trees. Four of Saunders' early books are enhanced with her drawings; more would have been but for her untimely passing in 1910.

Saunders' journey west was an eye-opener. He and Elisabeth were completely captivated by the fascinating flora of Southern California — the abundant wildflowers, the thorny but fragrant chaparral, the unique desert plants. In 1906 they moved permanently to Southern California, ostensibly for Elisabeth's fragile health; another reason was their total enthrallment with the region. They bought a home in Pasadena, and wasted no time in exploring and enjoying the great Southwest.

Saunders' facile pen produced a half-dozen books during the ensuing decade, covering his three main new-found interests — the flora of the Southwest, the missions and the Indians. Several of these, most notably *The California Padres and Their Missions* (1915), in which he collaborated with J. Smeaton Chase, were best sellers.

During these years, Saunders often rested from his literary chores by slinging a knapsack over his back and, with one or more friends, hiking into the nearby mountains. Out of these outdoor adventures came *The Southern Sierras of California* (1923), the best of his eighteen books.

In the book, Saunders recounts his rambles through the verdant heart of the Sierra Madre, up such lofty summits as Old Baldy and San Gorgonio, across the desert-influenced Santa Rosas to the San Diego back country, and into the gentle hills behind Santa Barbara. With him usually was "The Professor," a fictitious character who sometimes represented a friend, sometimes a hiking acquaintance, sometimes himself.

Many of Saunders' descriptions are timeless. Here is how he described his and "The Professor's" crossing of the Devil's Backbone enroute to Old Baldy: "It was like walking some bridge of the gods, so uplifted above the earth was it, so sweet and buoyant the air that drew across it, so remote seemed the world. And it was a bridge that led us into quite a new land, treeless save for an occasional flattened tamarack or lowly clump of chinquapin, and rising easily by barren, gravelly undulations flecked with lingering snow-banks here and there, until we came out upon a wide, wind-swept expanse of shale and broken rock — a desert on a mountain peak."

Other accounts are of mountain landmarks long vanished, casualties to modern highways that allow easy entry. Colby's Ranch, once a hikers' hostelry deep in the Sierra Madre run by Delos and Lillian Colby, was described as "the little Canaan of the Sierra Madre — a land of milk and honey, of cherries and figs, of apples and pears and berries, of rhubarb pies and peaches and cream." Buckhorn Flat, now a busy public campground off the Angeles Crest Highway but in Saunders' time deep in the wilderness, was "a thicket from whose heart the music of running water rose, . . . an entrancing spot where silver firs, yellow pines, and incense cedars four and five feet in diameter made a contemplative twilight." Here, one Sunday morning long ago, Saunders and his friends held a Quaker meeting: "We all four sat together for an hour or so in worshipful silence beneath the great firs, hoping to experience the reality of the Lord's assurance . . . In such primeval temple, without priestly mediation, the ripple of the brook and the song of birds for anthem and the perfume of the lilies for incense, we made spiritual sacrifice to the universal Lord of life."

Among the large collection of Saunders' papers in the Henry E. Huntington Library are many little notebooks he kept on his outings. In them are bare notations, listing flora and fauna and giving directions, distances and travel times. A comparison of these skimpy field jottings with the finished book bears striking testimony to Saunders' creative power. Simple listings of names, places and numbers are, to paraphrase Lawrence Clark Powell,

Will Thrall (1873-1963) spent most of his life hiking and camping in the mountain ranges of southern California. He put his philosophy of outdoor living to work as editor of *Trails Magazine,* published by Los Angeles County during the years 1933 to 1939. Here he poses near Kellys Camp, with Old Baldy in the background, used on the cover of *Trails Magazine,* Spring 1939. – HENRY E. HUNTINGTON LIBRARY

expanded by knowledge, illumined by imagination, and transformed into literature.

The Southern Sierras of California remains today the best book about the Southern California mountain country and a worthy complement to Muir's *The Mountains of California.* If your library is to contain just a single volume on the local mountains, this should be the one.

Hikers in the San Gabriels during the 1920s and 1930s often came upon a short, wiry gentleman dressed in khaki, wearing a wide-brimmed hat and World War I-type leggings. After a few cheerful words of greeting, the elderly man would bound off up the trail, moving at a vigorous pace, and disappear from view as he scrambled up a nearby summit. The startled hikers had just met Will H. Thrall, the energetic editor of *Trails Magazine* and author of a host of articles on the San Gabriel Mountains.

To Thrall, the acme of enjoyment and inspiration was experienced in traveling a forest trail or scrambling up a lofty summit. He believed the essence of life was found in the beauty and simplicity of nature. Hand in hand with his love of the wilderness, Thrall believed in the benefits of strenuous physical activities associated with mountain hiking. "There is no exercise so beneficial, physically, mentally or morally, nothing which gives so much of living for so little cost, as hiking our mountain and hill trails and sleeping under the stars," he wrote.

Will Thrall put his philosophy of outdoor living to work as editor of *Trails Magazine,* published under the auspices of the Los Angeles County Department of Recreation Camps and Playgrounds during the years 1933 to 1939. The magazine became a hit with hikers and campers from the start. Included in each issue were descriptions of mountain landmarks, road and trail directions, news of outing activities by various outdoor organizations, maps and illustrations. Beginning with the Winter 1936 issue, *Trails Magazine* became a major source of information on mountain history with its "Cabin Landmarks of the

Angeles" series. At Thrall's request, Lloyd Austin, proprietor of Switzer's Camp in the Arroyo Seco, wrote the story of the resort. Each subsequent issue contained one or more articles of historical interest, written either by early mountain pioneers still living or by Thrall, based on interviews and research. The material thus preserved will always be of priceless value to historians of the San Gabriel Mountains.

As Thrall became better known as an authority on the local mountains, the *Los Angeles Times* invited him to contribute a weekly column on mountain trails. His popular feature "Today's Hike" ran every Sunday in the *Times* from October 21, 1934 through November 2, 1941. Thrall personally checked out the trails every week, often covering some 20 or 30 miles on foot, to insure that the directions given in "Today's Hike" were accurate.

When *Trails Magazine* folded, Thrall was 65 years old, retirement age for most men. But for a man of his vitality, retirement from an active life was a temperamental impossibility. Until he reached 80, he continued to take weekly hikes in the San Gabriels. Questioned about this strenuous activity on his 78th birthday, he said, "Hiking is the world's finest exercise. I'm not as fast as I once was, but I can still scale those peaks. I'll never stop hiking. It's life to me." Besides his outdoor activities, Thrall continued to collect mountain history and authored a number of articles for such publications as *Westways* and the *Southern California Quarterly.* He gave many talks to historical and conservation organizations on the saga of the San Gabriels.

Will Thrall passed away on February 20, 1963 at the golden age of 89. As a fitting memorial to this man whose deep love of the mountains and gift of communication allowed him to convey this passion to others, the United States Board on Geographic Names, at the request of the Forest Service and hundreds of Thrall's friends, bestowed the name "Will Thrall Peak" on a 7845-foot forested summit on the north side of the San Gabriel Mountains.

Few have written more beautifully, or with more feeling, about the San Gabriel Mountains than Russ Leadabrand. Leadabrand's free, easy-flowing style has been enjoyed by thousands of readers of the *Pasadena Star-News, Westways* magazine, and the Ward Ritchie Press guidebook series over the past two decades. A good portion of his writings have been concerned with the San Gabriels — the history, the natural appeal, the highways and byways, the current problems of fire, flood and overuse.

Leadabrand, a native of California's great San Joaquin Valley, got his local start as a reporter with the *Pasadena Star-News,* but it was his immensely popular "Let's Explore A Byway" series in *Westways,* running from 1961 until the late 1970s, that made his name a household word among Southern California travel buffs. Every month Leadabrand would guide his readers along highway and byway through lowland, mountain and desert — just about anywhere it was possible to drive in Southern California. Among his trips were many into the San Gabriels — the Angeles Crest Highway, Big Tujunga, San Gabriel Canyon, San Antonio Canyon, Lytle Creek and the back side country of Wrightwood, Big Pines and Devil's Punchbowl.

Russ Leadabrand writes beautifully about the mountains and deserts of southern California. His *Guidebook to the San Gabriel Mountains* was published in 1963.

Leadabrand's "Let's Explore A Byway" columns caught the eye of publisher Ward Ritchie. At Ritchie's request, Leadabrand authored a shelf of compact little guidebooks, the first of which was *Guidebook to The San Gabriel Mountains of California* (1963). In easy-going, disarming prose, Leadabrand imparts a great deal of knowledge about the mountains and the byways leading into them. He tells of the historical landmarks, the resorts, the campgrounds and picnic spots, the many attractive views. "But," Leadabrand writes, "the best thing about the San Gabriel Mountains is the mountains themselves: rockribbed, burned over or green with young chaparral, sharp-etched against the blue winter sky or misty and phantom in the creeping, canyon-following arms of smog. The sights and sounds, the wash of winds, the medicinal and restoring scents — these are the things that have lured the traveler into the range for hundreds of years. May it ever be thus."

Appendix

In 1977 *The San Gabriels: Southern California Mountain Country,* covering the western part of the range, was published by Golden West Books. Since then, information has come to light that necessitates some corrections. The writer wishes to thank Glen Owens of Arcadia, Kenyon De Vore of Monrovia and Viola Carson of La Crescenta for pointing out errors in the original edition.

Page 108: Commodore Perry Switzer was the full name of the founder of Switzer's Camp in the Arroyo Seco. "Commodore" was not a nickname.

Page 119: Sturtevant's first name was Wilbur, not William. He was born in Ohio in 1841 and died in Los Angeles in 1910.

Page 122: Newcomb's first name was spelled Lewis, not Louis. He was usually called "Louie," however.

Page 131: The first trail resort reached by the hiker on the Sturtevant Trail from Sierra Madre was Ernest Benjamin Gray's Little Gray Inn, located on the ridgetop a half mile before Joe Clark's Halfway House. Gray operated his little trail hostelry from about 1910 to 1926.

Page 146: The grizzly bear killed by Cornelius Johnson in Big Tujunga on October 18, 1916 was apparently an escapee from the Los Angeles Zoo at Griffith Park, not a wild animal.

Page 154: The derivation of Mt. Lukens' original name, Sister Elsie Peak, is clouded in uncertainty. Exhaustive research into Catholic Church records fails to find any evidence of a nun named Sister Elsie nor an orphanage named El Rancho de Dos Hermanas. The name first appeared on the Wheeler Survey Atlas sheet in 1878.

Page 187: The story of Chilao receiving its name from the bear-killing exploits of one of Tuburcio Vasquez's men is a pleasant legend with no basis in fact. The late Lindley Bynum of the Huntington Library turned up information that the flats were named for one Chileo Silvas, who reportedly herded cattle and lassoed bears there for some forty years.

Bibliography

BOOKS

Austin, Mary, *California: Land of the Sun.* London: Adam and Charles Black, 1914.

Beattie, George William and Helen Pruitt, *Heritage of The Valley: San Bernardino's First Century.* Oakland: Bio-Books, 1951.

Black, Esther Boulton, *Rancho Cucamonga and Dona Merced.* San Bernardino: San Bernardino County Museum, 1978.

Black, Esther Boulton, *Stories of Old Upland.* Upland: Chaffey Community Cultural Center, 1979.

Clary, William W., *History of The Law Firm of O'Melveny and Myers, 1885-1965.* Los Angeles: privately printed, 1966.

Cleland, Robert G., *The Cattle on A Thousand Hills.* San Marino: The Henry E. Huntington Library, 1951.

Fisher, Pearl Comfort, *The Mountaineers.* San Bernardino: San Bernardino County Museum, 1972.

Fisher, Pearl Comfort, *The Wrightwood Women.* Wrightwood: privately printed, 1978.

Fultz, Francis M., *The Elfin Forest.* Los Angeles: Times-Mirror Press, 1923.

Graves, Jackson, *California Memories, 1857-1930.* Los Angeles: Times-Mirror Press, 1930.

Gudde, Erwin G., *California Place Names.* Berkeley: University of California Press, 1969.

Holder, Charles Frederick, *Life in The Open: Sport With Rod, Gun, Horse and Hound in Southern California.* New York: G.P. Putnam's Sons, 1906.

Hoover, J. Howard, *Profile of San Dimas.* San Dimas: San Dimas Press, 1961.

Jackson, Sheldon, *A British Ranchero in Old California: The Life and Times of Henry Dalton of The Rancho Azusa.* Glendale: The Arthur H. Clark Co., 1977.

Johnson, Frank, *The Serrano Indians of Southern California.* Banning: The Malki Museum Press, 1965.

Johnston, Bernice, *California's Gabrielino Indians.* Los Angeles: The Southwest Museum, 1962.

Kinney, Abbot, *Forest and Water.* Los Angeles: The Post Publishing Co., 1900.

Leadabrand, Russ, *Guidebook to The San Gabriel Mountains of California.* Los Angeles: The Ward Ritchie Press, 1964.

Lockmann, Ronald F., *Guarding The Forests of Southern California: Evolving Attitudes Toward Conservation of Watershed, Woodlands, and Wilderness.* Glendale: The Arthur H. Clark Co., 1981.

Muir, John, *The Mountains of California.* New York: The Century Co., 1894.

O'Melveny, Henry W., *William G. Kerckhoff: A Memorial.* Los Angeles: privately printed, 1935.

O'Melveny, Stuart, *It's Best to Divide With Friends.* Los Angeles: privately printed, 1955.

Pflueger, Donald, *Glendora: The Annals of A Southern California Community.* Claremont: Saunders Press, 1951.

Robinson, John W., *Mines of The San Gabriels.* Glendale: La Siesta Press, 1973.

Robinson, John W., *Mines of The East Fork.* Glendale: La Siesta Press, 1980.

Robinson, John W., *The San Gabriels: Southern California Mountain Country.* San Marino: Golden West Books, 1977.

Robinson, John W., *Trails of The Angeles.* Berkeley: Wilderness Press, 1971.

Robinson, W.W., *The Forest and The People: The Story of Angeles National Forest.* Los Angeles: The Title Insurance and Trust Co., 1946.

Saunders, Charles Francis, *The Southern Sierras of California.* Boston: Houghton-Mifflin Co., 1923.

Shinn, G. Hazen, *Shoshonean Days: Recollections of a residence of five years among the Indians of Southern California, 1885-1889.* Glendale: The Arthur H. Clark Co., 1941.

Truman, Ben C., *Semi-Tropical California.* San Francisco: The A.L. Bancroft Co., 1874.

Van Dyke, Theodore S., *Flirtation Camp, or, The Rifle, Rod, and Gun in California: A Sporting Romance.* New York: Ford, Howard, and Hulbert, 1881.

Van Dyke, Theodore S., *Southern California: Its Valleys, Hills, and Streams; Its Animals, Birds, and Fishes; Its Gardens, Farms, and Climate.* New York: Ford, Howard, and Hulbert, 1886.

Vosburg, Keith, *Azusa, Old and New.* Azusa: Azusa-Foothill Citrus Co., 1921.

Whitney, Josiah D., *Geology, Volume I: Report of Progress and Synopsis of The Field Work From 1860 to 1864.* Philadelphia: Caxton Press of Sherman and Co., 1865.

Wiley, John L., *History of Monrovia.* Pasadena: The Star-News Press, 1927.

PERIODICALS

Baker, C.C., "Don Enrique Dalton of The Azusa," *Annual Publication of The Historical Society of Southern California,* 1917.

Battle, Don, "Ancients of The Angeles Forest," *Westways,* October 1962.

Battle, Don, "Down to Crystal Lake," *Westways,* September 1962.

Belden, L. Burr, "Gold Rush Feuds Mark Early Days for Lytle Creek," *San Bernardino Sun-Telegram,* April 11, 1954.

Bidwell, Belle J., "Our Camp in The Canon," *Overland Monthly,* August 1887.

Black, Esther Boulton, "Ranch Life in San Antonio Canyon in the 1870's," *Pomona Valley Historian,* Spring 1975.

Burt, Arthur W., "Adventures in Light and Power," *Pomona Valley Historian,* July 1966.

Clark, Alfred, "The San Gabriel River: A Century of Dividing The Waters," *Southern California Quarterly,* June 1970.

Dawson, Glen, "Ascents of Mount San Antonio," *Trails Magazine,* Summer 1938.

Dawson, Muir, "Mining in Upper San Antonio Canyon," *Southern California Quarterly,* March 1948.

Gay, Thomas and Samuel Hoffman, "Mines and Mineral Deposits of Los Angeles County, California," *California Journal of Mines and Geology,* July-October 1954.

Graves, J.A., "Sportsmen of the '90s," *Touring Topics,* June 1929.

Grinnell, Joseph, "California's Grizzly Bears," *Sierra Club Bulletin,* April 1938.

Guinn, J.M., "The Gold Placers of Los Angeles," *Land of Sunshine,* July 1896.

Harmon, Ginger, "Angeles National Forest: Our Next Big Urban Resort?" *Los Angeles Magazine,* March 1971.

Heald, Weldon F., "There'll Always Be A Baldy," *Westways,* April 1956.

Hellmers, Henry, "The San Gabriel Mountains — Man and Nature in Conflict," *Cal Tech Quarterly,* Winter 1962-63.

Hoffman, Abraham, "Angeles Crest: The Creation of A Forest Highway System in the San Gabriel Mountains," *Southern California Quarterly,* September 1968.

Hoffman, Abraham, "Mountain Resorts and Trail Camps in Southern California's Great Hiking Era, 1884-1938," *Southern California Quarterly,* Fall 1976.

Hoffman, Abraham, "The Bridge to Nowhere," *The Branding Iron,* September 1975.

Hoffman, Dr. J.W., "Azusa Canon Pictographs," *4th Annual Report of The Bureau of Ethnology, 1882-1883,* J.W. Powell, Director. Washington: Government Printing Office, 1886.

Holt, Raymond M., "Dr. Baldwin's Bright Vision," *Westways,* March 1957.

Jackson, Sheldon G., "Henry Dalton's Water War on The San Gabriel," *Mt. San Antonio Historian,* Summer 1978.

Kern, J.C., "A Few Leaves from The Campground History Book," *Trails Magazine,* Spring 1936.

Kern, J.C., "Public Camp Development in the Angeles National Forest," *Trails Magazine,* Summer 1935.

Leadabrand, Russ, "Crossing Cajon Country," *Westways,* September 1971.

Leadabrand, Russ, "From Wrightwood to La Canada," *Westways,* November 1966.

Leadabrand, Russ, "Highway Into History," *Westways,* March 1958.

Leadabrand, Russ, "Into Mount Baldy Country," *Westways,* October 1967.

Leadabrand, Russ, "Into Old Baldy Country," *Westways,* November 1963.

Leadabrand, Russ, "San Antonio Canyon Entices," *Westways,* July 1974.

Leavens, George F., "By Way of The Devil's Backbone," *Land of Sunshine,* August 1896.

Littleboy, Jeff, "Gold in The San Gabriels," *Westways,* November 1955.

Lummis, Charles F., "The Mother Mountains," *Land of Sunshine,* August 1895.

Manker, Fletcher and Dan Alexander, "At The Foot of Mt. San Antonio," *Trails Magazine,* Spring 1937.

Maynard, Glyde, "The Development of San Antonio Canyon," *Pomona Valley Historian,* January, April, July 1965.

Mears, Joe, "California's New Gold Rush Is On," *Westways,* May 1934.

Mendenhall, William V., "Mountain Recreation," *Trails Magazine,* Spring 1938.

Michelson, A.A., "Measurement of The Velocity of Light Between Mt. Wilson and Mt. San Antonio," *Astrophysical Journal,* January 1927.

Miller, William J., "San Gabriel Glacier Sites Located," *The Grizzly Bear,* October 1928.

Mueller, A.J., "Road Development in The Angeles National Forest," *Trails Magazine,* Spring 1936.

O'Melveny, Henry W., "The San Gabriel: Sportsmens' Rendezvous of Half A Century Ago," *Westways,* May 1944.

Peck, Sedley, "Colorful Old Days on The Upper San Gabriel," *Trails Magazine,* Summer 1938.

Pemberton, J.E., "Early Fire Control in Los Angeles County," *Trails Magazine,* Spring 1936.

Roberts, Jim, "Hydraulic Mining of Early Canyon Days Described," *Azusa Herald,* October 20, 1937.

Robinson, John W., "A Fine, Shaggy Excursion: John Muir in The San Gabriels," *Pacific Historian,* Fall 1979.

Robinson, John W., "Baldy Summit Inn," *Pomona Valley Historian,* April 1970.

Robinson, John W., "Charles Francis Saunders: A Quaker Botanist in Southern California," *Southern California Quarterly,* Summer 1978.

Robinson, John W., "Eldoradoville: Forgotten Southern California Mining Camp," *Pomona Valley Historian,* Spring 1976.

Robinson, John W., "Gold Rush in The San Gabriels," *Desert Magazine,* September 1971.

Robinson, John W., "The Great Hydraulic Race," *Desert Magazine,* October 1977.

Robinson, John W., "History of Dalton and San Dimas Canyons and The San Dimas Experimental Forest," *Mt. San Antonio Historian,* Spring and Summer 1980.

Robinson, John W., "History of San Gabriel Canyon," *Pomona Valley Historian,* Spring, Summer, Fall 1977; *Mt. San Antonio Historian,* Winter, Spring 1978.

Robinson, John W., "Mt. San Antonio: Man and The Mountain," *Pomona Valley Historian,* October 1972.

Robinson, John W., "San Antonio Canyon Before 1880," *Pomona Valley Historian,* Fall 1973.

Rodman, Willoughby, "The Ascent of San Antonio," *Sierra Club Bulletin,* June 1904.

Rolfe, Frank, "Gold Mining Days in San Gabriel Canyon," *Southern California Quarterly,* June 1953.

Sears, W.L., "History of Angeles National Forest," *Trails Magazine,* Spring, Summer 1936.

Sinclair, J.D., "Watershed Management Research: The San Dimas Experimental Forest," *Trails Magazine*, Spring 1936.

Smith, Cornelius, "The Old San Gabriel and Some of Those Who Made Its History," *Trails Magazine*, Summer 1936.

Thrall, Will H., "Browns Flat," *Trails Magazine*, Summer 1938.

Thrall, Will H., "Days of Gold," *Trails Magazine*, Summer 1935.

Thrall, Will H., "Lytle Creek Canyon from Indian Days to 1900," *Southern California Quarterly*, September 1950.

Thrall, Will H., "Nectar of The Gods," *Trails Magazine*, Autumn 1941.

Thrall, Will H., "Our Unusual Rains," *Pomona Valley Historian*, Fall 1977.

Vernon, Charles Clark, "A History of The San Gabriel Mountains," *Southern California Quarterly*, March, June, September, December 1956.

Wharton, Mel, "Soil Sleuths of San Dimas Canyon," *Westways*, January 1937.

Woodford, A.O., "Why San Gabriels?" *Westways*, February 1936.

PAMPHLETS

Alexander, Dan P., *Tales and Trails of San Antonio Canyon.* Camp Baldy: Alexander's Studio, 1924.

Dawson, R.W., *Souvenir of Cold Brook Camp.* Paintings by A. Franklin Fields. San Gabriel Canyon: Cold Brook Camp, n.d. (ca. 1908).

Fisher, Pearl Comfort, *A Trip Into Wrightwood's Past.* Wrightwood: Mountaineer Publishing and Printing Co., 1977.

UNPUBLISHED MANUSCRIPTS

Baden, Beverly, "Origin of Place Names of San Antonio Quadrangle, California," Claremont Colleges, typescript, 1940.

Baldwin, Cyrus, papers and photographs, Honnold Library, Claremont.

Clark, Alfred, "War Over The San Gabriel," Senior thesis, Cal Poly Pomona, 1968.

Coleman, Edward A., "The San Dimas Saga," San Dimas Experimental Forest, typescript, 1938.

Froelich, Donald R., "San Gabriel River — Morris Reservoir," Metropolitan Water District, typescript, 1974.

Hill, Lawrence W., "The San Dimas Experimental Forest," U.S. Forest Service, mimeograph, 1963.

Johnson, Eunice B., "Gold Mining in San Gabriel Canyon," MA thesis, La Verne College, 1964.

Kushner, Ed, "History of Big Pines Park," Senior thesis, Cal Poly Pomona, 1963.

Los Angeles County Fire Department, Forestry Division, reforestation and fire control files.

McNaughton, D.A., "Geology of the Eastern San Gabriel Mountains," Cal Tech, unpublished typescript, 1934.

Noble, Dorothy Evans, "Charles Vincent Dougherty," typescript, Big Pines Ranger Station.

Peck, Sedley, papers and photographs, Follows Camp, San Gabriel Canyon.

Praskins, Wayne, "Water Rights In and Around San Antonio Canyon," Senior thesis, Claremont College, 1979.

San Dimas Experimental Forest, files, Glendora.

Show, S.B., "History of Angeles National Forest," U.S. Forest Service, typescript, 1945.

Thrall, Will H., papers and photographs, Henry E. Huntington Library.

Wheeler, Frank, scrapbooks, Honnold Library, Claremont.

Widman, Florence, "Memories of 50 Years in Coldwater Canyon," typescript, 1976.

NEWSPAPERS

Azusa Herald, 1929-1946 (October 20, 1937 is special issue on San Gabriel Canyon)
Azusa Pomotropic, 1889-1924
Claremont Courier, 1908-1929
Glendora Gleaner, 1904-1909, 1911-1932
Glendora Press-Gleaner, 1933-1938
Glendora Signal, 1887-1889
Los Angeles Star, 1851-1864, 1868-1876
Los Angeles News, 1862-1872
Los Angeles Times, 1881-1980

Telegraph Peak and Coldwater Canyon from the North Fork of Lytle Creek. – C. W. MCLAUGHLIN

Pomona Daily Review, 1904-1908
Pomona Progress, 1889-1890
Pomona Weekly Times, 1892-1904
San Bernardino Guardian, 1867-1876
San Bernardino Times, 1875-1879
San Bernardino Times-Index, 1879-1880
San Bernardino Sun-Telegram, 1925-1977
San Dimas Press, 1918-1938
Southern Vineyard (Los Angeles), 1858-1859
Wrightwood Mountaineer, 1970-1980

Index

Alexander, Dan, 140, 146
Allison, John James, 39
Allison Mine, 39-40
Applewhite, James, 190
Asuksangna, 10
Austin, Mary, 210
Azusa, Rancho, 11, 15, 45-48
Azusa Water Development & Irrigating Co., 46-49

Baden-Powell, Mt., 38, 112, 114
Baldwin, Cyrus G., 51-54
Baldy Summit Inn, 169-170
Banks, James, 24-25
Bauwens, George, 173, 175
Baynham, Charles, 50, 140-141
Bear Canyon Resort, 142, 148
Beatty, "Doc", 92
Big Dalton Canyon, 13, 49, 59, 115-117
Big Dalton C.C.C. Camp, 126
Big Horn Lodge, 194
Big Horn Mine, 38-39
Big Pines, 200-206
Bonita Falls, 195
Bradford, James, 138, 140
Branscome Camp, 97
Browns Flat, 188-121
Buell, "Uncle" Dave, 34
Burnham, Mount, 112
Burns, Ruth Curry, 153-156

Cajon Pass, 11-12
Camp Baldy, 141-145, 150-156
Camp Bonita, 96
Camp Rincon, 10, 11, 89-92
Camp, John Bradford, 118-119
Chaffee, George, 50, 51
Champion, Douglas, 192
Chapman, Clarence Roy, 142, 147
Chapman Ranch, 142, 147
Circle Mtn. Cattle Co., 198
Civilian Conservation Corps (CCC), 77, 92, 94, 126-127, 156
Clark, Joe, 24
Clyde, Almon, 185-187, 196
Cogswell Dam, 66-68
Cogswell, Prescott, 69
Coldbrook Camp, 92-94
Committee of Nine, 48-49, 54
Covina Outing Club, 86
Creel Club, 83-85
Crespi, Fray Juan, 13, 207
Crystal Lake, 57, 105-107, 109-111
Cucamonga Peak, 180
Cucamonga, Rancho, 16, 190
Cucamonga Wilderness, 181-183
Curry, Foster, 150-153
Curtis, Ronald, 42

Dagger Point, 158
Dalton, Henry, 11, 15, 45-46
Davidson Arch, 201
Dawson, R.W., 46, 57, 90, 92, 105-106
Dear Park, 74-77
Delker, Henry, 147, 149
Dell, Fred, 138, 166-167
Dells Camp, 138-139
Devils Backbone, 165-166, 170
Dewey, William H., 28, 169, 170
Dougherty, Charles Vincent (see Vincent, Charles Tom)
Driver, Thomas, 19

Eagle Mine, 39-40
Earp, Wyatt and Virgil, 196
East Fork, San Gabriel Cyn., 18-20
Eaton, E.C., 59-66
Eckles, Almyra, 121
Eldoradoville, 18-20
El Encanto, 104
Electric Power Company, 57
Eleven Oaks, 142, 148
Emerson Flat, 73

Fairchild, Dr. B.H., 166-167
Falling Springs, 94, 96
Ferguson, William G. 32-34
Flintham, Stuart J., 123-124
Flood Control, 57-71
Follows Camp, 86-89
Follows, Ralph & Jennie, 86-89
Forest fires, 76-77, 98-99, 138, 159
Frederick, Lloyd A., Sr. & Jr., 192-193
Fultz, Francis M., 212

Gabrielino Indians, 10-13
Garces, Fray Francisco, 13-14
Gilman, Herbert S., 123, 125
Glendora Mountain Road, 121-122
Glenn Ranch, 187, 190-193
Glenn, Silas, 187, 190
Gold Dollar Mine, 39-41
Gold Ridge Mines, 28-29
Graveyard Canyon, 10

Hannager, Captain, 18
Happy Jack, 193
Hardy Harris Cabin, 78
Harpending Company, 21
Harwood Lodge, 158, 170
Harwood, Mount, 179
Hawkins, Mount, 92, 111
Hawkins, Nellie, 92
Headlee, Frank, 94
Heaton, William Tecumseh, 35, 36, 87
Hocumac Mines, 25-26
Hoffman, J.W., 11

Hogsback, 132, 134, 136-138, 140
Holder, Charles Frederick, 211-212
Holiday Hill, 206
Hooverville, 40, 42, 43
Howell, Cleves H., 68
Huntington, Henry E., 56
Hydroelectric Power, 51-57

Icehouse Canyon, 132-133
Icehouse Canyon Resort, 142, 147
Indian Trails, 11-12
Islip, Mount, 111-113

James, George Wharton, 209-210
Jarvi, Sim, 114
Joe Elliott Tree, 190, 194
Johnstone, William A., 123, 125
Justice, Oliver, 35, 36, 105

Kelly, John, 28, 147, 149
Kellys Camp, 28, 147, 149
Kelsey, Henry C., 30
Kelsey Silver Mine, 30-31
Kerckhoff, William, 54-56, 140
Kincaid, Madison Moses, 135, 136
Kinney, Abbott, 211

Leadabrand, Russ, 216
Leffler, Herb, 175-176
Leopold, Aldo, 181-182
Little Jimmy Spring, Camp, 108-109
Lookout Mounain, 173
Loop and Meserve Tract, 49
Los Angeles County Flood Control District, 57-71
Lummis, Charles, 210
Lytle Creek, 21-23, 185-195

Maley, Fred, 35
Manker Flat, 138
Monrovia Canyon, 73-79
Moose Retreat, 115
Morris Dam, 63-66
Mosauer, Dr. Walter, 174, 176
Mountainview Ranch, 82-83
Mountain High, 206
Mount Baldy (see San Antonio, Mount)
Mount Baldy Ski Lifts, Inc., 176-178
Muir, John, 207-208

Narrows Bridge, 102
Native Son Mine, 38
Negley Sisters, 106

Old Baldy (see San Antonio, Mount)
O'Melveny, Henry, 54, 81, 83, 86
Ontario Peak, 180
Overturff, Ben, 74-77

Pacific Light & Power Co., 55-56
Palomares, Ygnacio, 12, 15, 45
Pasadena Bait Club, 85
Persinger, Mary and Bates, 84
Pierce, Himan, 135
Pine Flat, 105-108
Pomona Land & Water Co., 49
Portwood, John Knox, 35, 37
Potter, Cornelius, 90
Potter, William, 82-83

Rankin, Edward Payson, 79
Rankins, Hibbard and family, 73-74
Reagan, John W., 57-59
Roberts, Henry C., 18, 32-34, 46, 87, 95
Roberts and Williams Stage Line, 18

San Antonio Canyon
 early days, 132-138
 hydroelectric power, 52-54
 resorts, 139-157
 water, 49-51
San Antonio Dam, 69-71
San Antonio Mines, 23-28
San Antonio, Mount, 10, 161-178
San Antonio Water Co., 26, 50-51, 138, 140-141, 150
Sanborn, Kate, 209
Sanborns Camp, 141
San Dimas Canyon, 11-12, 57, 115-118
San Dimas Experimental Forest, 123-131
San Gabriel Canyon
 Indians, 11-12
 Spanish, 13, 15
 mining, 18-20, 29-38
 water struggles, 45-49
 hydroelectric power, 54-57
 flood control, 57-71
 railroad, 60-62
 fishing, 81-82
 resorts, 83-98
 fires, 98-99
 roads, 99-103
San Gabriel Mission, 13-15

San Gabriel Mountains
 discovery, 13
 naming, 13-14
San Gabriel Wilderness, 181-183
San Jose Land & Water Co., 49
San Jose, Rancho, 12, 15-16, 49
San Sevaine Flats, 185, 188-190, 194
Saunders, Charles Francis, 213-215
Sawpit Canyon, 15, 73-79
Scotland, 188, 195
Scott, Jay Gardner, 96
Shady Oaks, 96-97
Sharp, Louis, 30, 46
Shay, Art, 151
Sheep Mountain Wilderness, 181-184
Shoemaker, Alonzo, 35
Sierra Club, 169-172, 177
Sierra Madre (see San Gabriel Mountains)
Sinclair, J. Donald, 125-126
Ski Sunrise, 206
Slover, Isaac, 196
Smith, Charlie, 39-40, 54, 90
Snowcrest Resort, 147, 148
Southern California Edison Co., 57
Spring Camp, 78-79
Squirrel Inn, 92
Stanley-Miller Mine, 38-40
St. Francis Dam disaster, 62
Stockton Flat, 188-189
Stoddard, William H., 136
Stoddards Camp, 136-137
Swarthout Lodge, 202, 205
Swarthout Valley, 196
Swinnerton, Jimmy, 92, 107-109
Sycamore Flat, 57, 118

Tally, Seymour & Barbara, 192
Tanbark Flats, 118, 123, 126-127, 131
Telegraph Peak, 179
Temple, F.P.F., 134
Texas Point Mine, 21-23, 186
Thrall, Will H. 215-216
Throop Peak, 112
Thunder Mountain, 179
Trask, Tallman, Boy Scout Camp, 77-80
Trogden, George, 35, 37, 56
Truman, Ben C. 208
Turk, George 23-24
Turner, Spence D., 123-124

Van Dyke, Theodore, 208
Vejar, Ricardo, 12, 15
Victoria Silver Mine, 30-31
Vincent, Charles Tom, 38, 163-164

Walton, Harry, 35
Water struggles, 45-71
Wawona Cabin, 107
Webers Camp, 97-98
Wheeler Survey, 24, 162-163, 165
Whitecomb Trail, 115
Widman Ranch, 98
Williams Camp, 96
Williamson, Mount, 111
Winston, Dr. James B., 29-30
Wixom, Nathan & sons, 186-187
Wolfskill Canyon, 118
Wolfskill Falls, 116, 118
Wolfskill Falls Camp, 117-118
Wright, Sumner Banks, 197-200
Wrightwood, 196-200

Zalvidea, Fray Jose Maria de, 14
Zapata, Francisco, 29-30
Zapata Silver Mine, 29-30

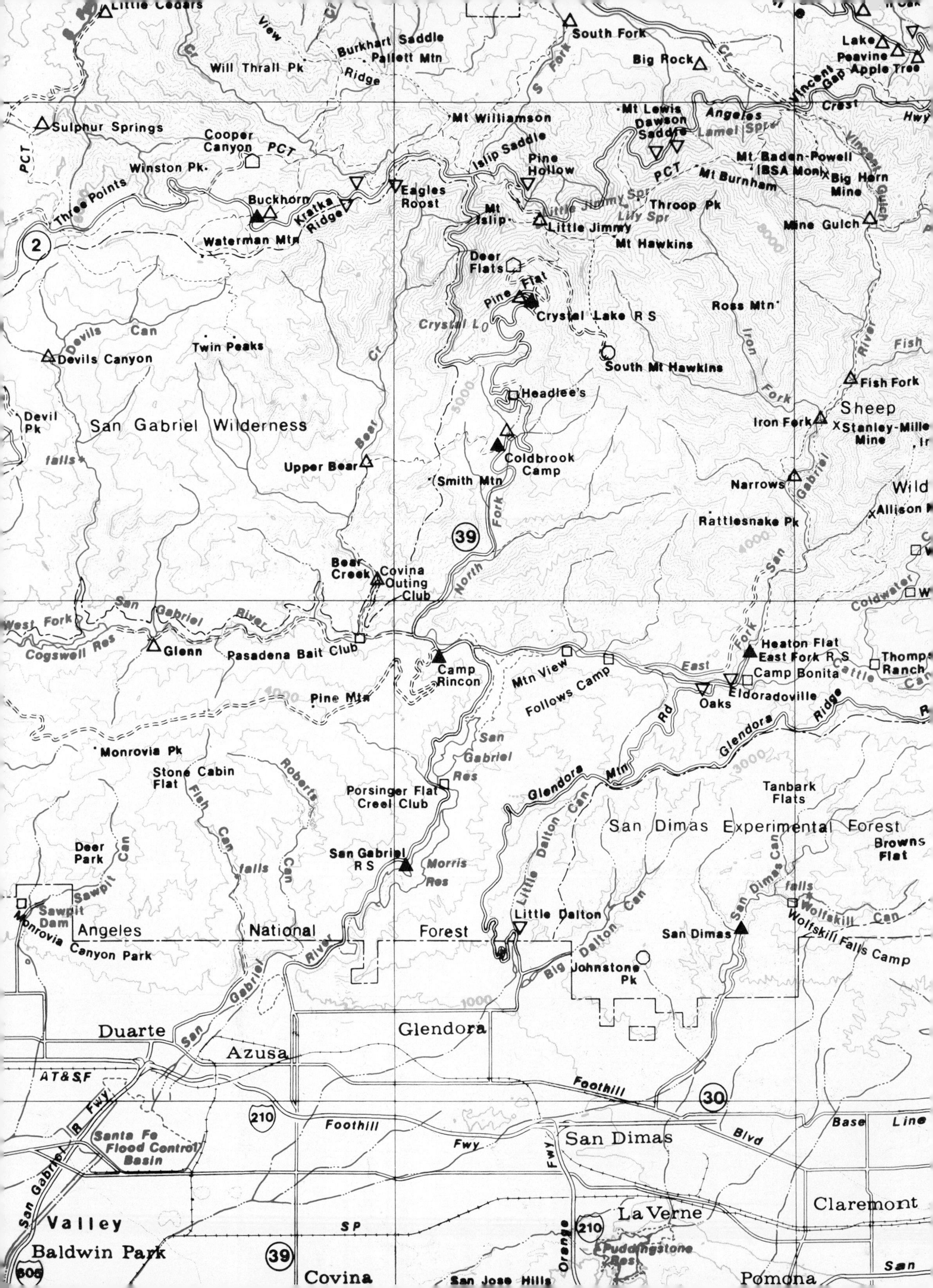

Little Cedars
South Fork
Burkhart Saddle
Pallett Mtn
Will Thrall Pk
Ridge
Big Rock
Lake
Peavine
Apple Tree
Vincent Gap
Crest
Hwy
Sulphur Springs
Mt Williamson
Mt Lewis
Dawson Saddle
Angeles
Lamel Spr
Cooper Canyon
PCT
Islip Saddle
Pine Hollow
Winston Pk.
Mt. Baden-Powell
(BSA Mon)
Big Horn Mine
Mt Burnham
Vincent Gulch
Three Points
Buckhorn
Kratka Ridge
Eagles Roost
Mt Islip
Little Jimmy Spr
Throop Pk
Lily Spr
Little Jimmy
Mine Gulch
Waterman Mtn
Mt Hawkins
2
Deer Flats
Pine Flat
Crystal Lake R S
Crystal L
Ross Mtn
Devils Can
Twin Peaks
Devils Canyon
South Mt Hawkins
Iron Fork
Fish
Fish Fork
Headlee's
Devil Pk
San Gabriel Wilderness
Sheep
Iron Fork
Stanley-Miller Mine
Bear
falls
Upper Bear
Coldbrook Camp
Smith Mtn
Narrows
Wild
Allison
Rattlesnake Pk
39
North Fork
Bear Creek
Covina Outing Club
San
Coldwater
West Fork
San Gabriel River
Cogswell Res
Glenn
Pasadena Bait Club
Camp Rincon
Mtn View
Follows Camp
East
Heaton Flat
East Fork R S
Camp Bonita
Eldoradoville
Oaks
Cattle Can
Thompson Ranch
Pine Mtn
Rd
Glendora Ridge
Monrovia Pk
San Gabriel Res
Stone Cabin Flat
Roberts
Fish Can
Porsinger Flat
Creel Club
Glendora Mtn
Tanbark Flats
San Dimas Experimental Forest
Browns Flat
Deer Park
Sawpit Can
falls
Can
San Gabriel R S
Morris Res
Little Dalton Can
Dalton Can
San Dimas Can
falls
Wolfskill Can
Sawpit Dam
Monrovia Canyon Park
Angeles
National
Forest
Little Dalton
San Dimas
Wolfskill Falls Camp
Big Dalton Can
Johnstone Pk
River
Gabriel
1000
Duarte
Glendora
Azusa
San
AT&SF
Foothill
30
R Fwy
210
Foothill
Fwy
Fwy
San Dimas
Blvd
Base Line
Santa Fe Flood Control Basin
San Gabriel
Valley
Claremont
SP
Orange
210
La Verne
Baldwin Park
39
Puddingstone Res
605
Covina
San Jose Hills
Pomona
San